CARLA VIVIANA CORDOVA

SHAPING VISUAL STRUCTURES

THE ART OF COMPOSITION, MOVEMENT AND SPACE IN GRAPHIC DESIGN

BIS PUBLISHERS

TEXT, DESIGN & ARTWORK
BY CARLA VIVIANA CORDOVA
TYPEFACES FRANKLIN GOTHIC
ATF, FUTURA, FUTURA PT, AND
FUTURA PT CONDENSED

ISBN 978 90 636 9909 3

BIS PUBLISHERS
TIMORPLEIN 46
1094 CC AMSTERDAM
THE NETHERLANDS
bis@bispublishers.com
www.bispublishers.com

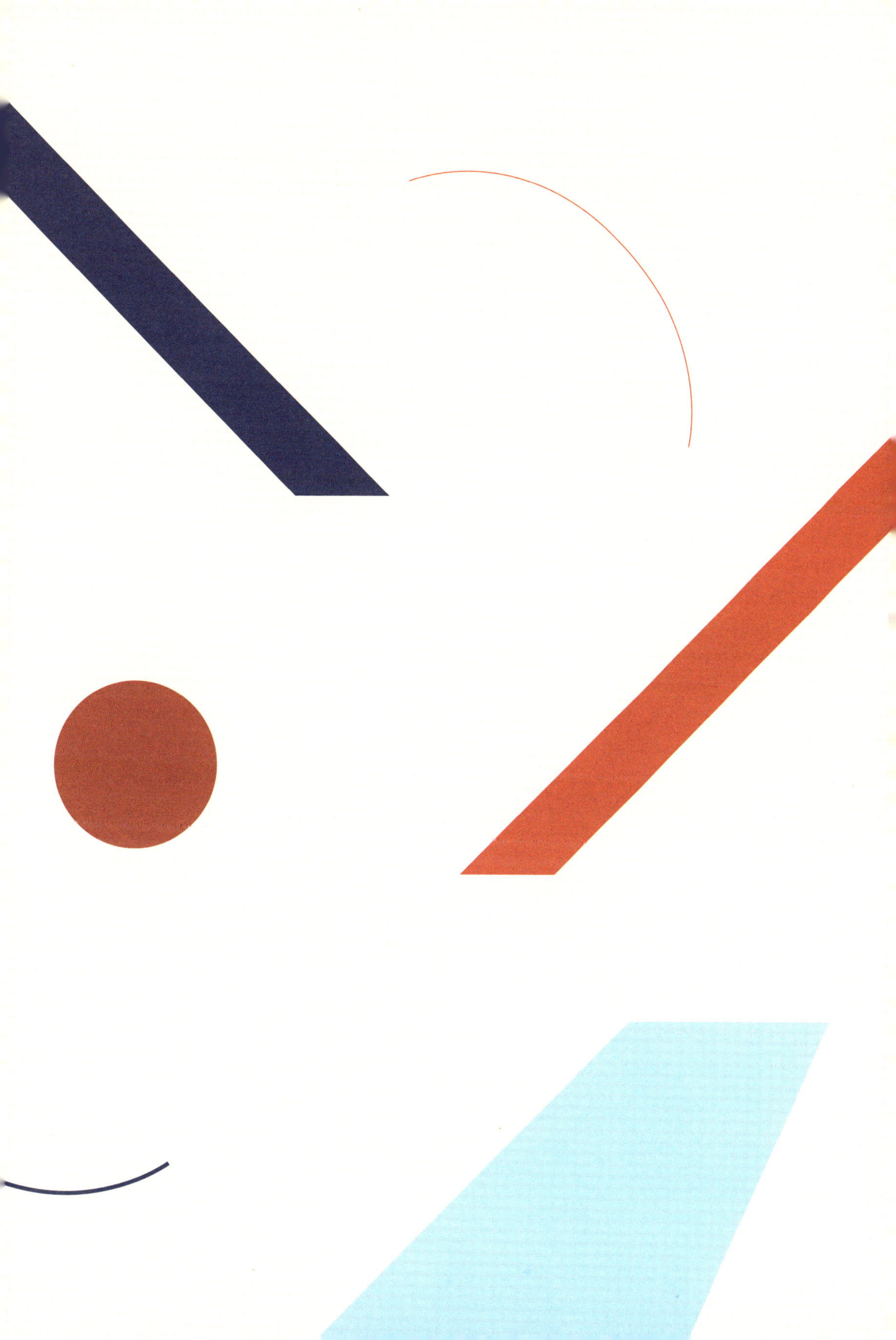

"Shaping Visual Structures presents a process-oriented approach to graphic design, emphasizing the dynamic interplay of composition, movement, and space. The book invites designers to blend digital precision with hands-on experimentation, fostering creativity and personal discovery."

Ben Hannam, Associate Professor and Department Chair, Elon University, North Carolina, USA

"This is an exceptional and much needed book. Viviana Cordova has developed an engaging and interactive publication that covers important information that helps shape our understanding of the underlying structures of design. The exercises are fun, engaging and informative and you will find this book helpful, whether you are a design student, design educator or practicing designer. I highly recommend this book."

Bernard Canniffe, Professor, Iowa State University, USA

"The book as a guided tool for experimentation and exploration both digital and analog promises to be essential in becoming well versed in visual language. The principles of visual arrangement of shapes are broken down to basic organizational principles and invites the reader to explore further. The book is fun, colorful, and inviting."

Alma Hoffmann, Associate Professor, University of South Alabama, USA

"A 'Design Playbook' to inspire experimentation. Simple assignments, explained in an easy-to-understand way, encourage you to start playing with shapes. Carla Viviana Cordova Chacon helps readers grasp the fundamentals of composition. And more! These basic exercises can also be applied to other areas, such as designing logos. Play!"

Sven Ingmar Thies, author of the book "Teaching Graphic Design", University of Applied Arts Vienna, Austria
thiesdesign.com
linkedin.com/in/sven-ingmar-thies

This book has been inspired by sketching, thinking, and designing elements that are part of the constant work in progress we go through as designers. Embracing thoughts and experimental endeavors that allow us to push boundaries and also understand how our design methods can change, diverge, evolve, and even go back to previous inspirational thinking. Our visual senses absorb the abstraction of our surroundings all the time.

I want to thank my daughter Luz who inspires me everyday, and my father Oscar and brother Oscar, who encourage me daily.

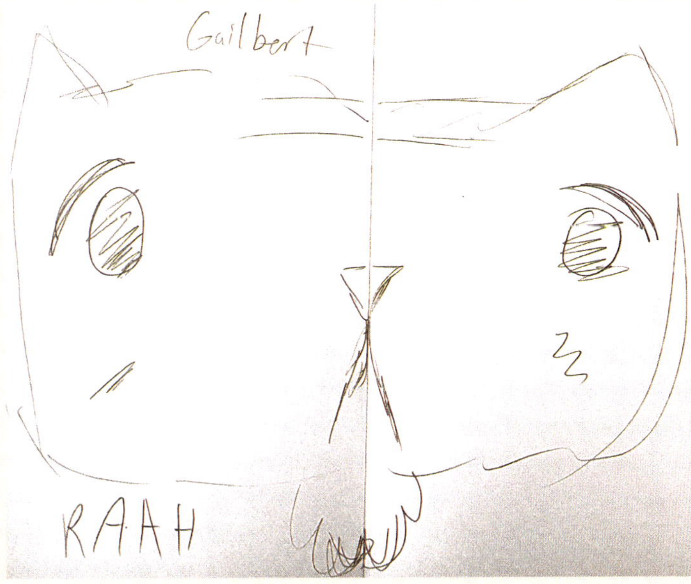

TABLE OF CONTENTS

1.introduction

Humans have communicated through graphics since 50 000 BC, starting with cave paintings of animals, hunting, people, and their lifestyle. During the Industrial Revolution, when communication became commercialized through graphic design, this came to be called commercial art. This transition from handmade products to manufacturing started in 1760 and continued to 1840 and brought about drastic changes and speed. Humanity started to crave a fast paced lifestyle during the Second Industrial Revolution, also known as the Technological Revolution, which ranged from 1817 to 1914.

The current Revolution we are experi–encing is the Information Age, which began in 1946 with computing and became more accessible in 1974 through Smalltalk, the first graphical user interface that allowed graphics on the computer screen. The advancement of graphic design has evolved because it has always been influenced by technology. The work in this book was influenced by the following Art and Design movements, including Dada 1916–1923, Bauhaus 1917–1932, and De Stijl 1917–1938. The content has inspirational visual exercises and methods of thinking and features an abstract approach, providing creative systems that are easy to understand and access.

Understanding how we work with structure and how elements are organized is essential to visual brainstorming. The content explores a vast range of topics, such as movement, experimental, spontaneity, etc. This explorative work will inspire students, professionals, and other enthusiasts to create their own designs.

shapes

geometric

irregular

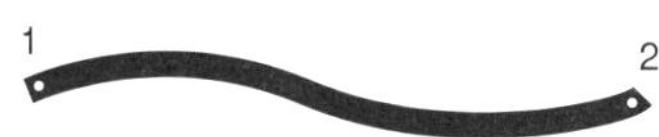

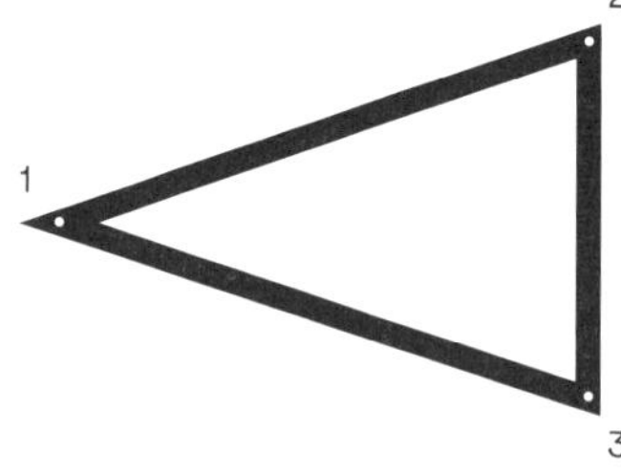

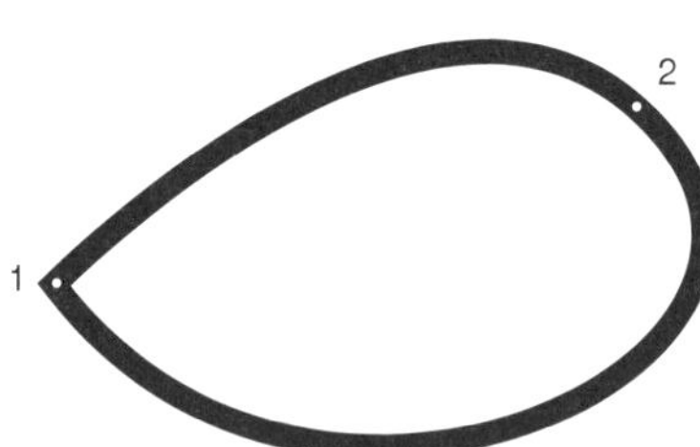

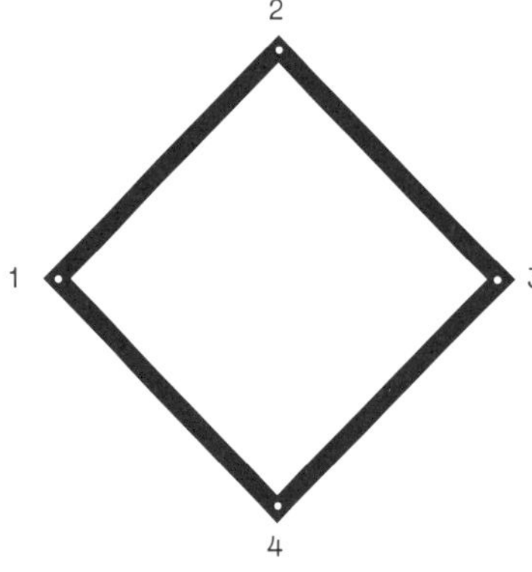

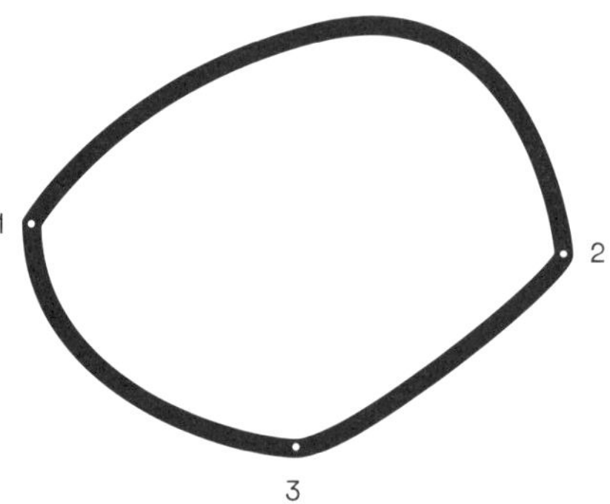

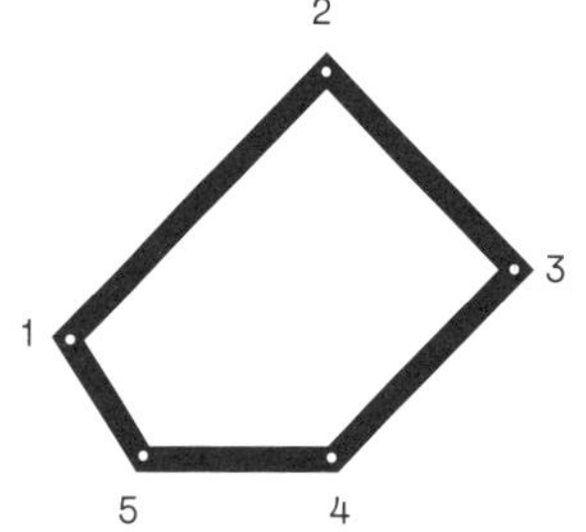

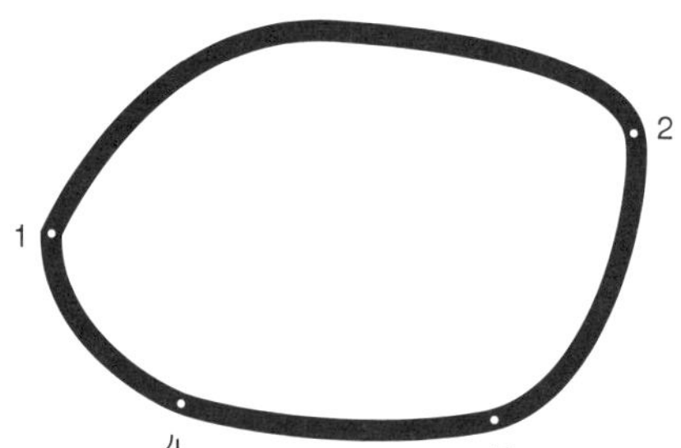

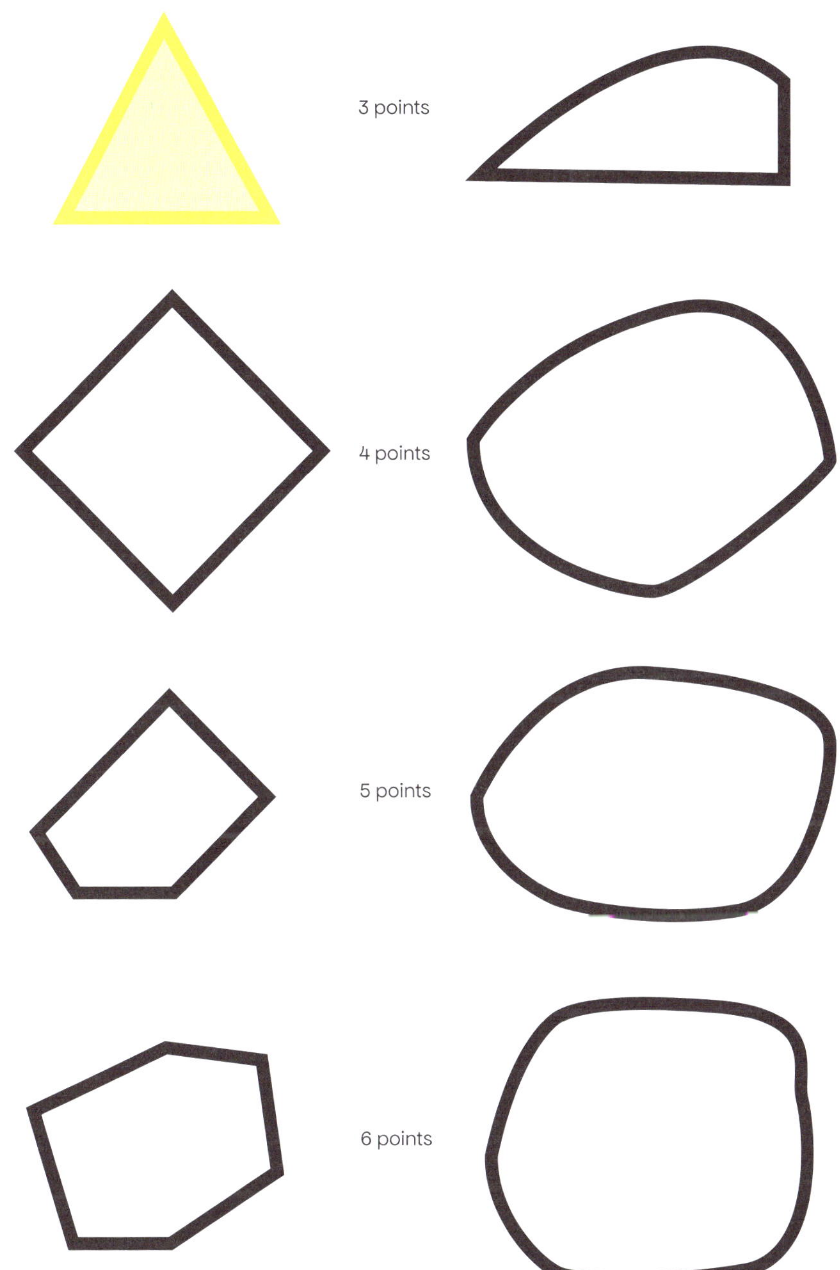
3 points
4 points
5 points
6 points

brainstorming and shape creation

Creating shapes can seem very easy because they are so primitive. By connecting points, we can easily form straight lines, curves, diagonals, and more complex systems using repetition, rotation, reflection, refraction, and other limitless actions. The simplest shapes are inspired by geometry—created using three, four, five, six, seven, eight, or even more points. Some shapes are very well-known: triangle, circle, trapezoid, hexagon, and so on. At the same time, we can explore abstract, free-form shapes that can be drawn with complete freedom.

Shapes can also be combined to create more complex forms that generate surfaces and textures—not only digitally, but also through hand drawing. Computing and digital tools have deeply influenced how mathematical our design process and thinking have become. Many graphic designers prefer to program and design using algorithms, fractals, and pre-made shapes, which offer convenience in our fast-paced world. However, exploring other mediums can generate fresh imagery and new modes of expression. Working both outside the computer and with digital tools is equally important.

Ancient tools such as pencils, brushes, unknown objects, and even our fingers are still in use and continue to inspire the creation of new shapes and forms. Also, various surfaces that we still use as canvas to create artwork and design. We should not limit ourselves—instead, we can combine and mix digital and physical processes to expand our creative possibilities.

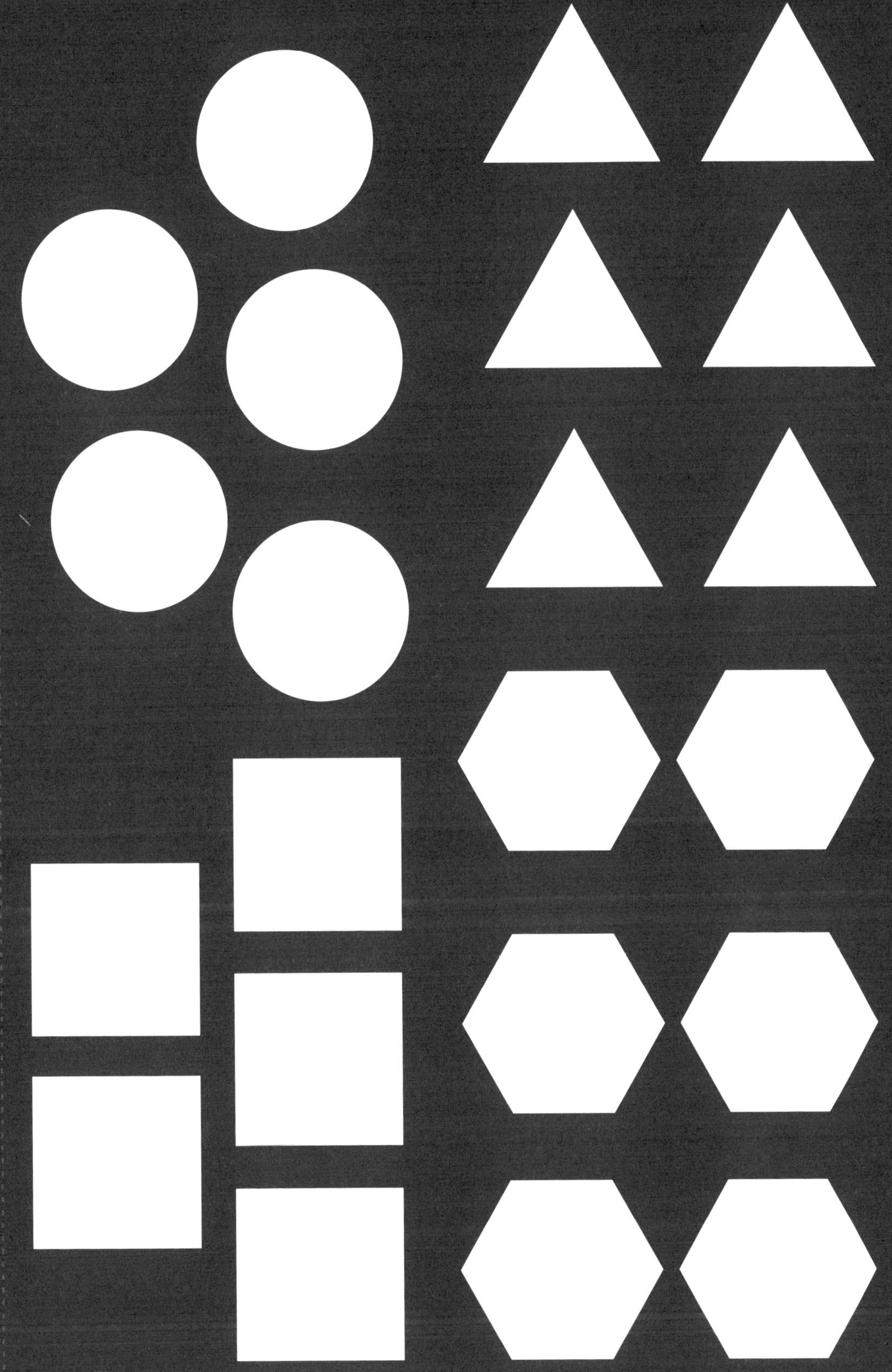

fold or cut here

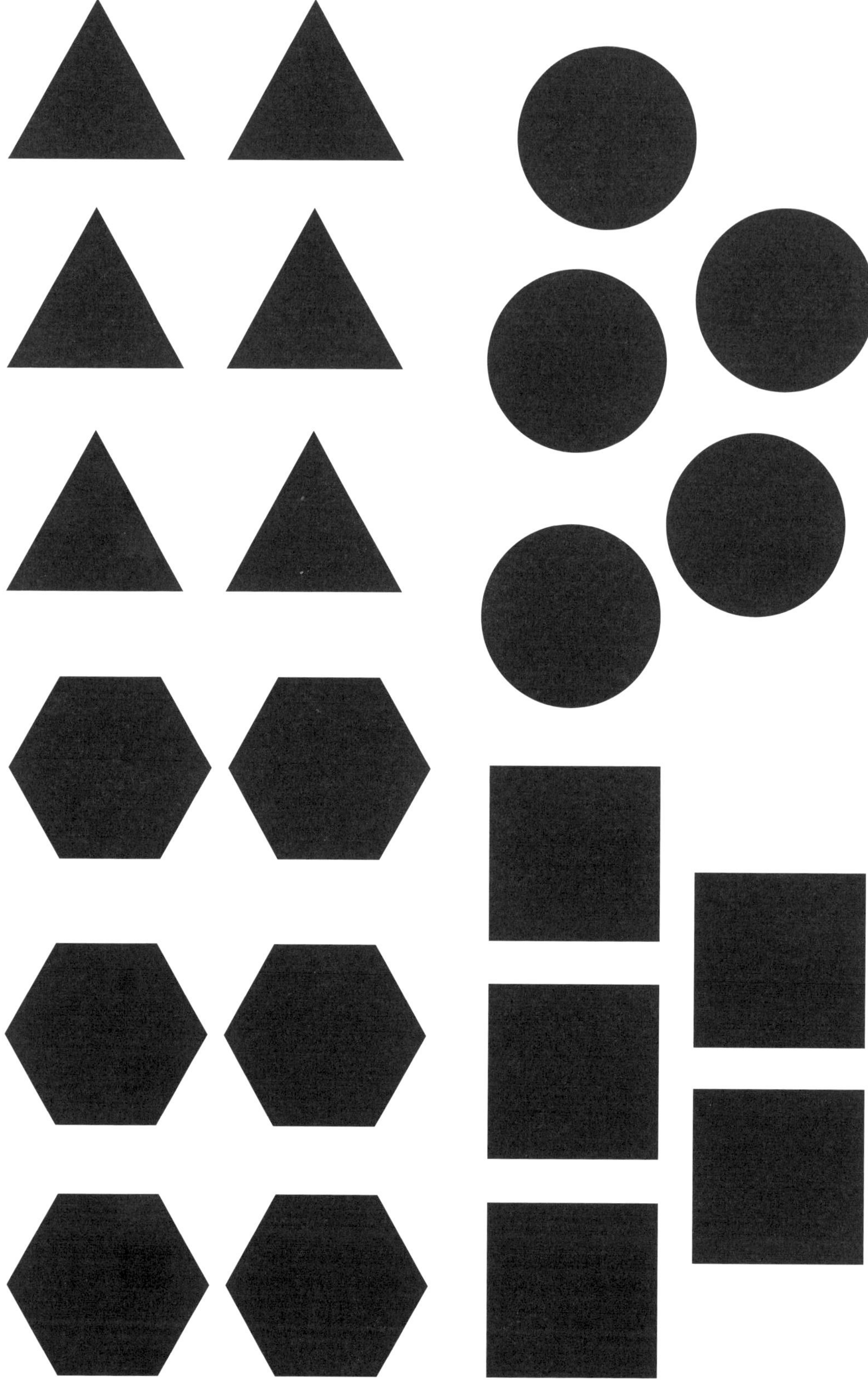

fold or cut here

exercise

Use the pages as a foundational start in this chapter to draw, cut, paste, etc. Be inspired to create and design using the shapes in the left page or the previous page to design in a separate sheet or sheets. Please feel free to use the space below as a canvas.

sketch, fold or cut here

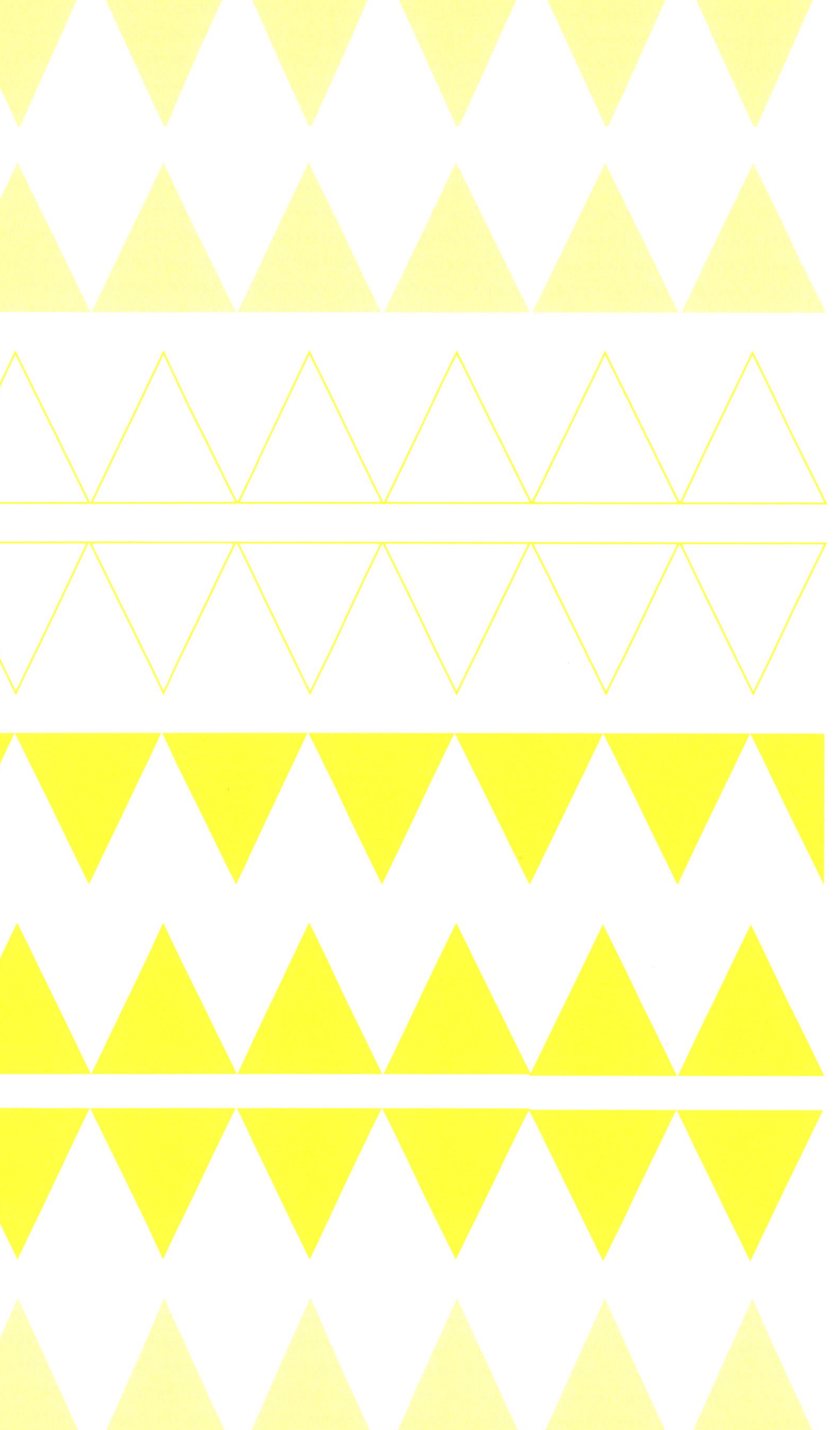

fold or cut here

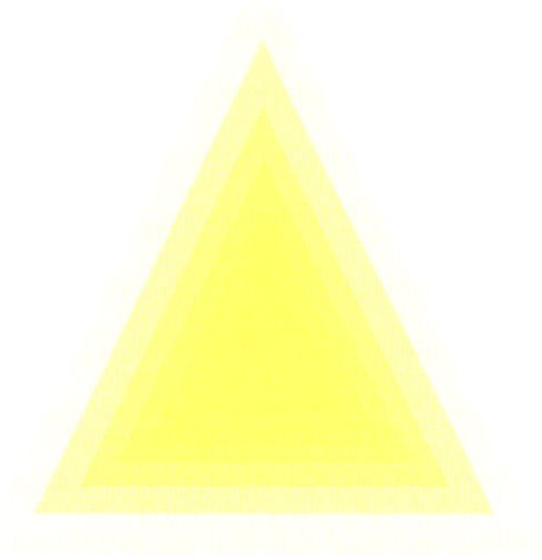

repetition, transparency,
and straight lines

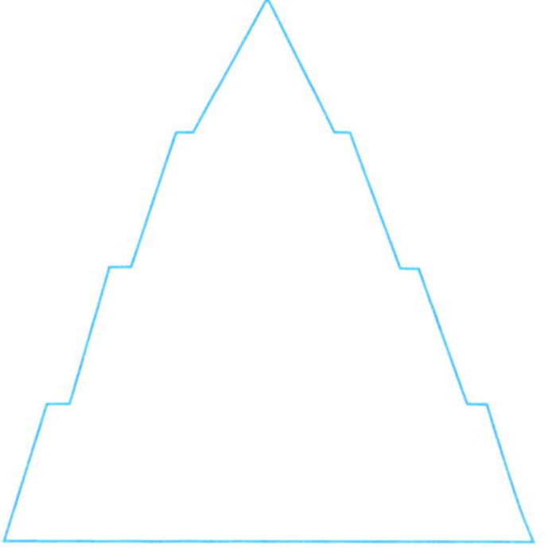

sharp edges, cyan outlines,
and angular lines

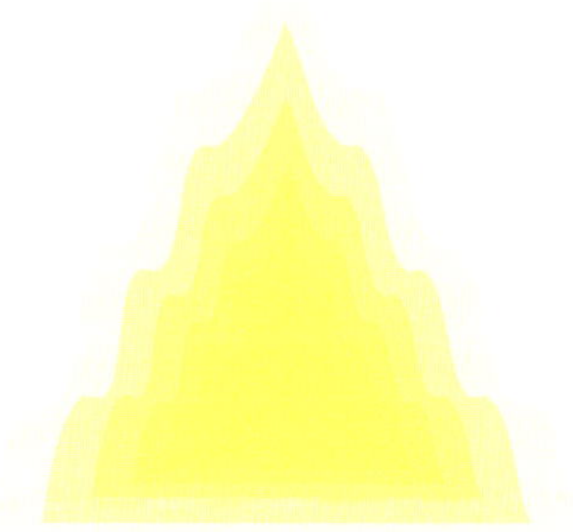

repetition, transparency,
yellow, and rounded edges

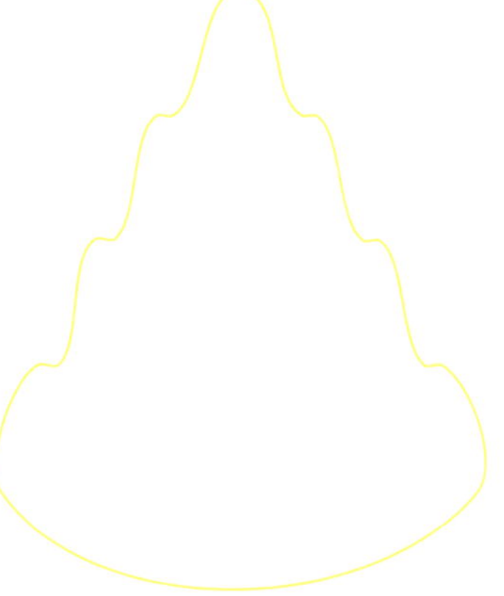

rounded stairs, yellow outline,
and triangle

fold or cut here

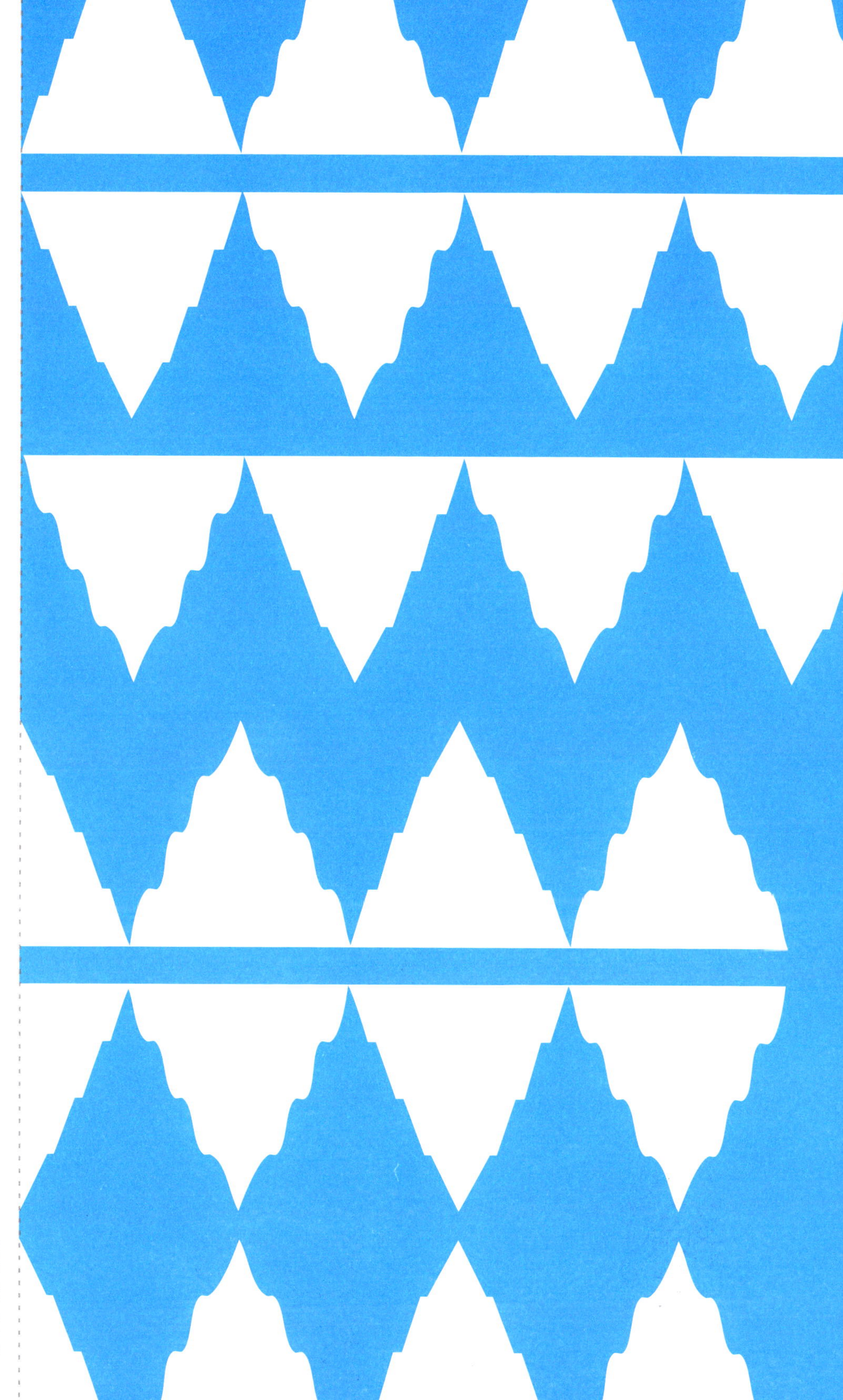

fold or cut here

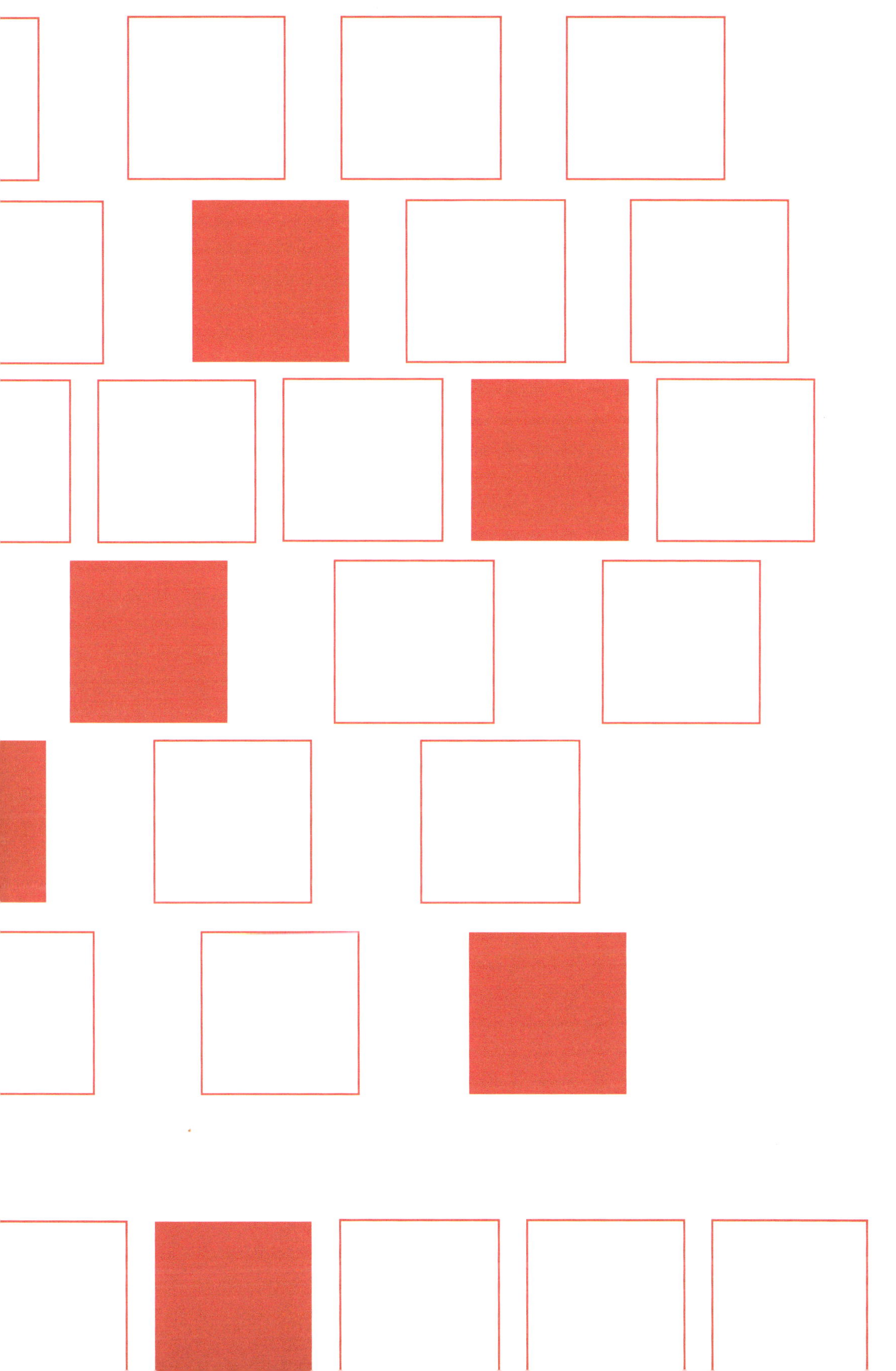

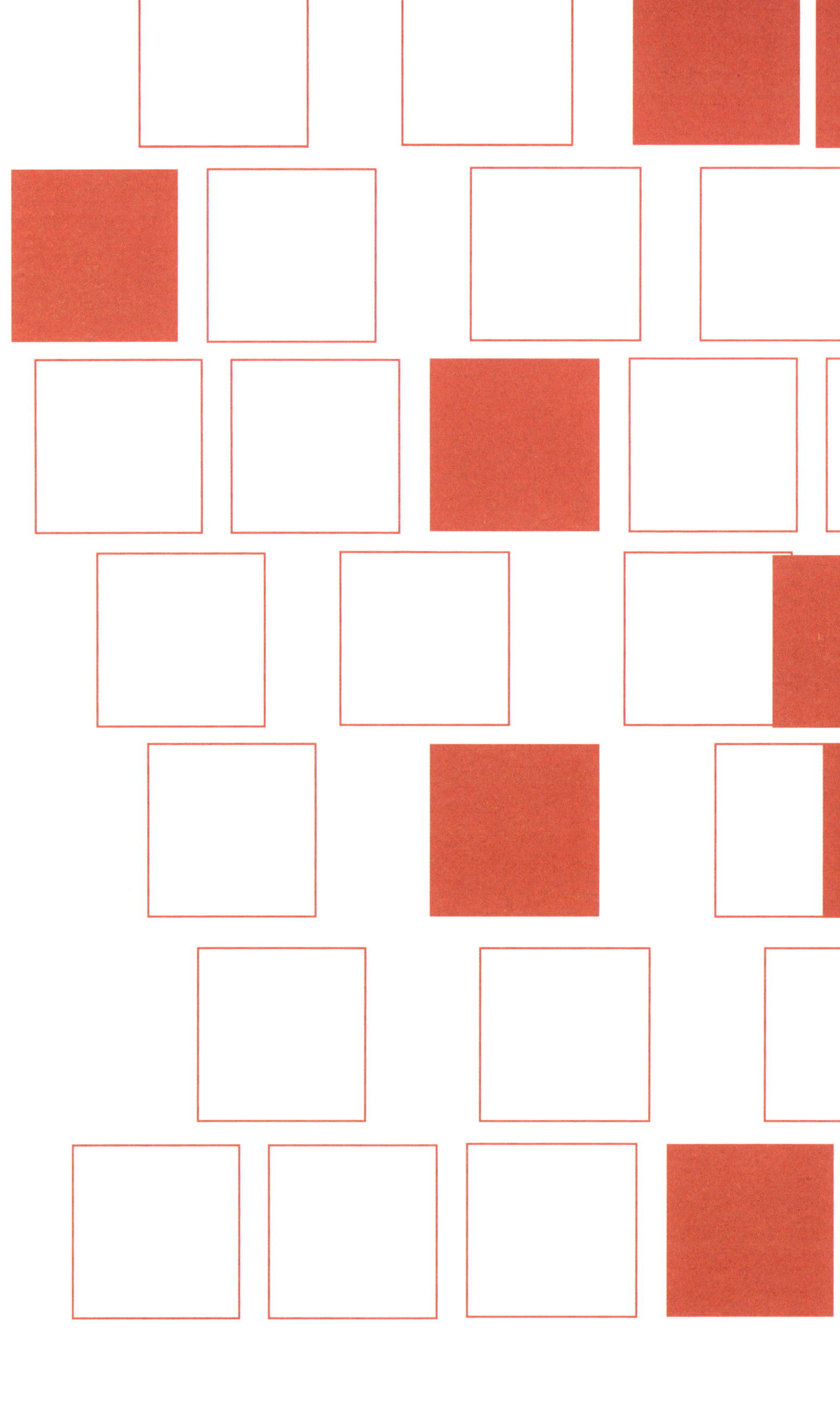

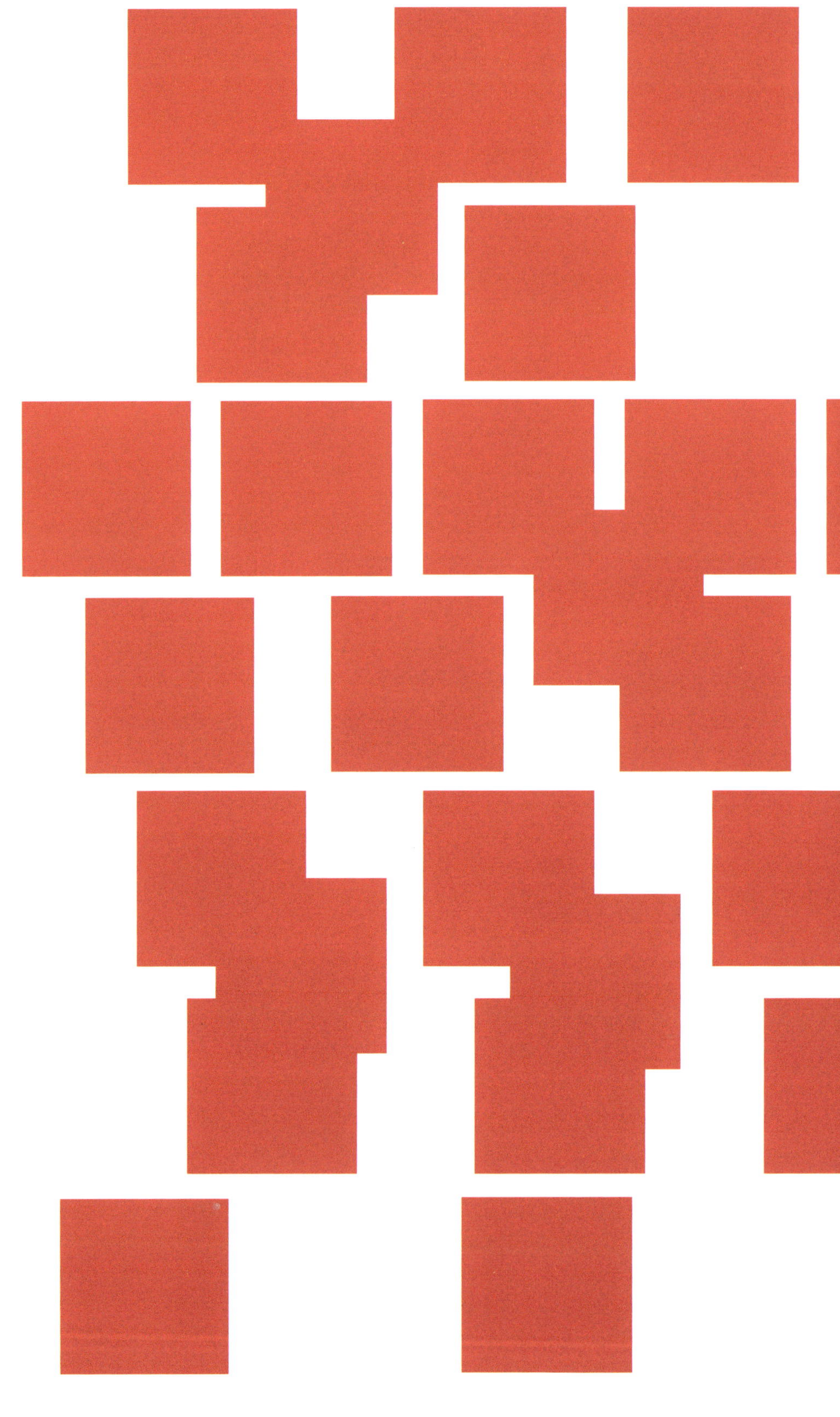

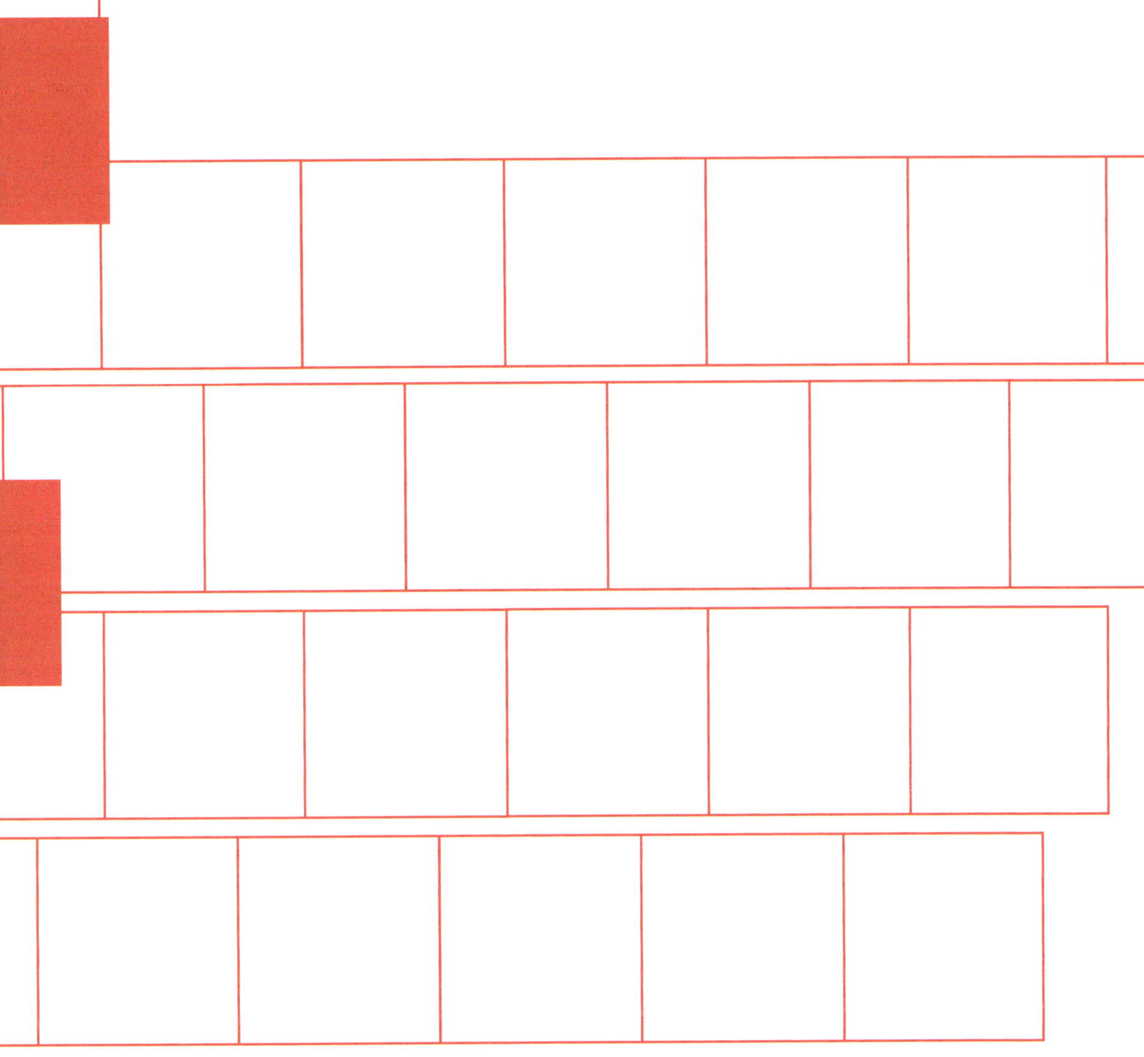

square and sequence

When squares are in use to create a pattern, whether they have negative and positive space, using color creates continouos lines that are vertical and horizontal.

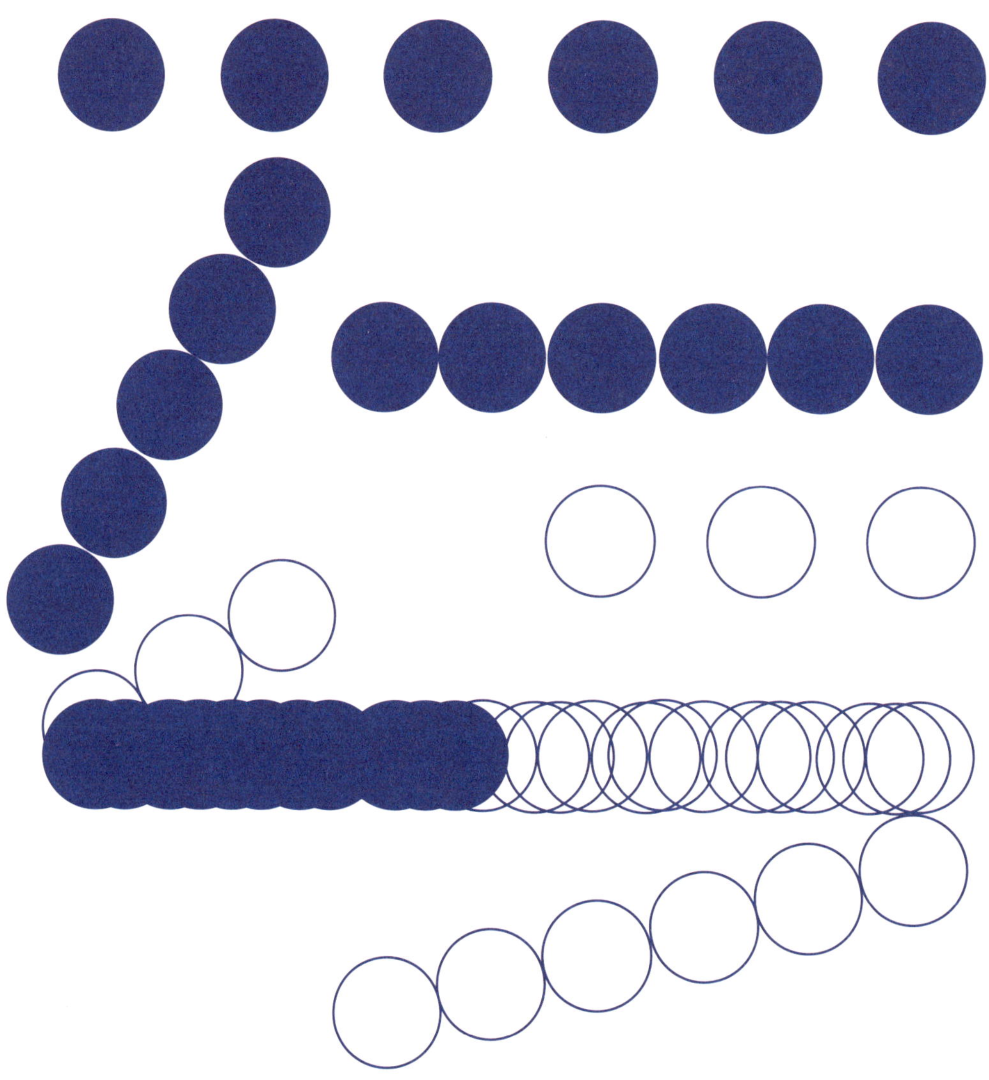

circle and grouping

When circles are in use to create spaces that have negative and positive space, using color creates continouos rotating angles and diagonals in many directions.

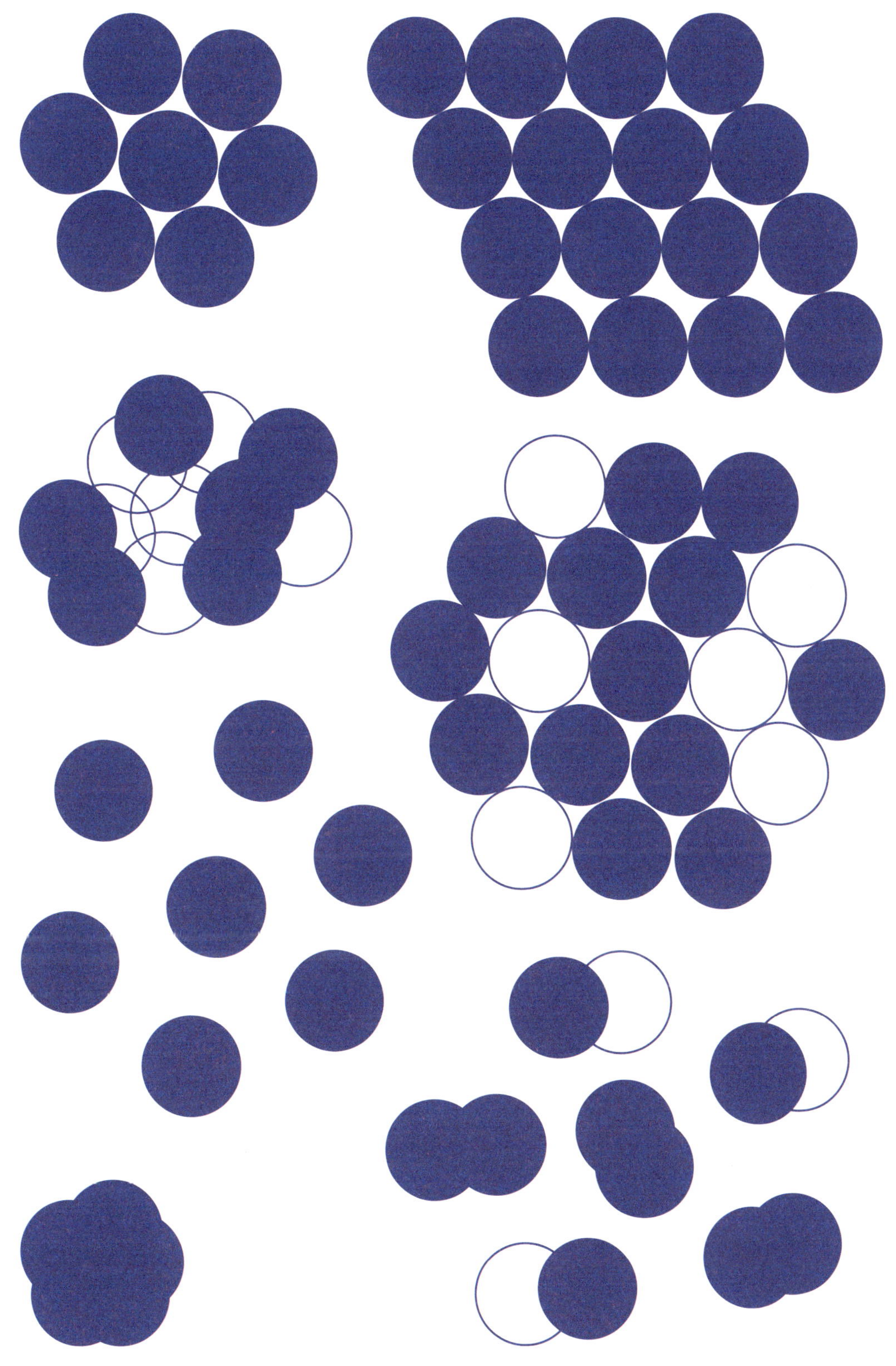

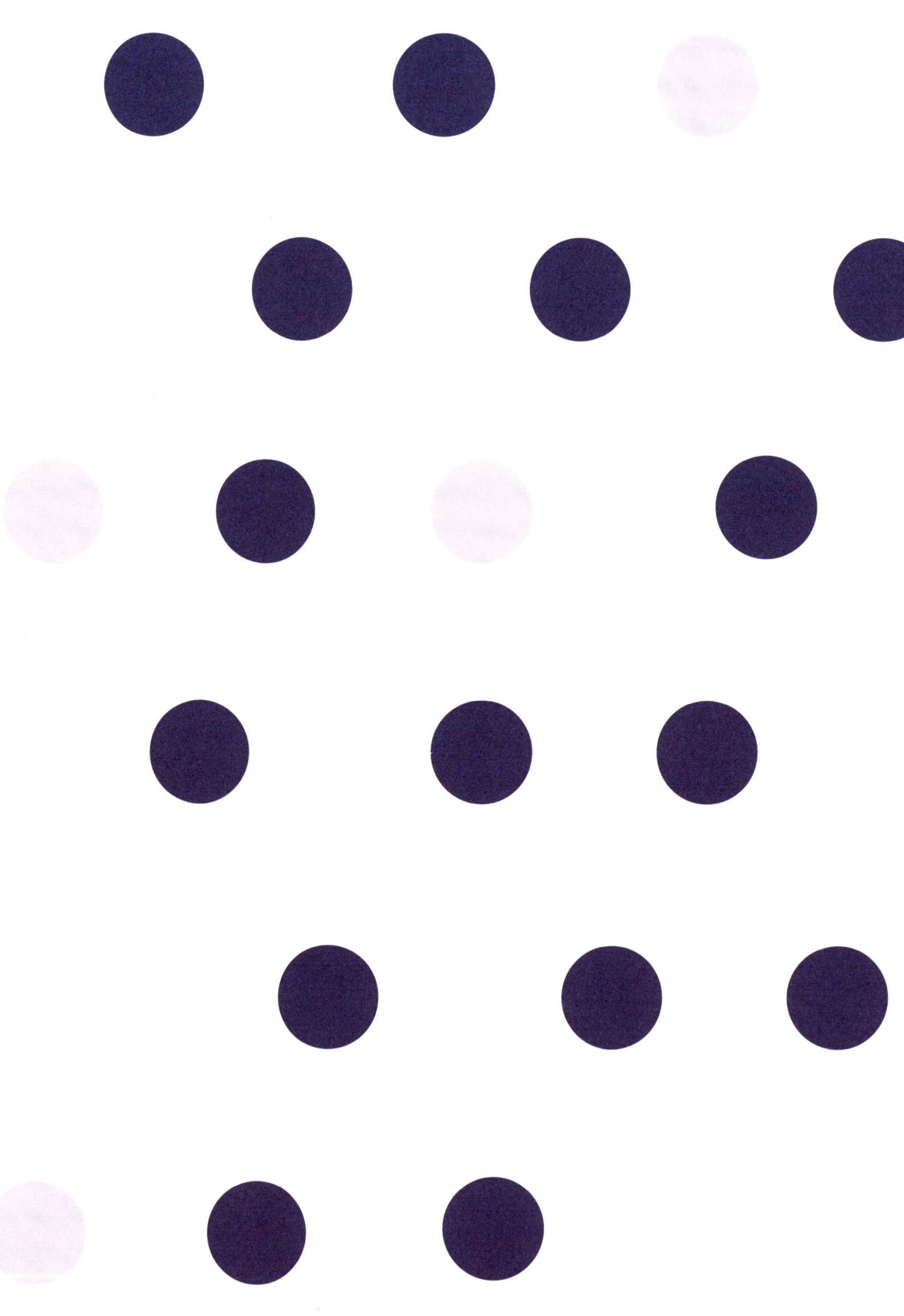

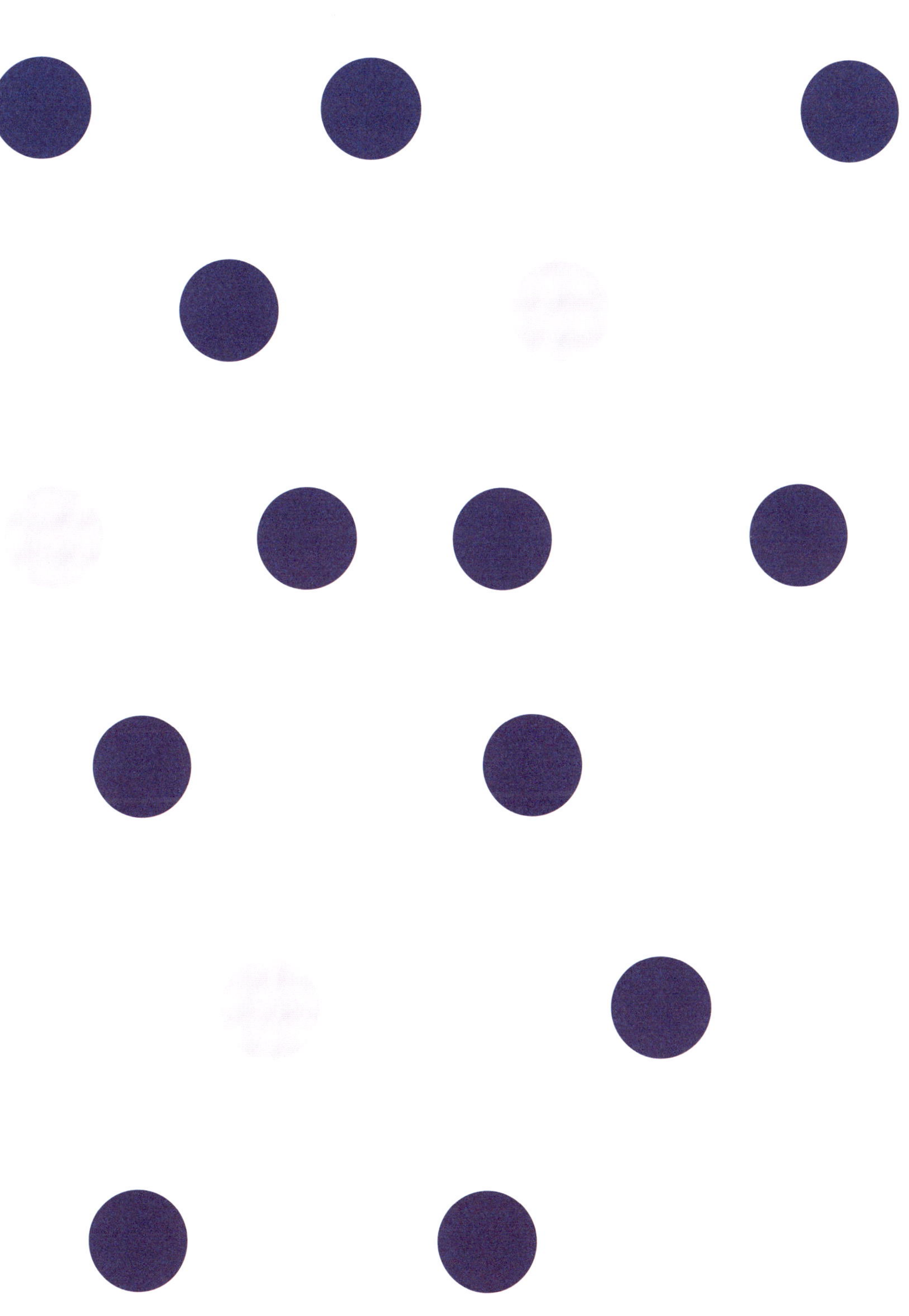

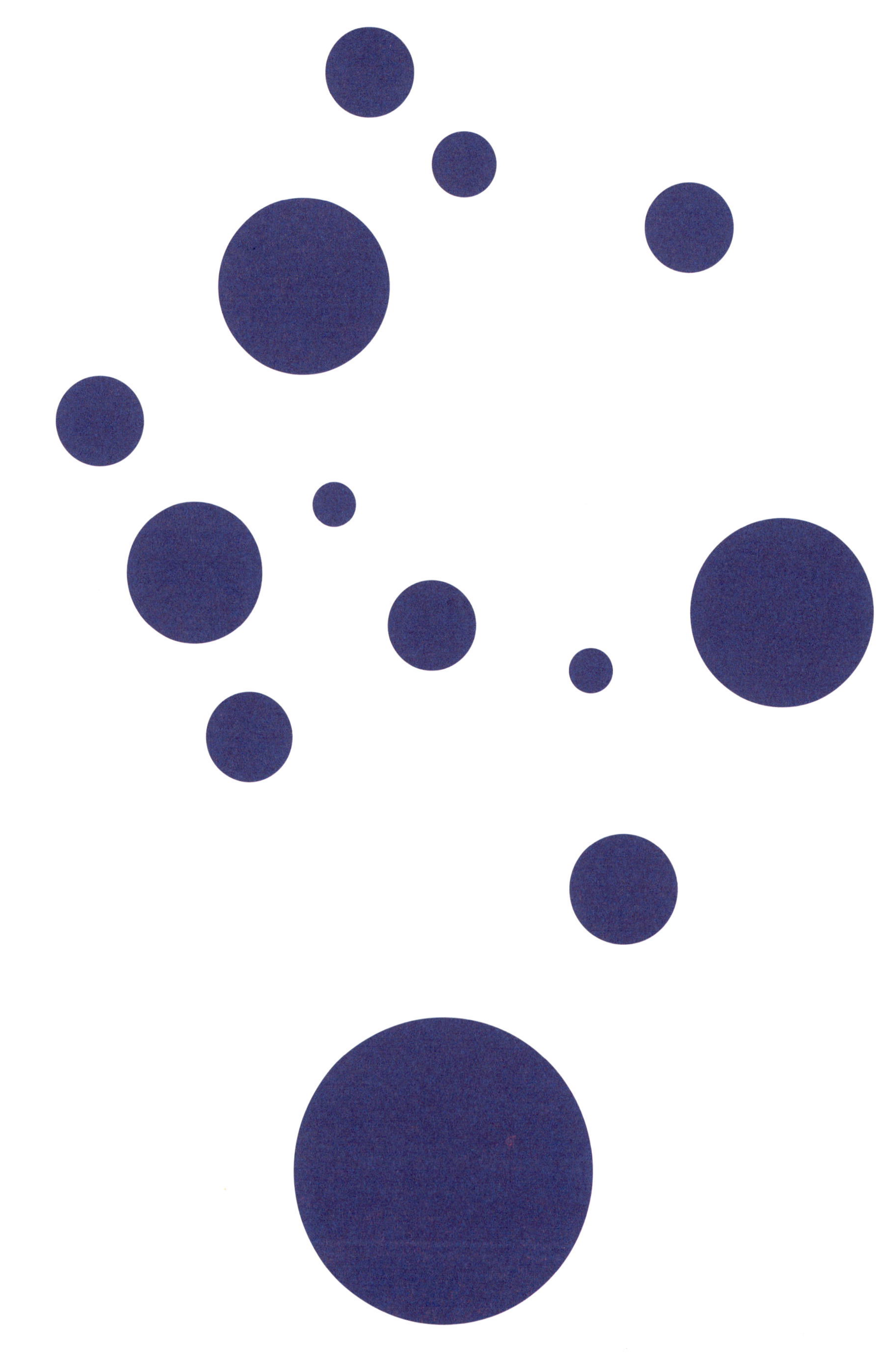

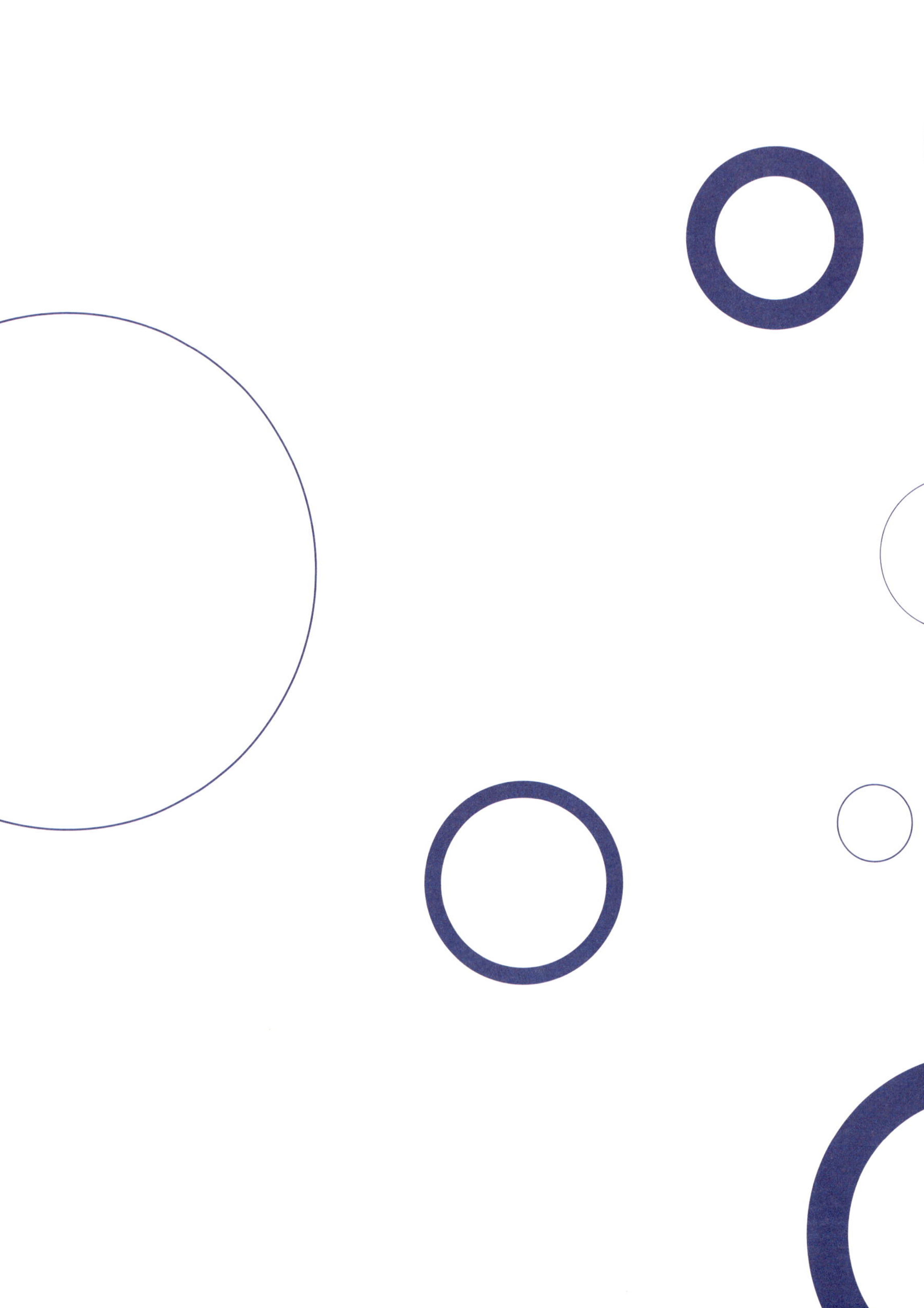

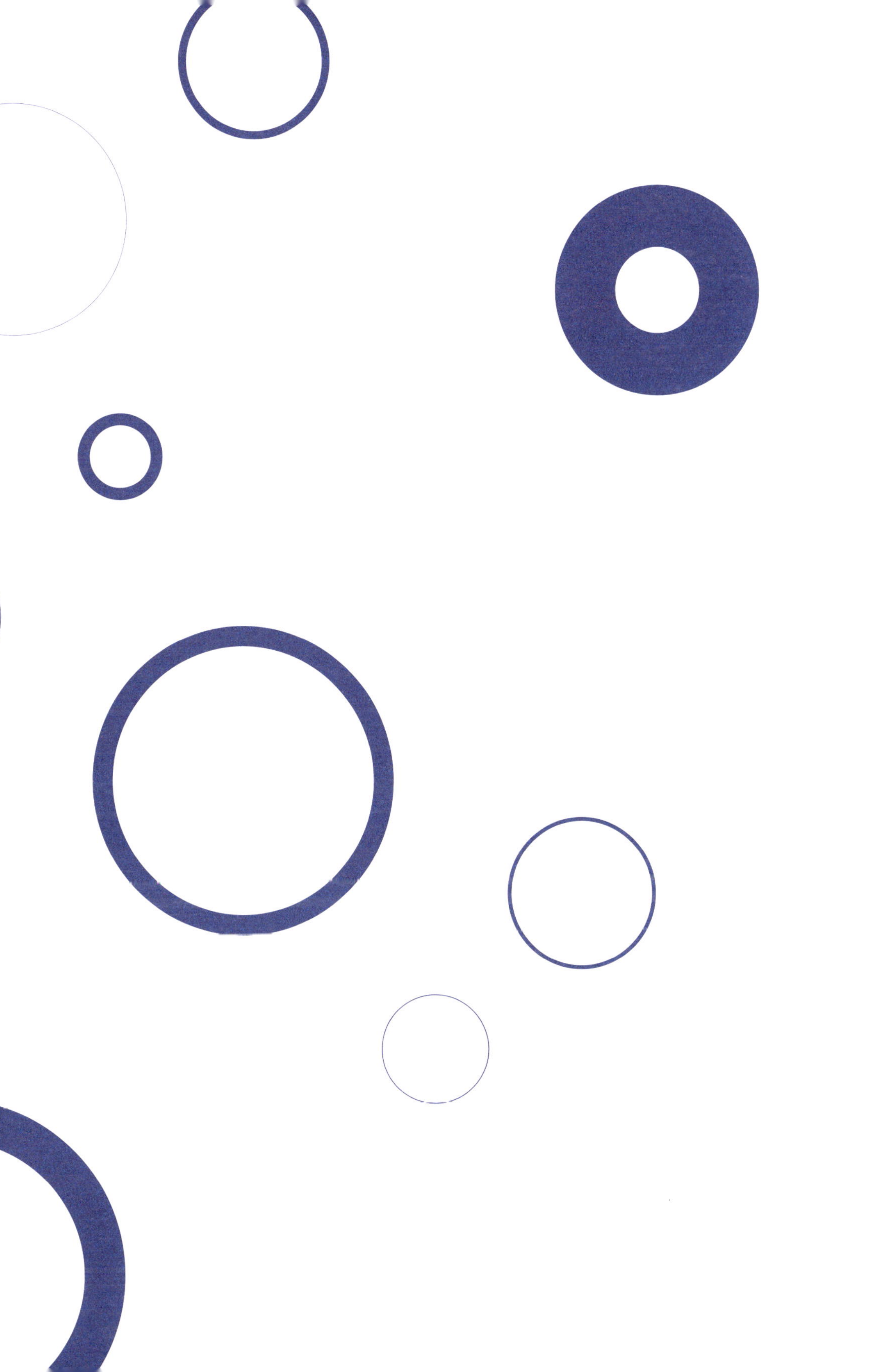

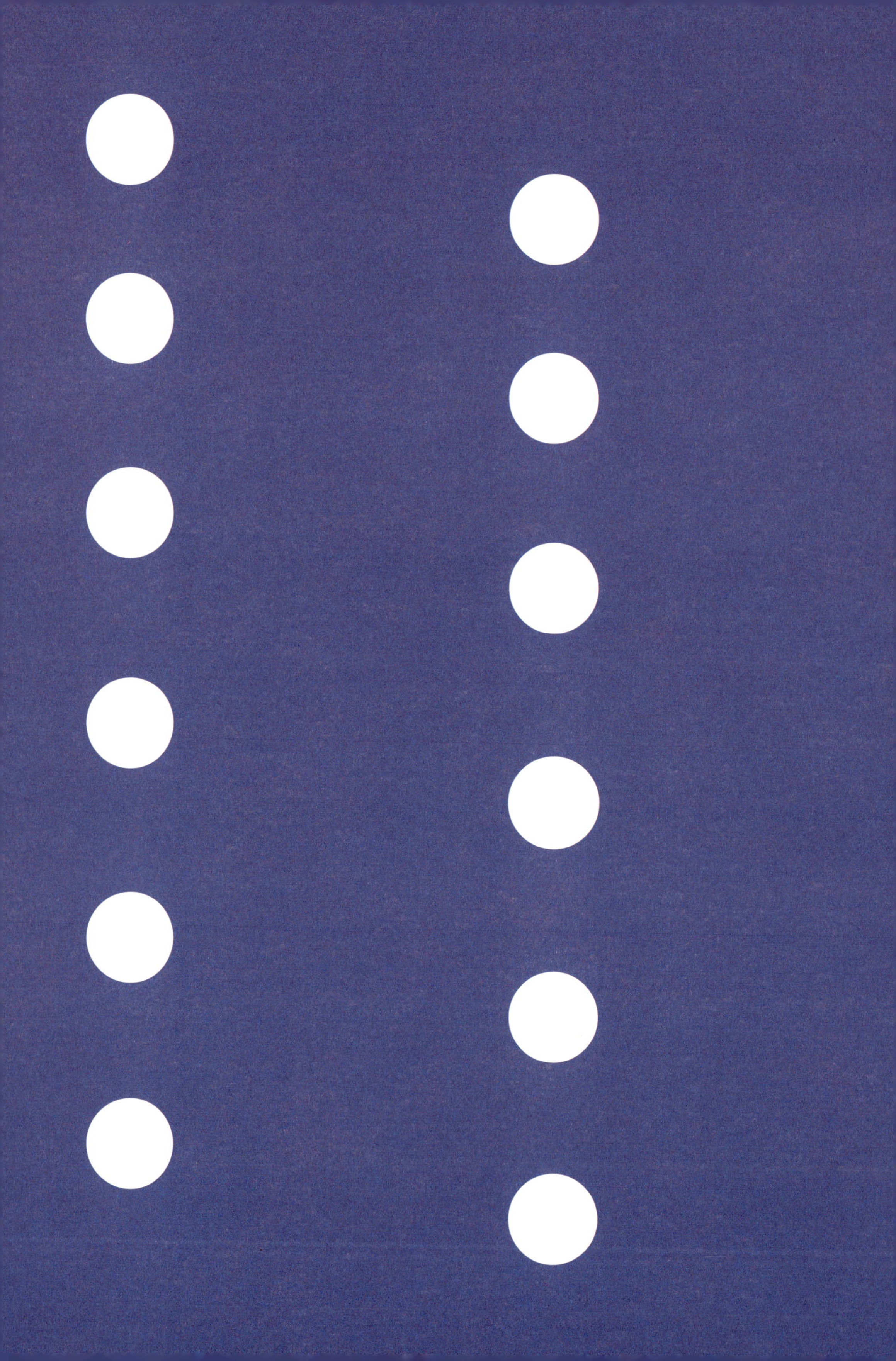

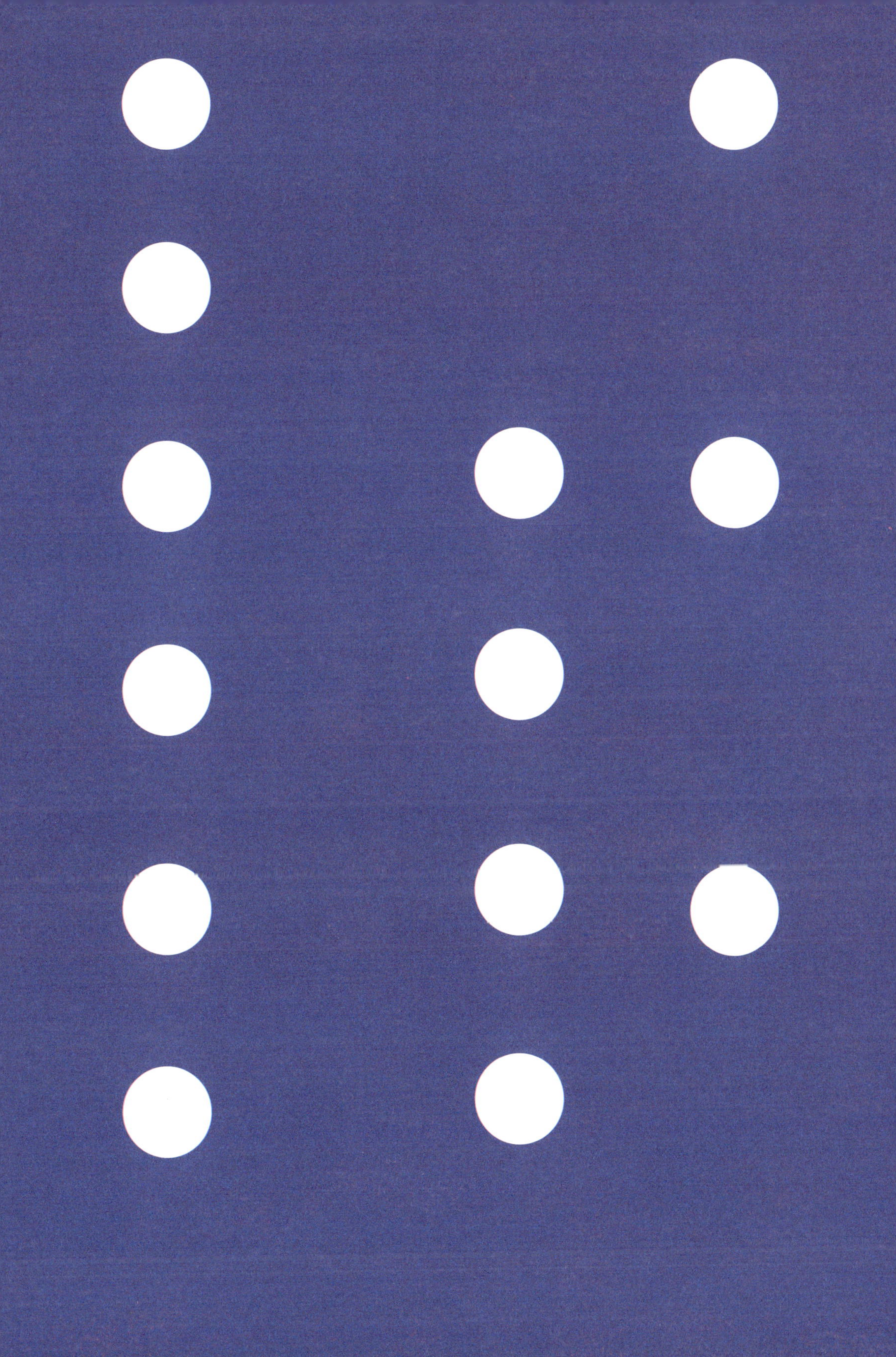

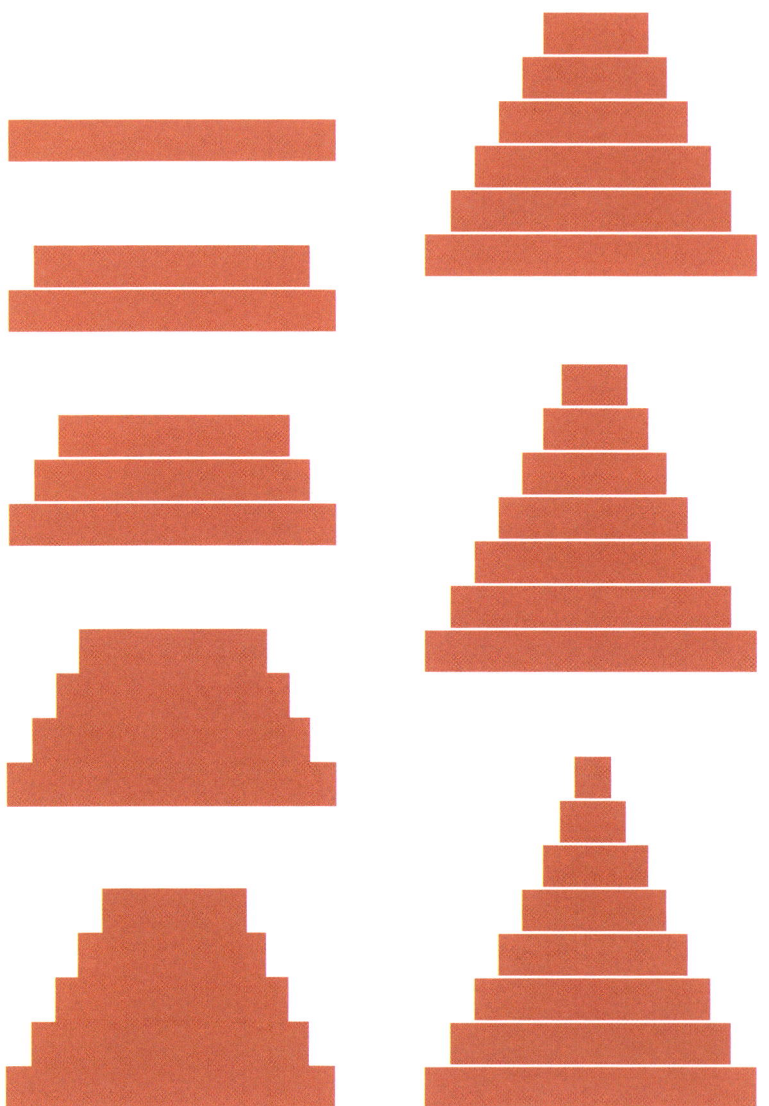

rectangles

These shapes are stacked to create a figure that has negative and positive space. Using color creates pyramids and staircases. Some shapes have white outlines which allows to create more dimension. Overall, it creates a vertical direction of growth as the shapes are smaller and smaller towards the top.

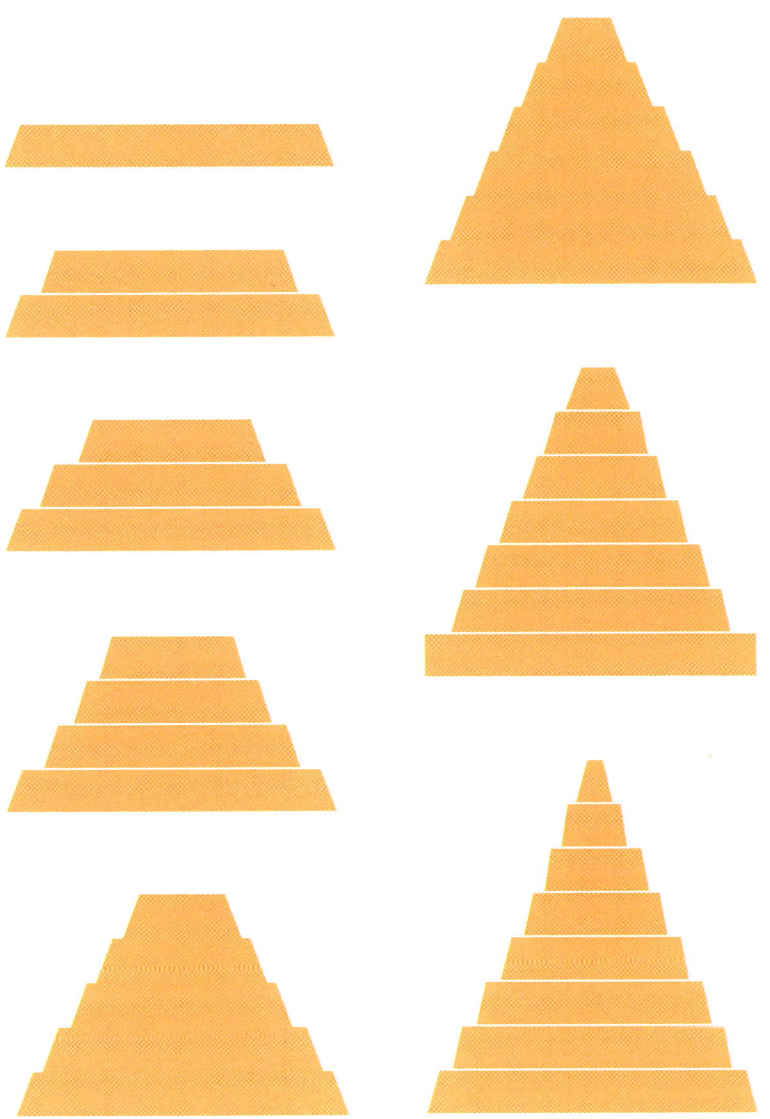

trapeze

Shapes that are being stacked creating piramids and or staircases. Some shapes have white outlines which allows to create more dimension. Overall, it creates a vertical direction of growth as the shapes create angles.

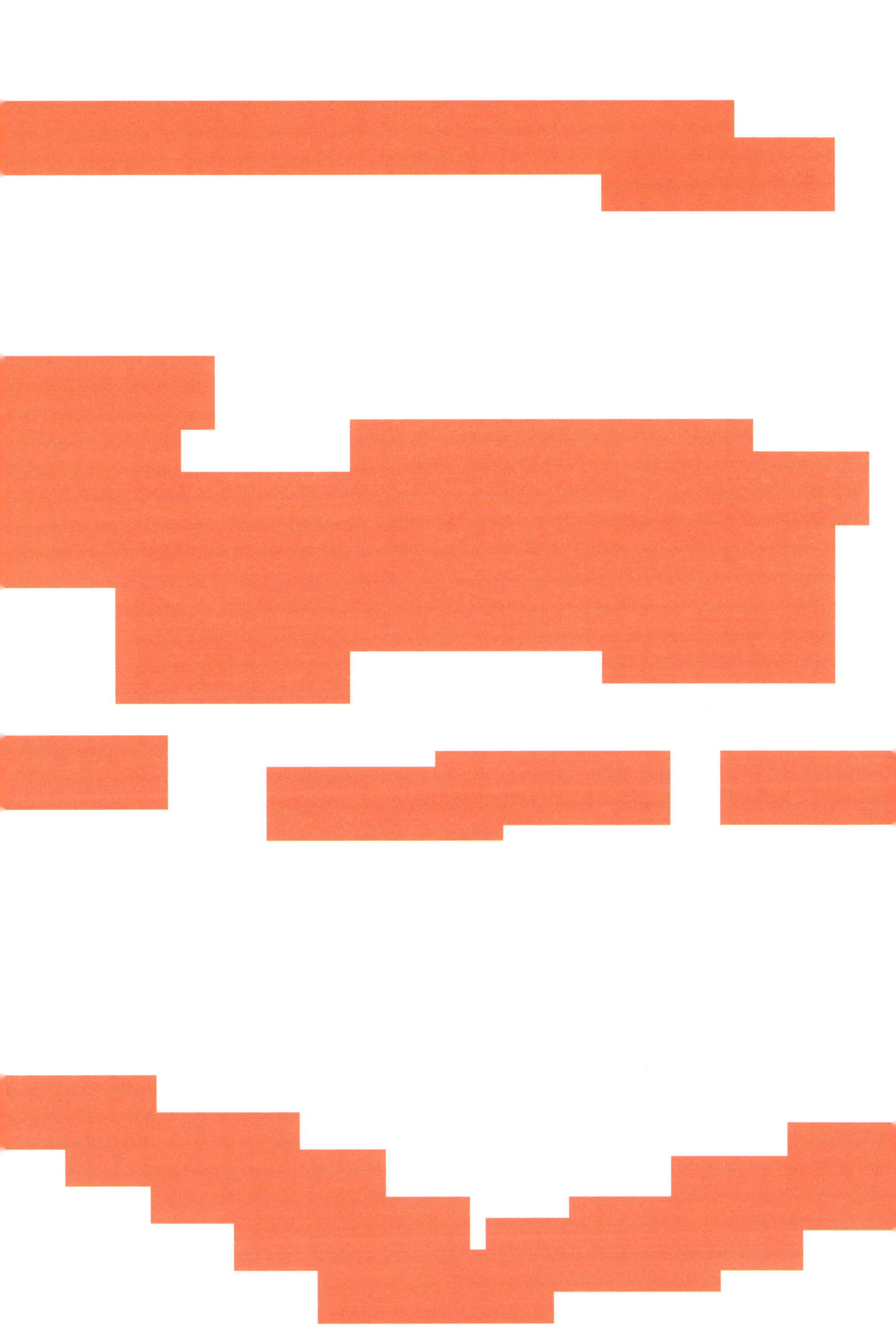

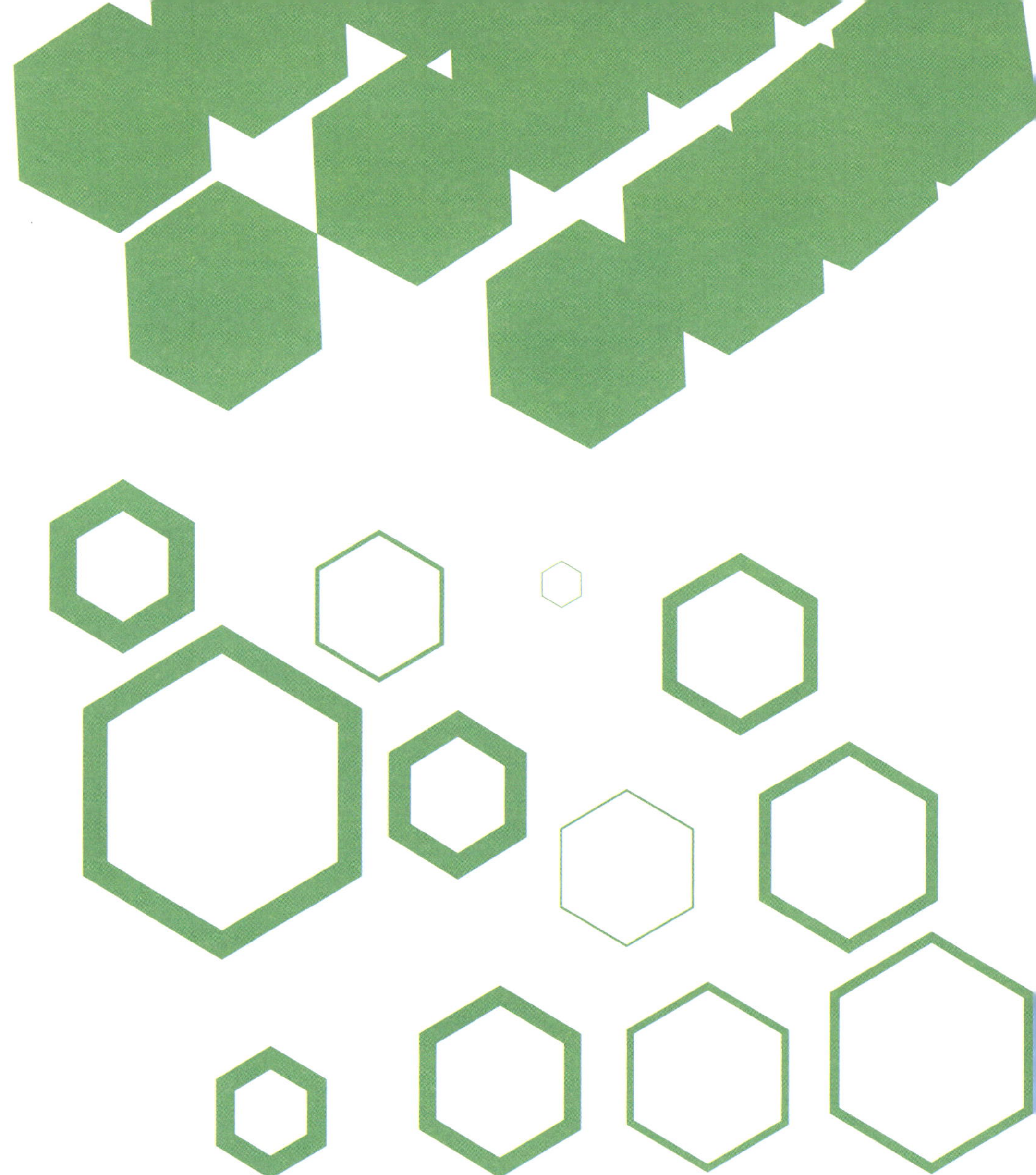

hexagon

This shape has six sides and four of them have angles and two sides are parallel to each other. In nature we can appreciate this in shapes such as honey beehive, bubbles, turtles shells, pineapples skin, etc. Also, hexagons can repeat and create patterns that give an illusion of 3D spaces.

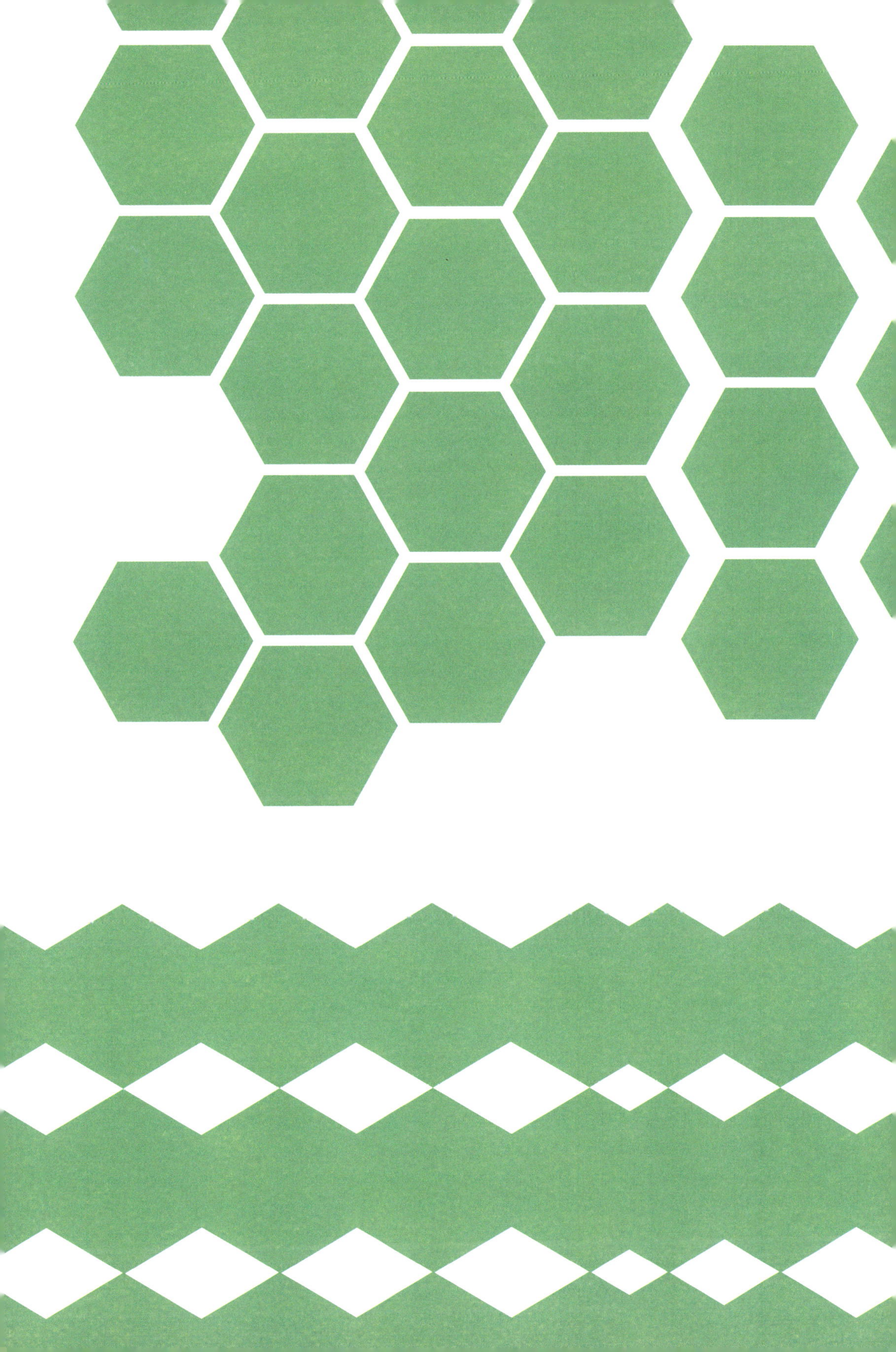

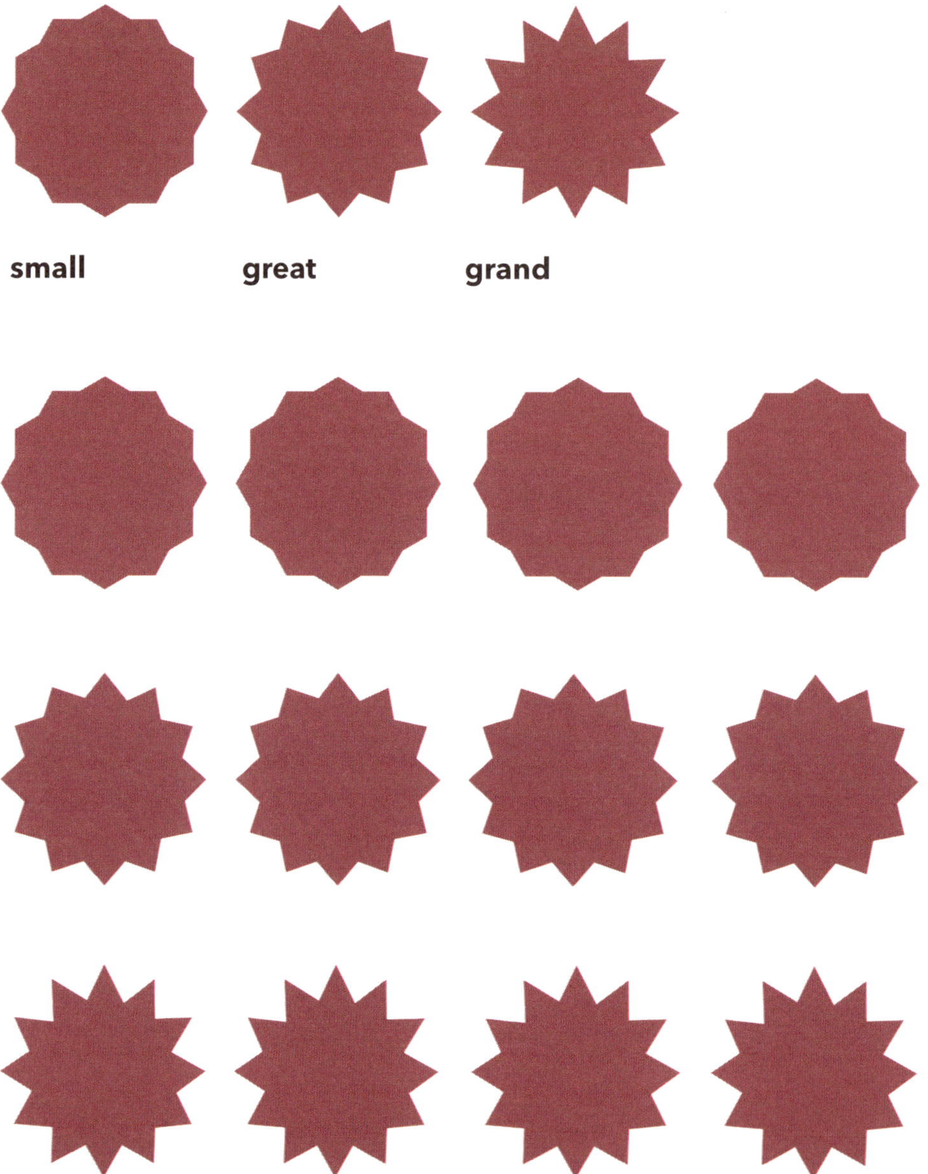

hendecagrams

This shape has eleven sides and there are many variations from small, great and grand as for example above. This shape is only one example of how a polygon can have so many sides and each side activates the space based on distance.

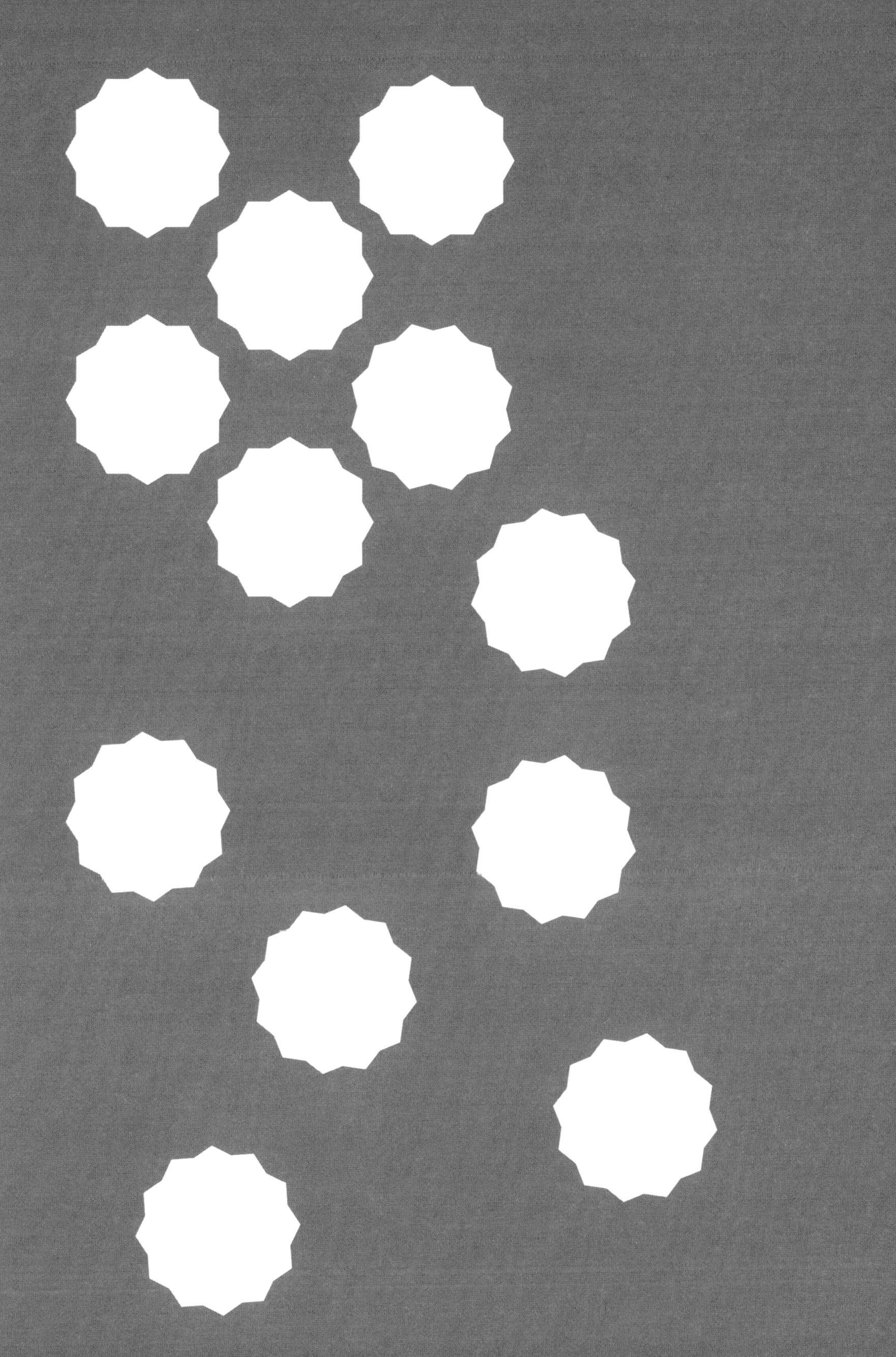

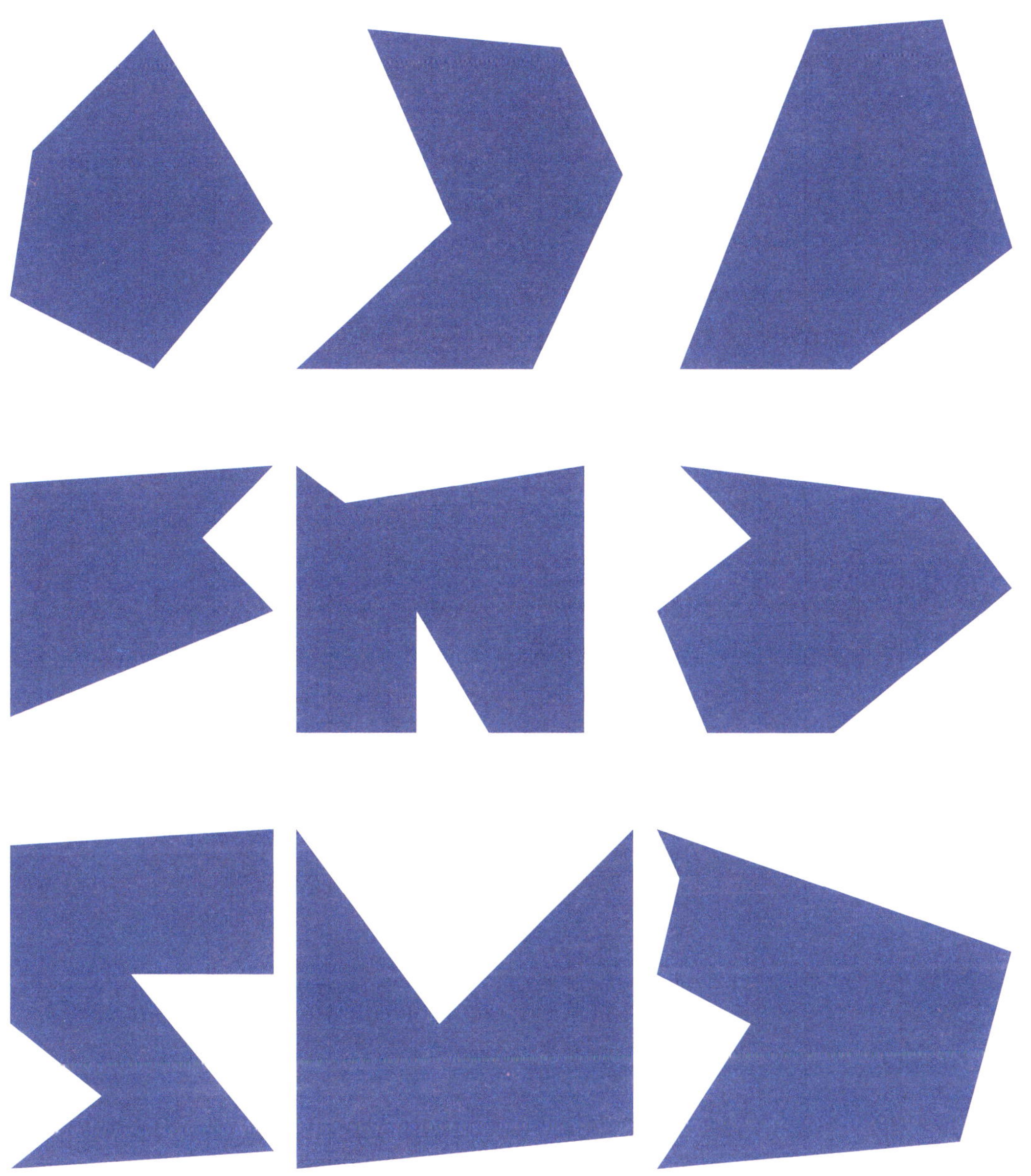

geometric irregular shapes

Shapes that are irregular can create negative and positive spaces of ambiguity and also abstract patterns. In the example above all of the shapes were created with straight lines and angles that are not equal at all.

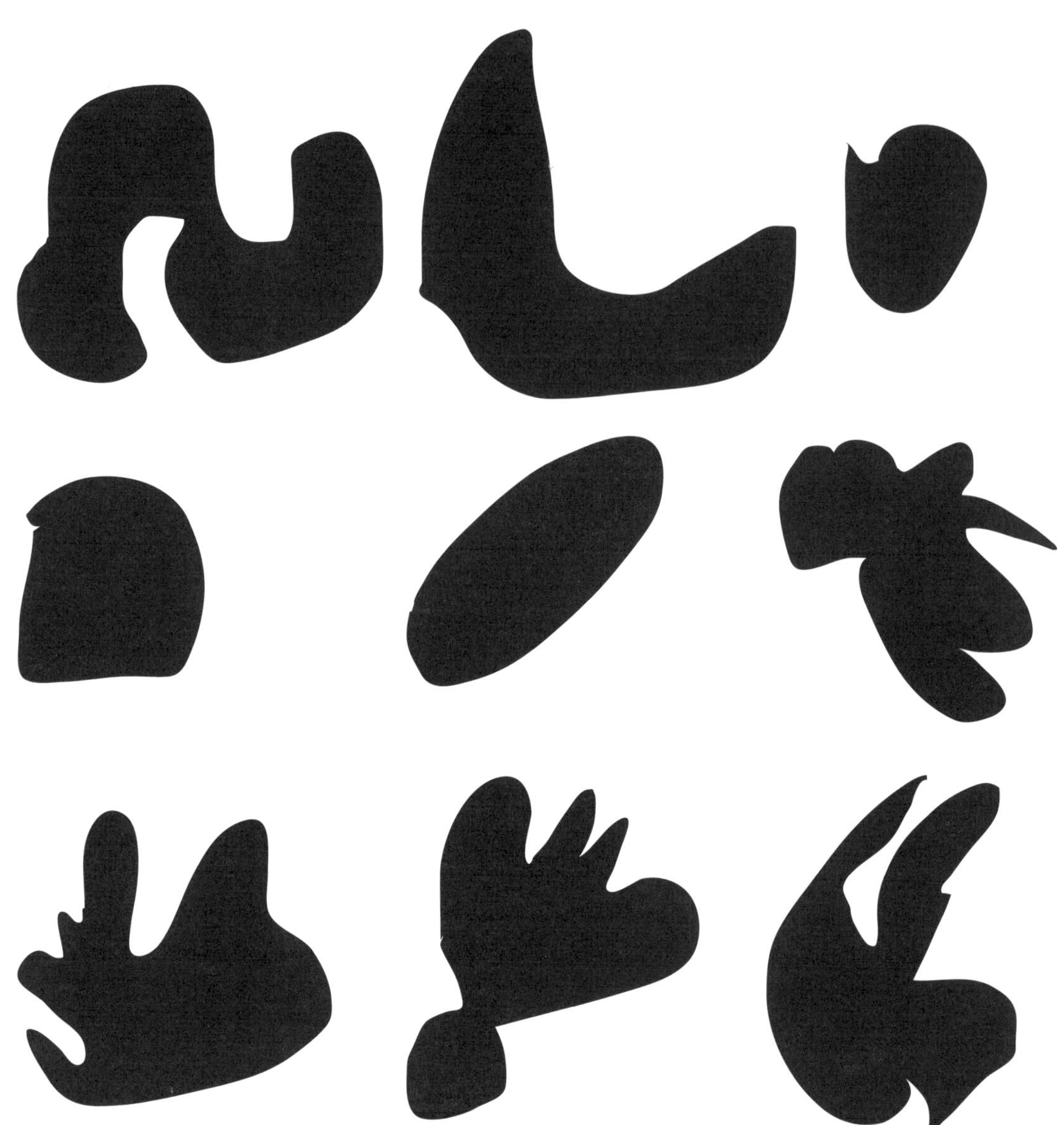

organic shapes

Shapes that are irregular can create spaces of ambiguity and also abstract patterns in many different ways. In the example above all of the shapes have their own particular form.

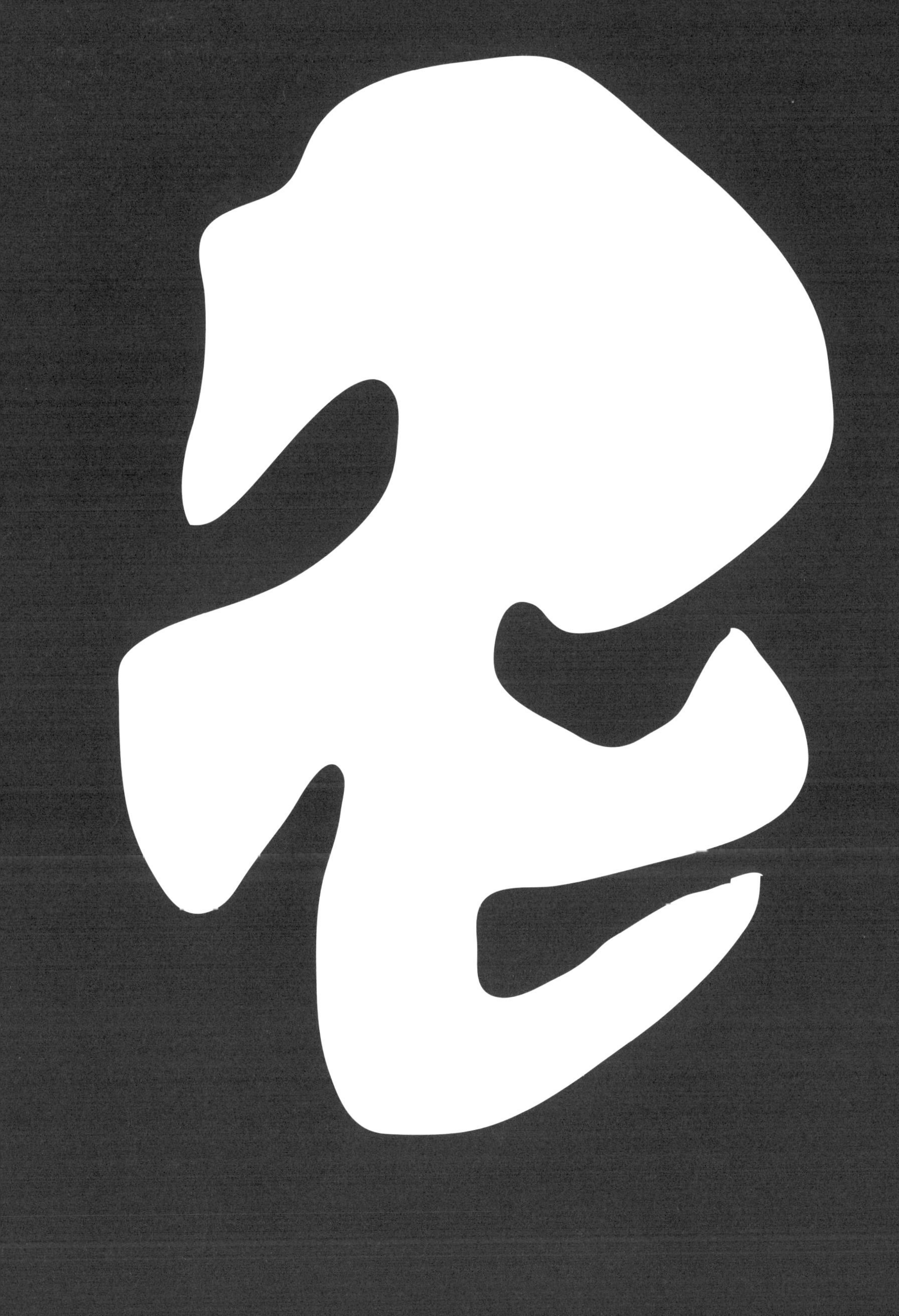

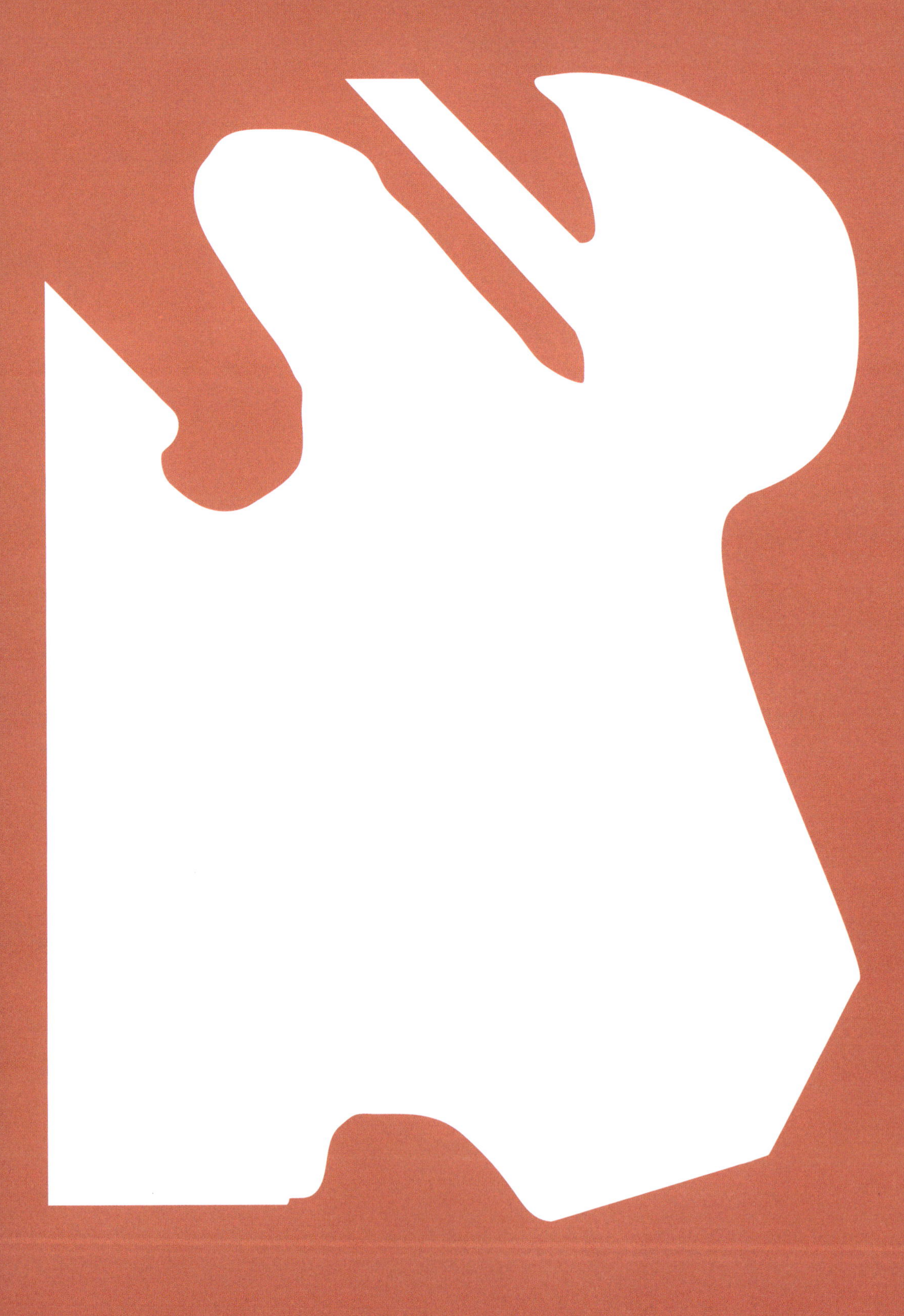

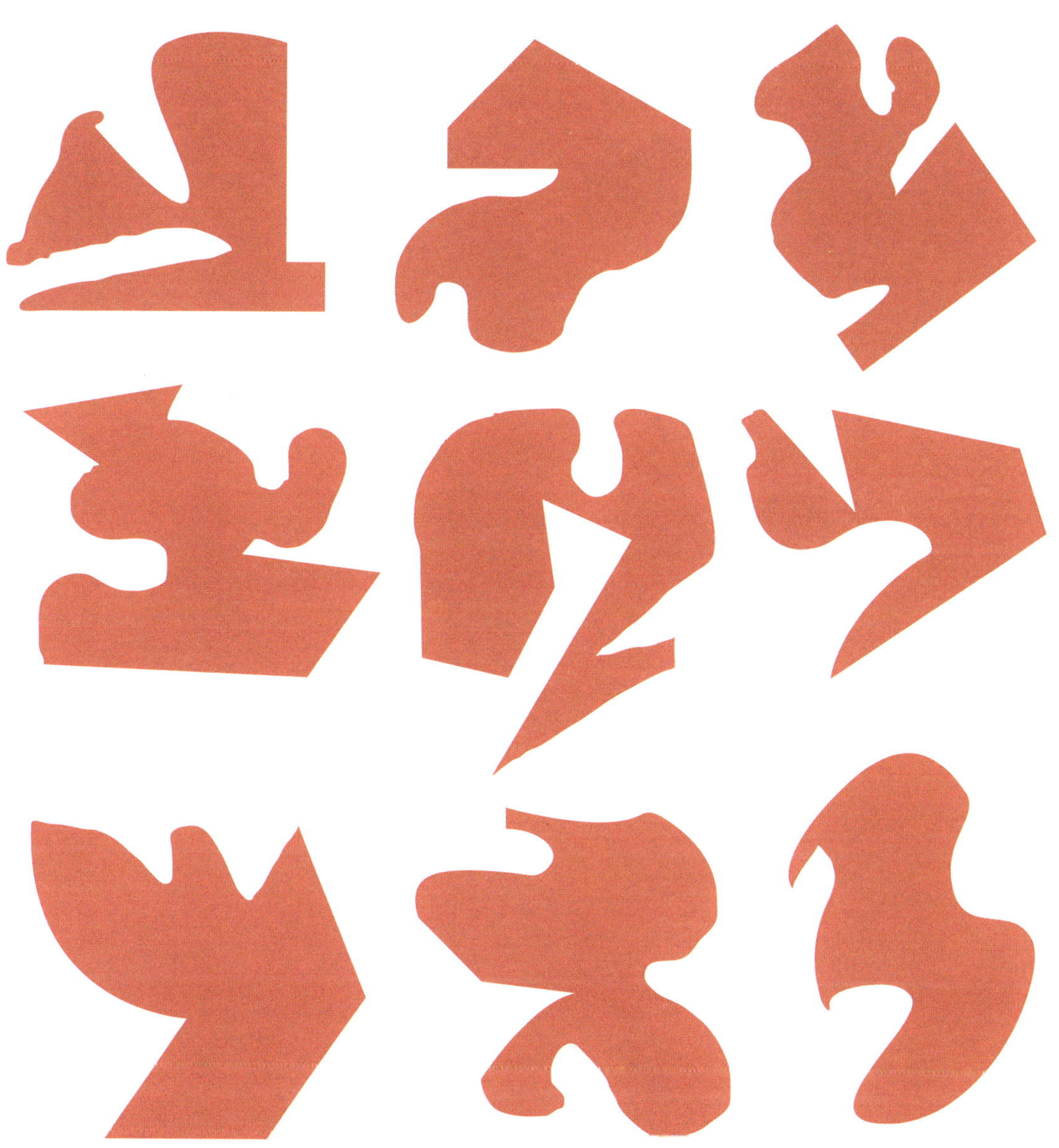

mixed geometric and organic irregular shapes

These shapes create ambiguous spaces and disrupt the uniformity of positive and negative space. These can easily be combined and create more uncertainty.

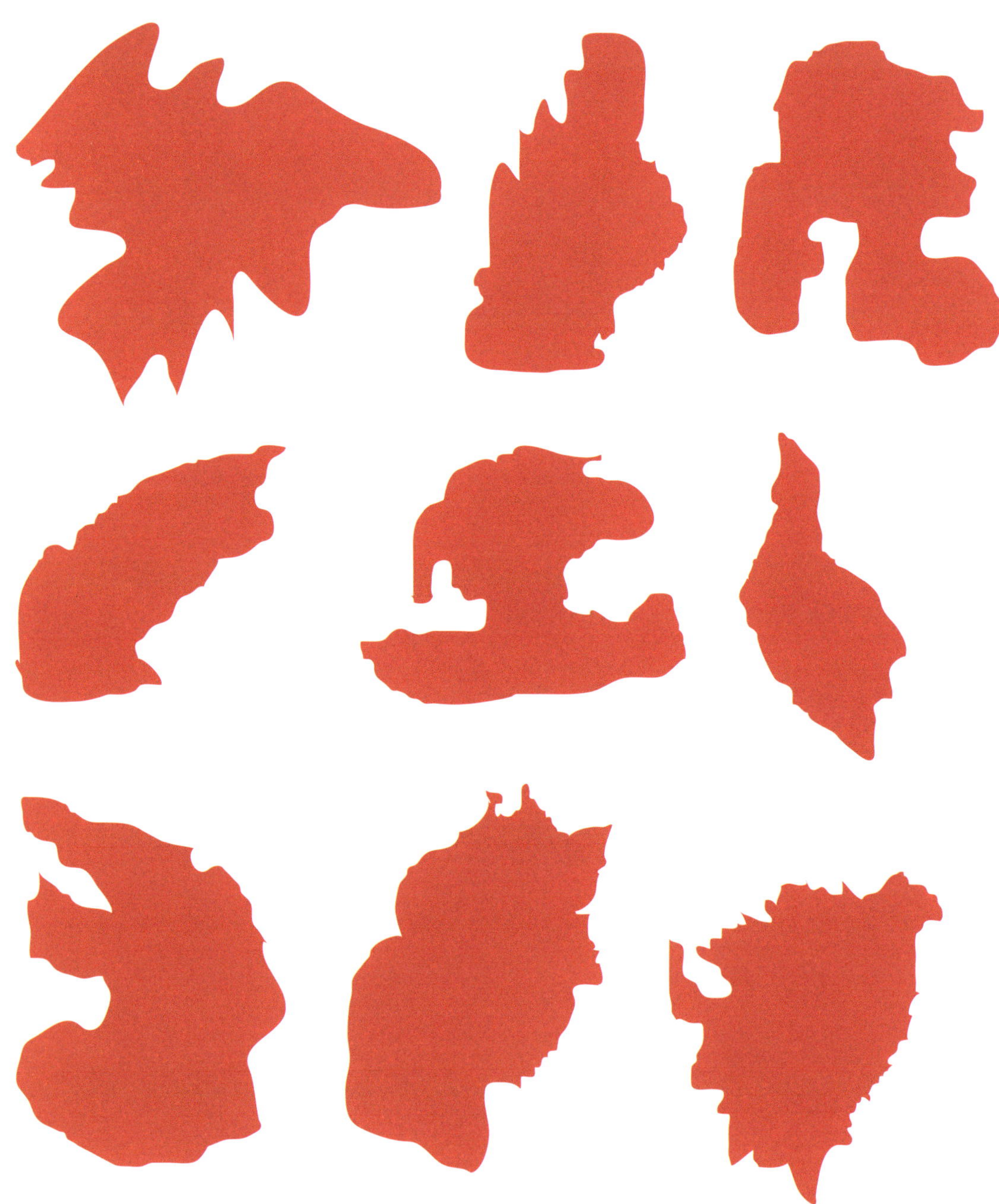

irregular shapes

These shapes cannot be measured in the blink of an eye. Angles, straight lines, curves, etc. are all mixed into the contour of the shape creating complex paths.

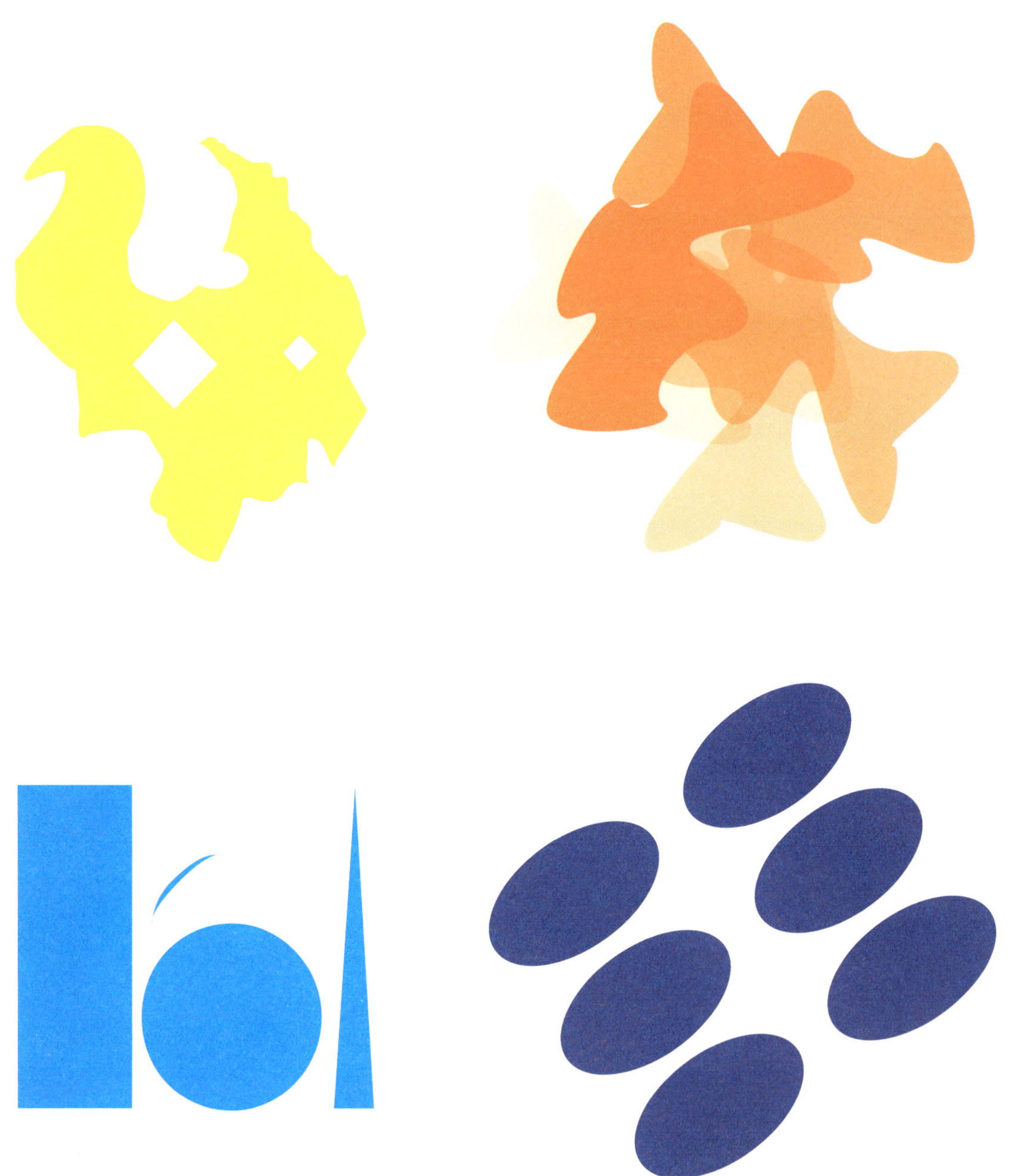

miscellaneous

Positive and negative shapes can create various levels of depth. These include layers and also foreground and background.

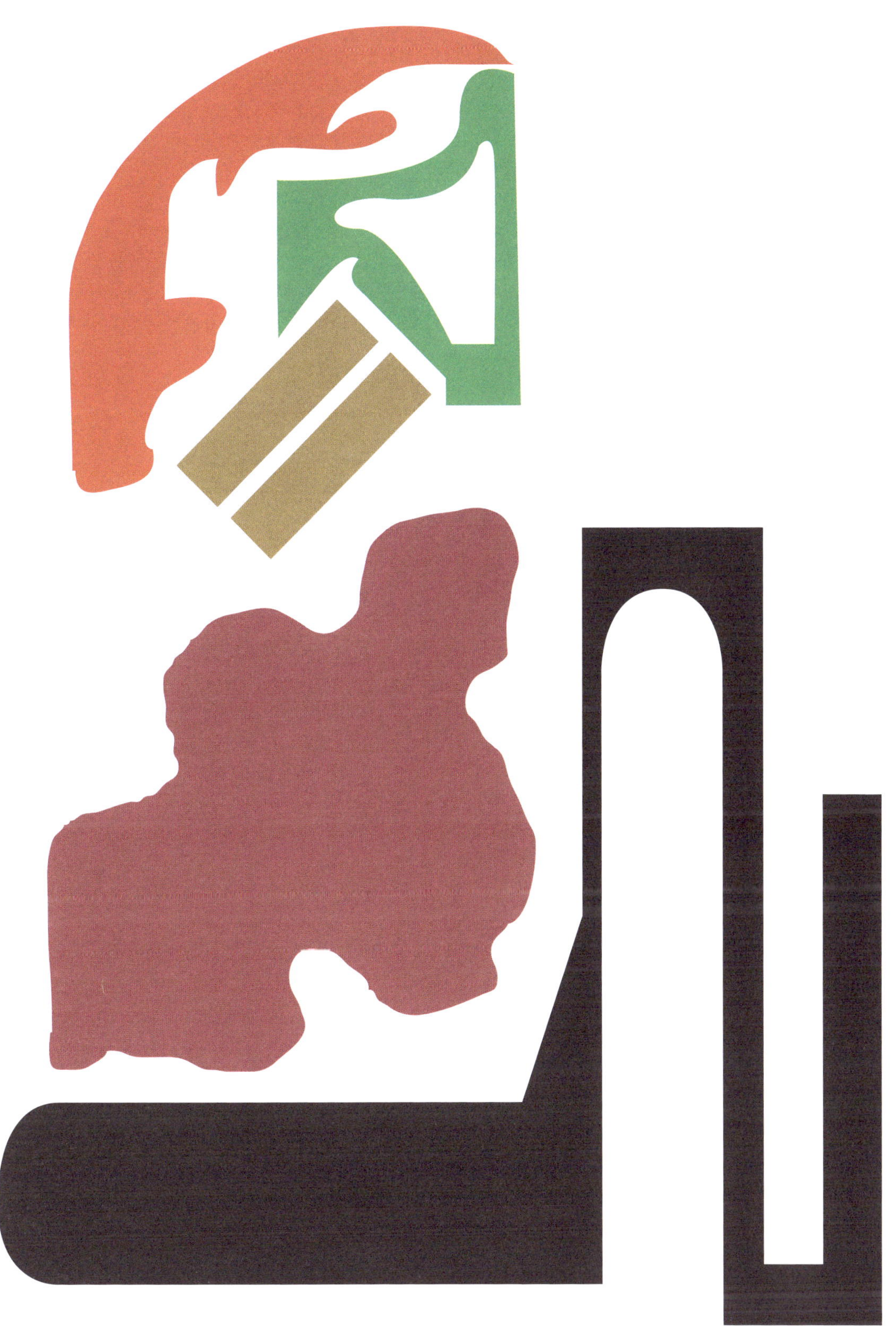

sketch, fold or cut here

exercise

Use this spread to draw, cut, paste, etc. Be inspired to create and design or take notes. Please feel free to use the space below as a canvas or a sketchbook.

sketch, fold or cut here

I COMPOSITION

2. systematic

The main structure is the organization of grids. There are many types of grids that a designer can work with in a space. This chapter presents examples for a broad range of options using grid, from basic modular arrangements to the complex layering of grids. Also, modularity is most important, but the chapter also shows other options and alternatives. This type of organization is cyclical, can be repeated according to the content, and should be easy to grasp. Meanwhile, Chapter 3 (Spontaneity) and Chapter 4 (Order and Disorder) explore more sporadic structures that also concentrate on destructuring.

Varying how the grid gets activated or deactivated is important to align content to the grid. The grid can have vertical rows and can go up to an unlimited number of rows and columns based on the medium and the format of the work.

Effectiveness in interconnecting forms of content is what leads to the successful outcome of a message, whether it is a simple abstract message or a complex set of messages. Overall, understanding structural spaces and refining the content is essential to this practice.

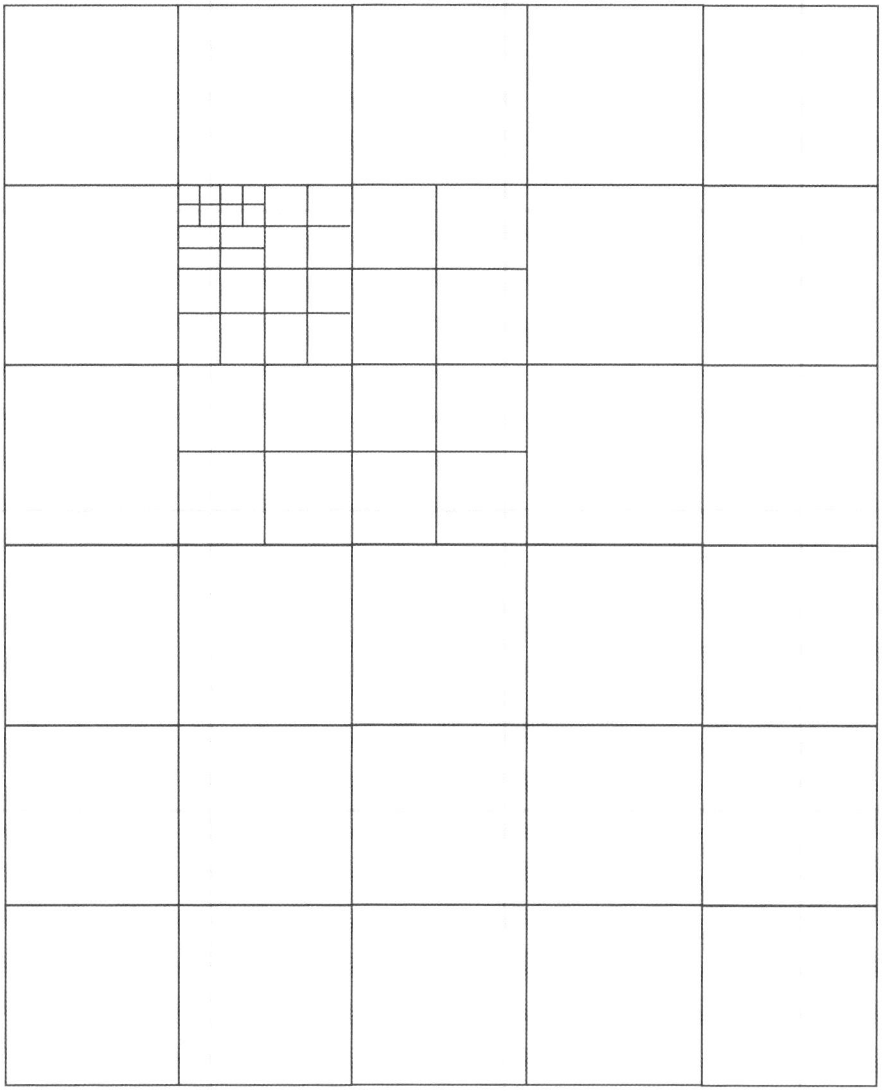

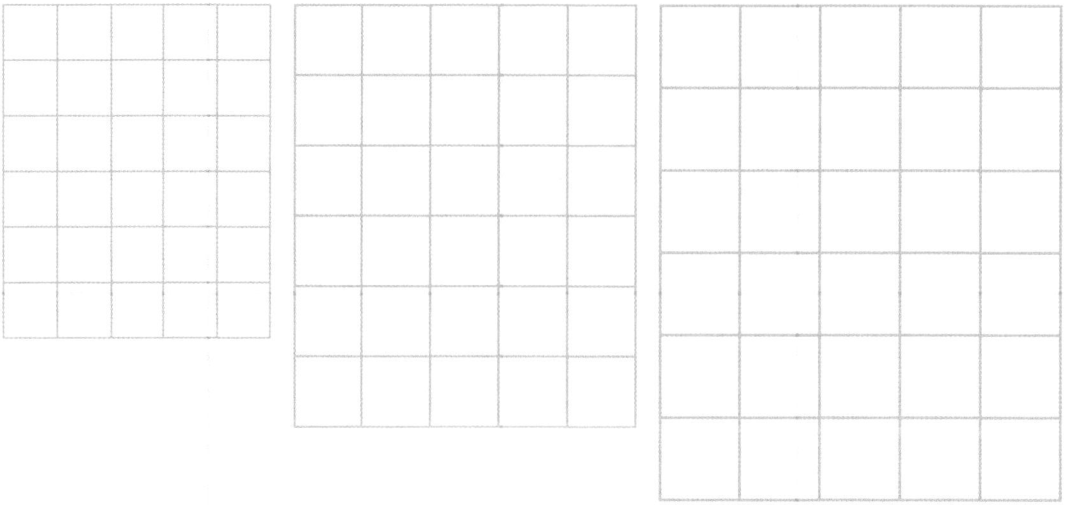

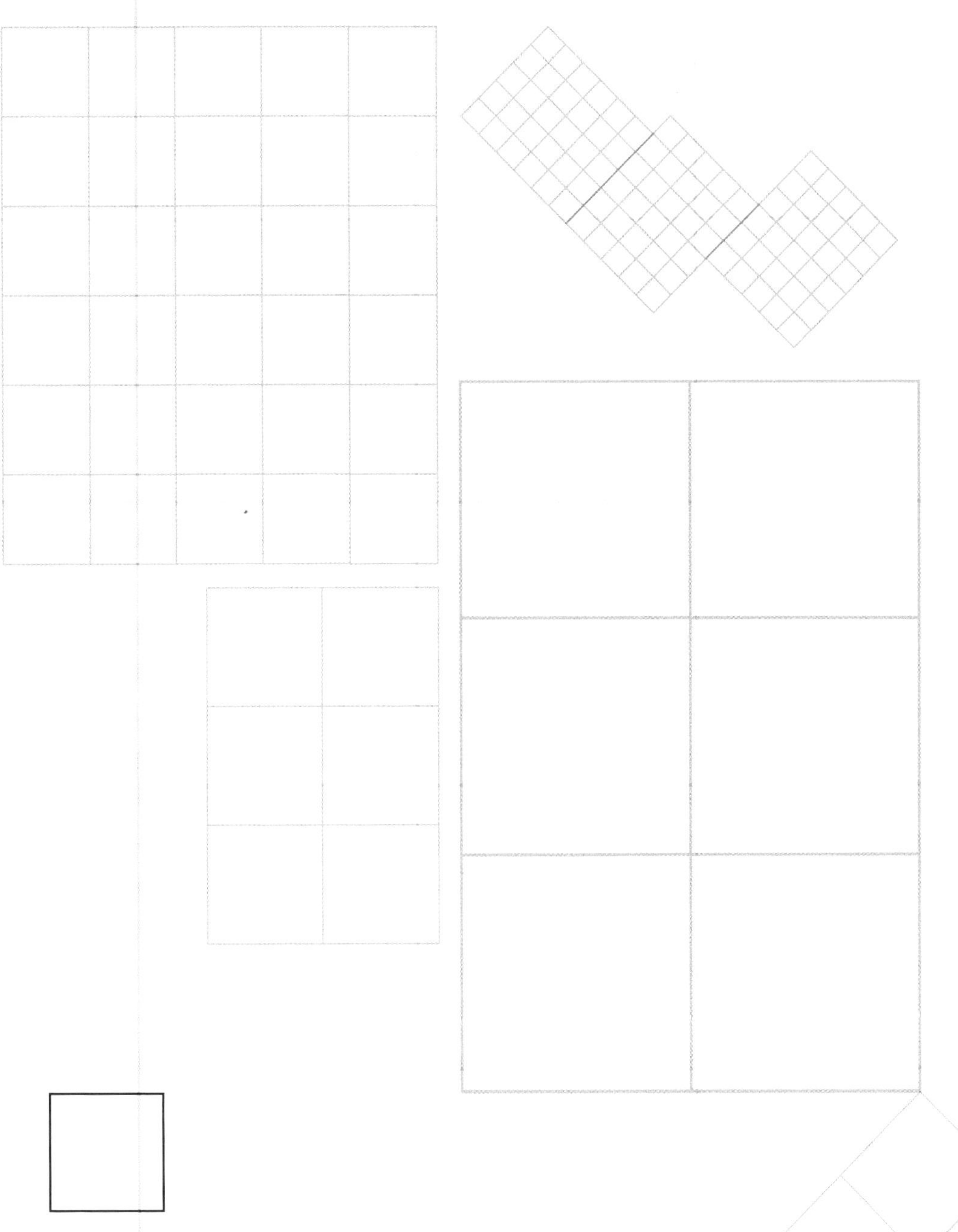

grids within grids

Examples of modular grids that are overlapping, creating other levels of organization that can be helping adjust scale, proportion, and rotation in these examples. This is a great way to explore and create other levels of grids.

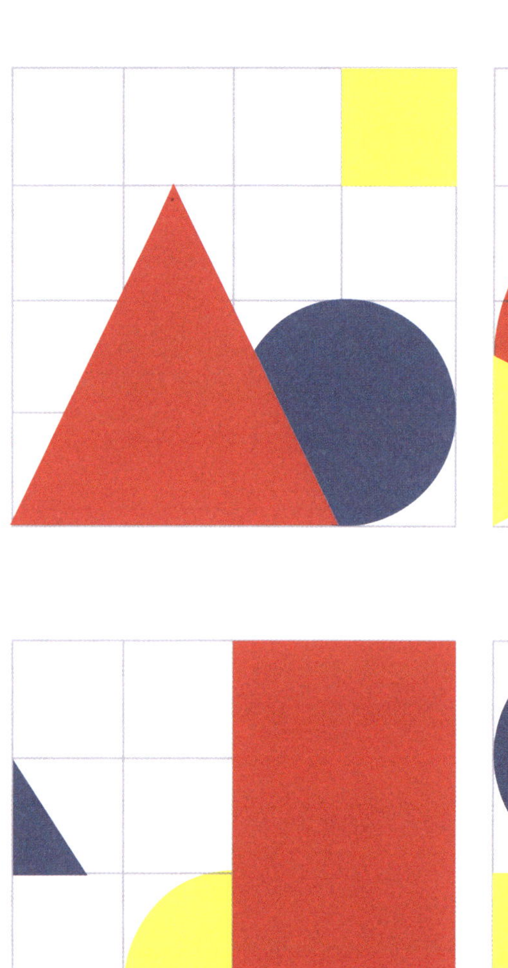
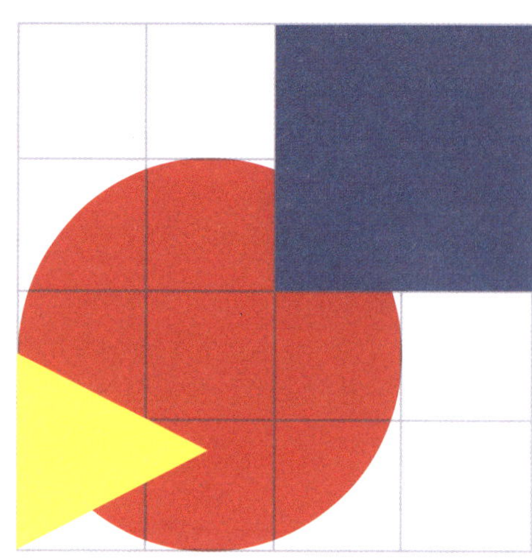
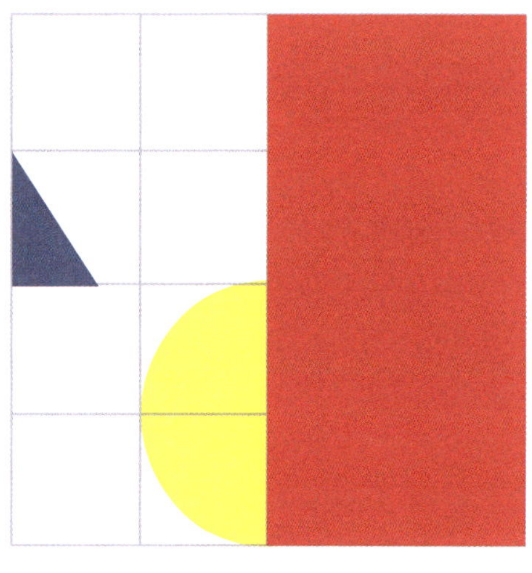
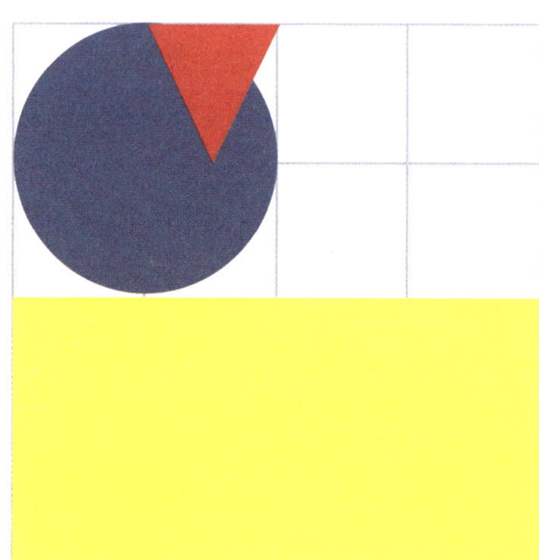
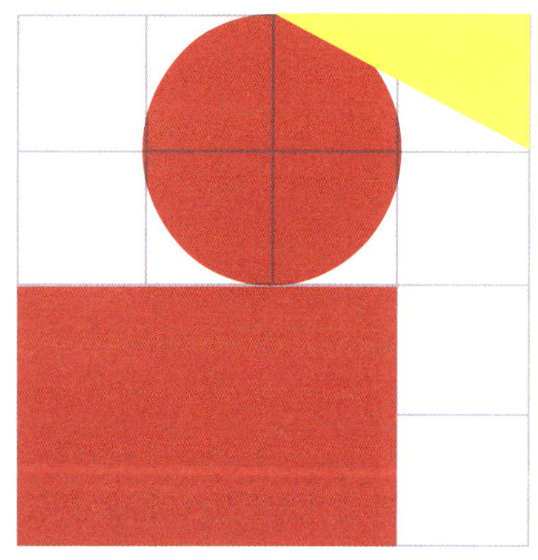
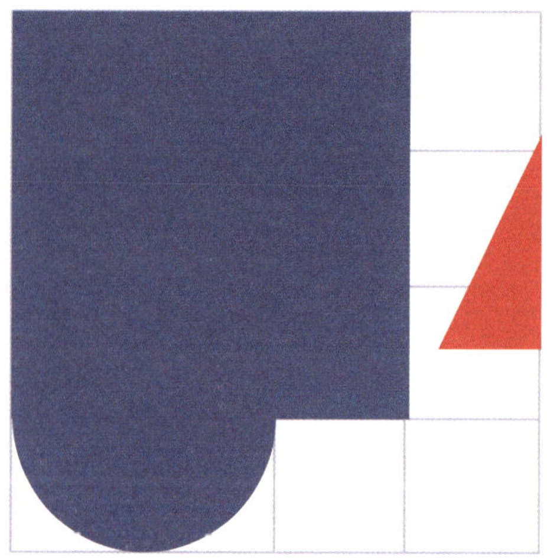

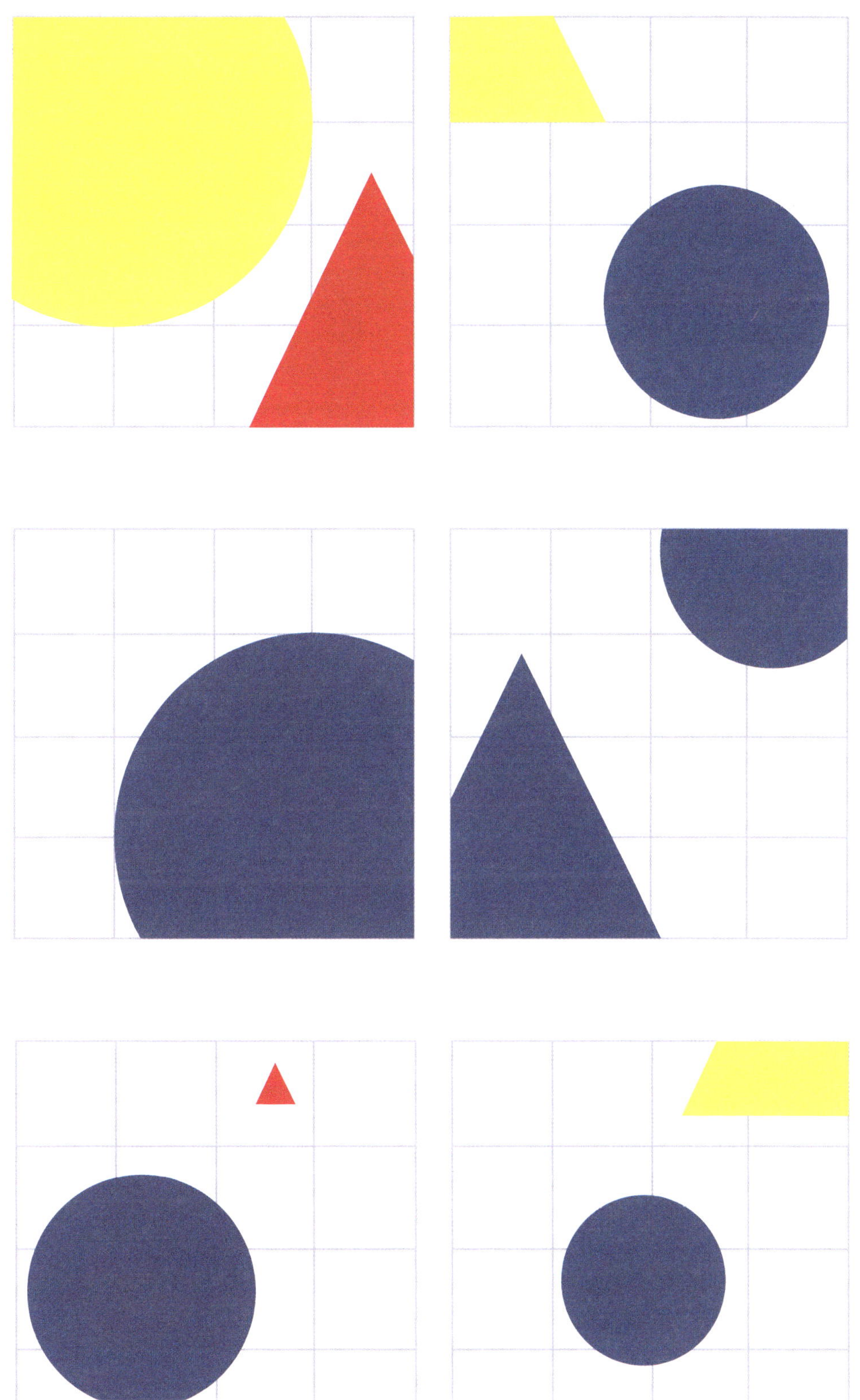

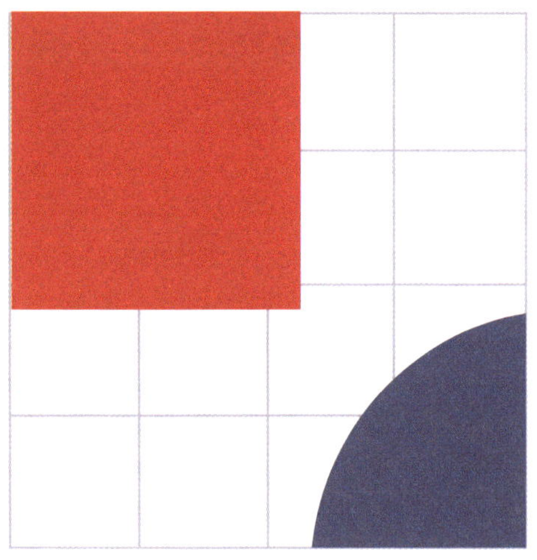
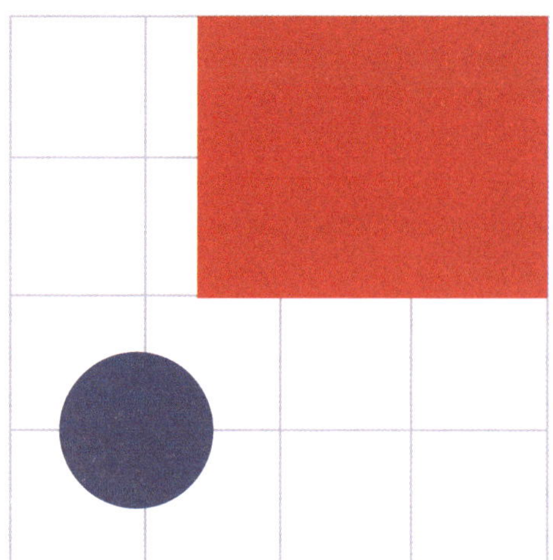
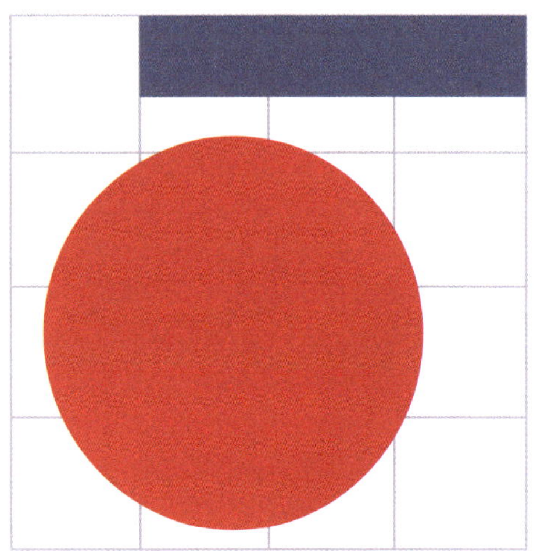
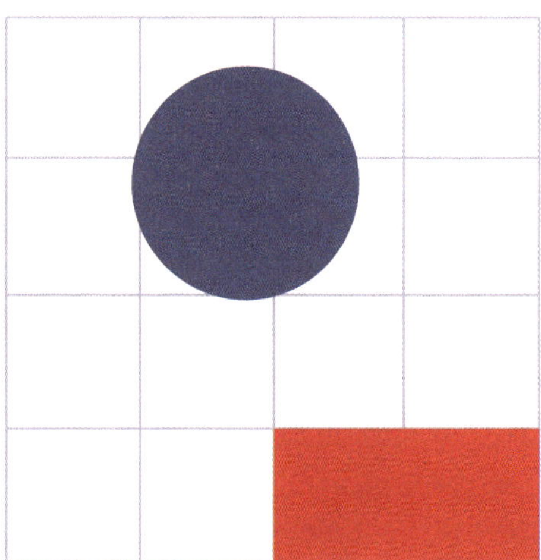

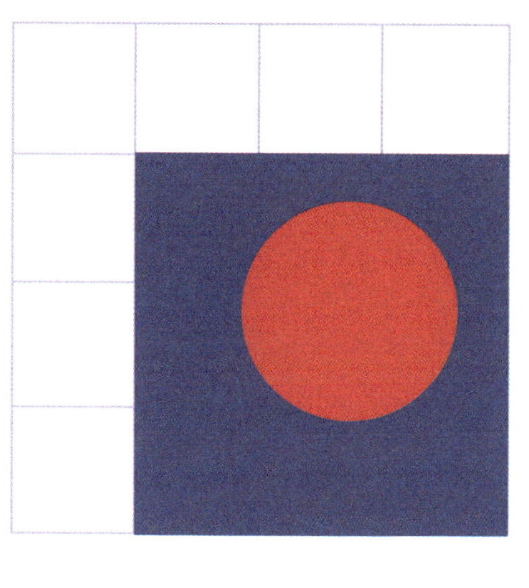
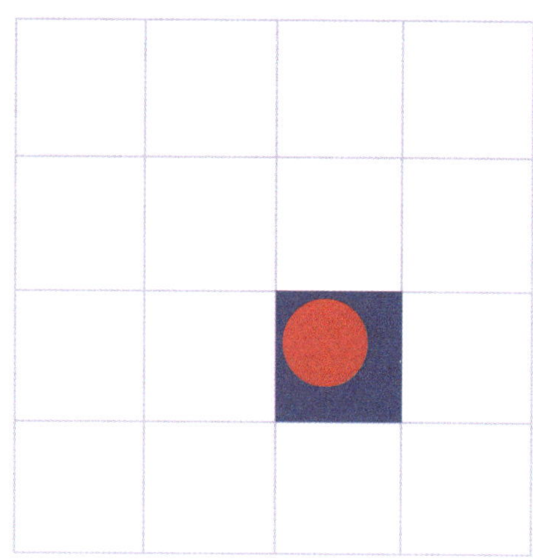

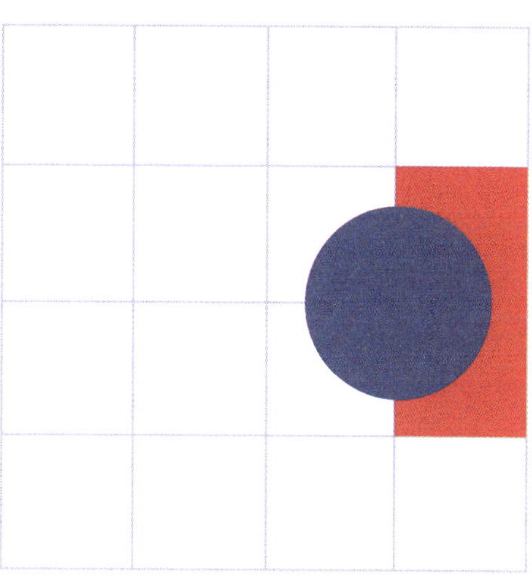
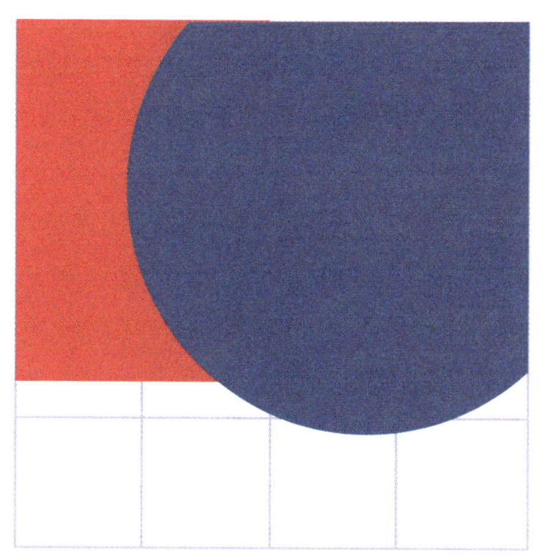
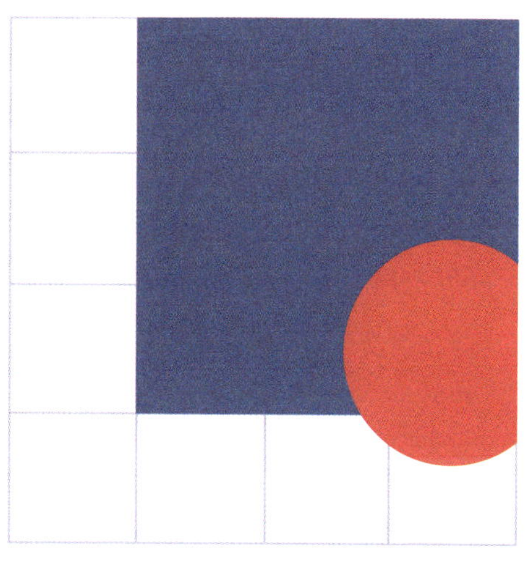

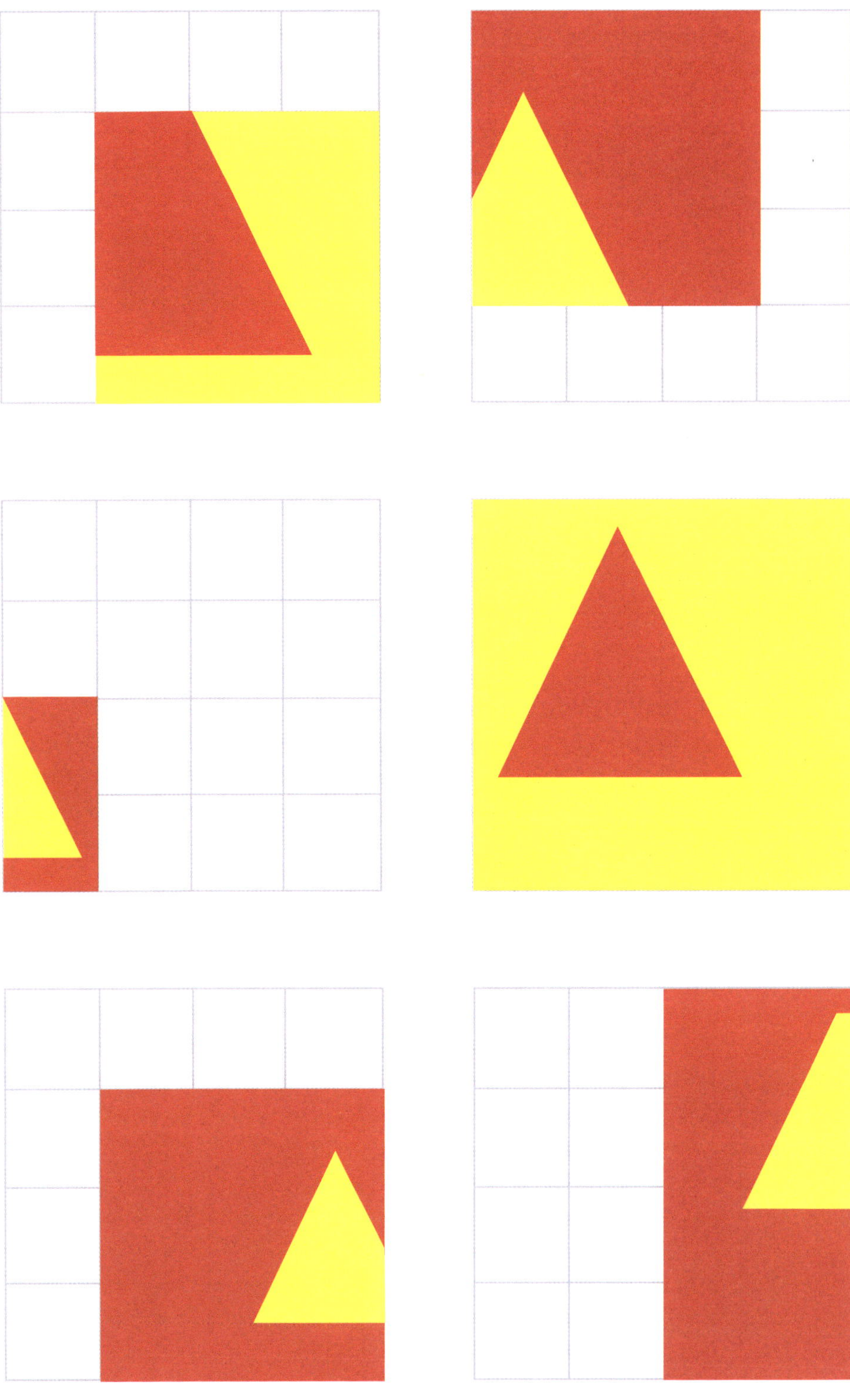

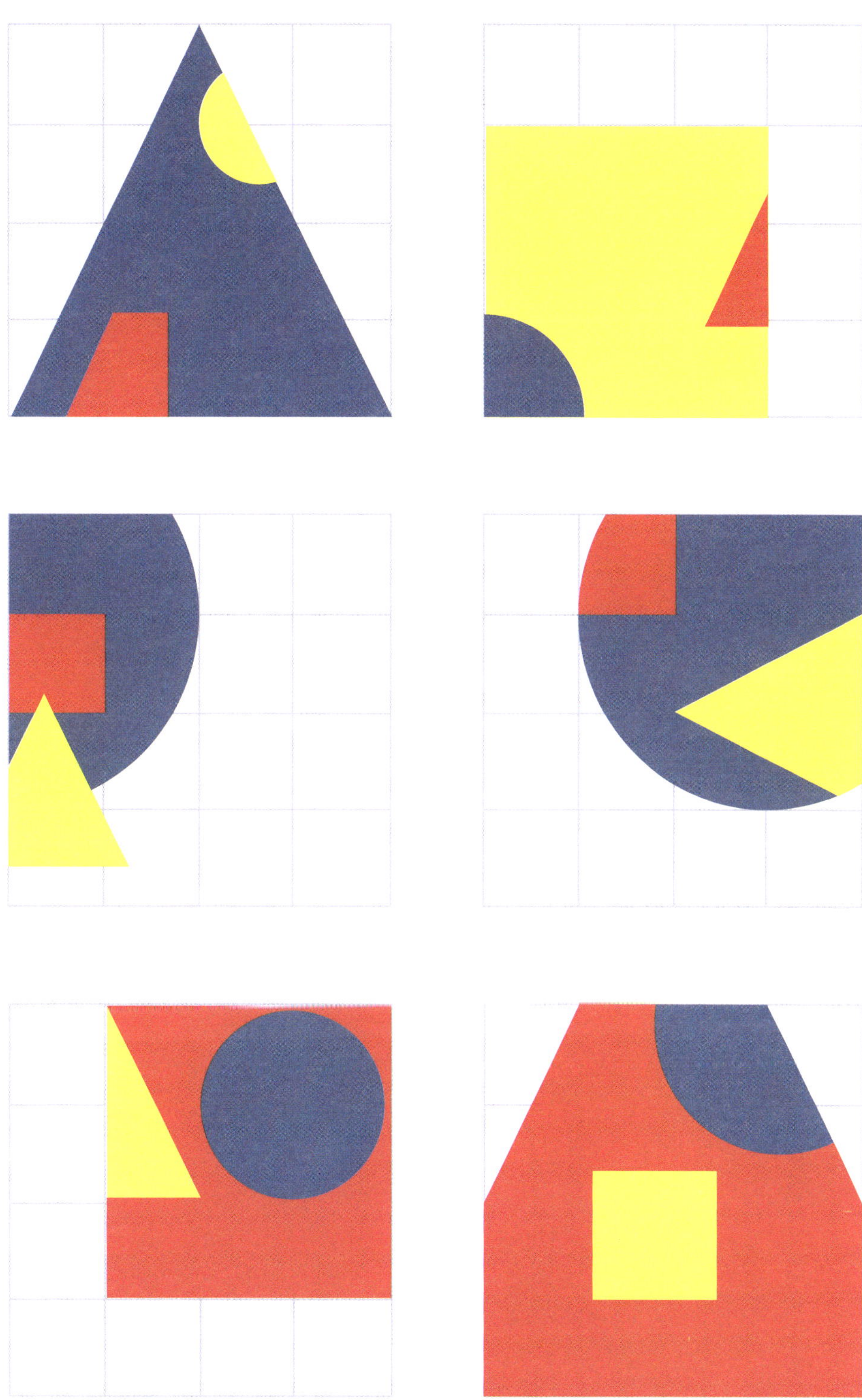

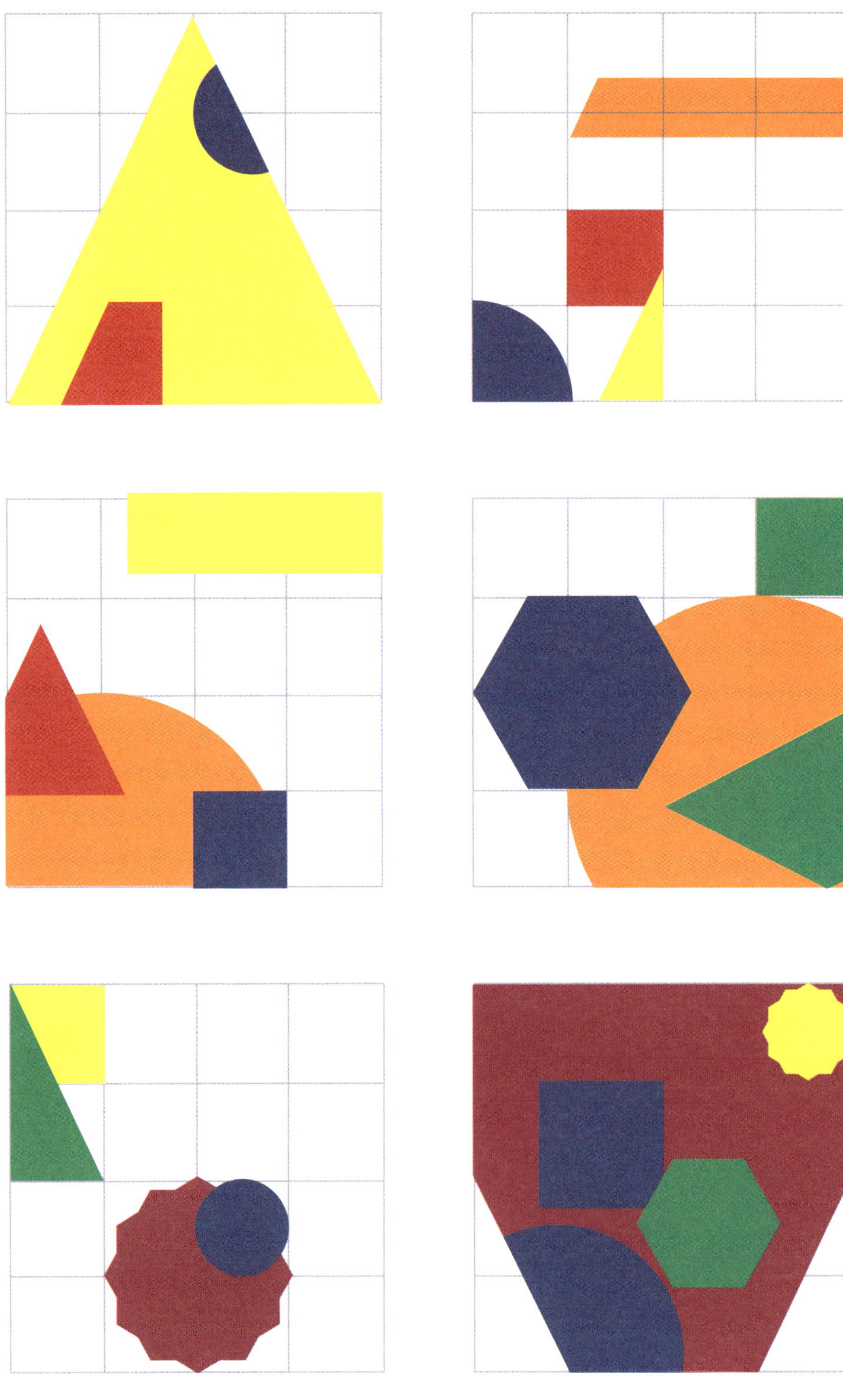

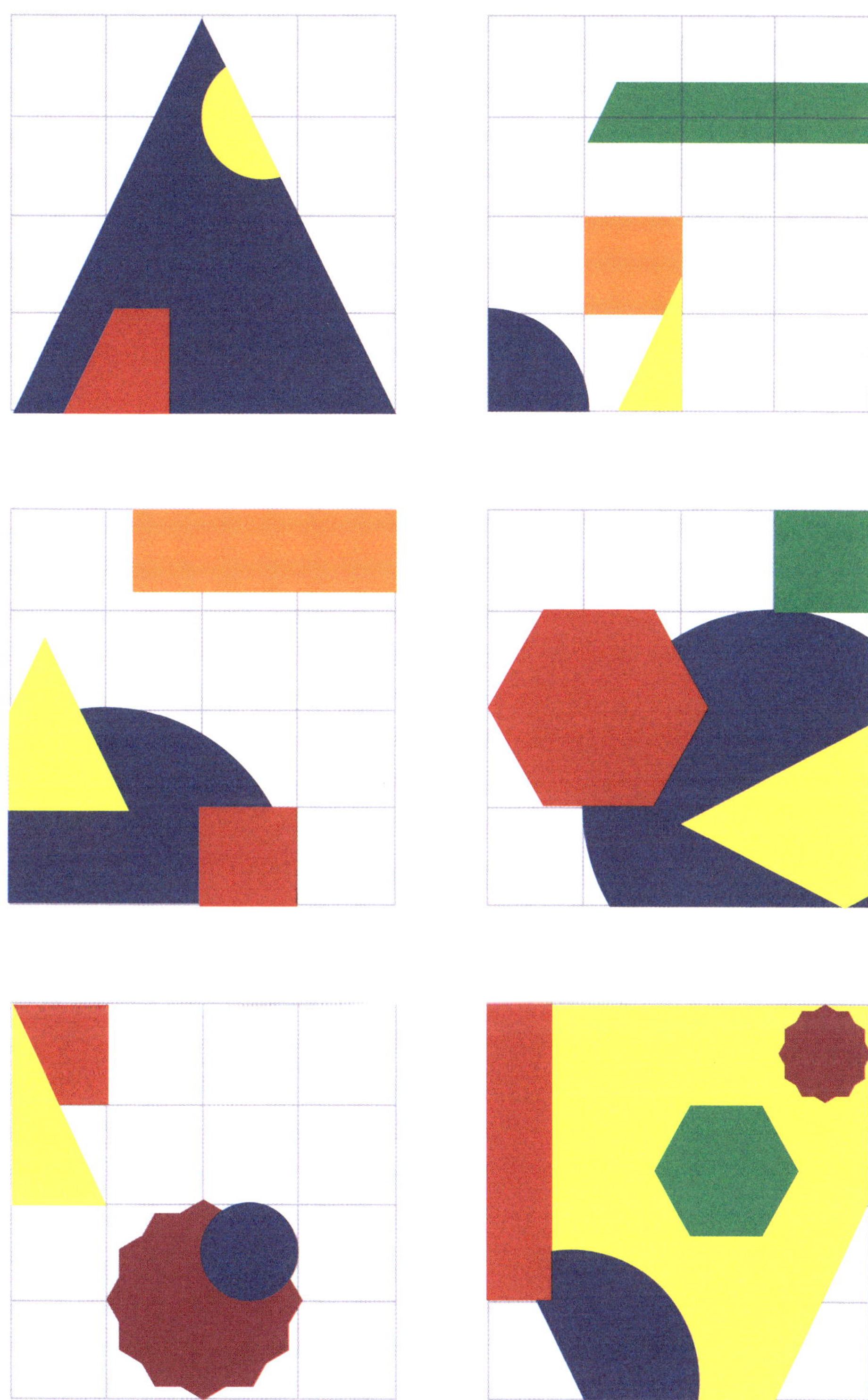

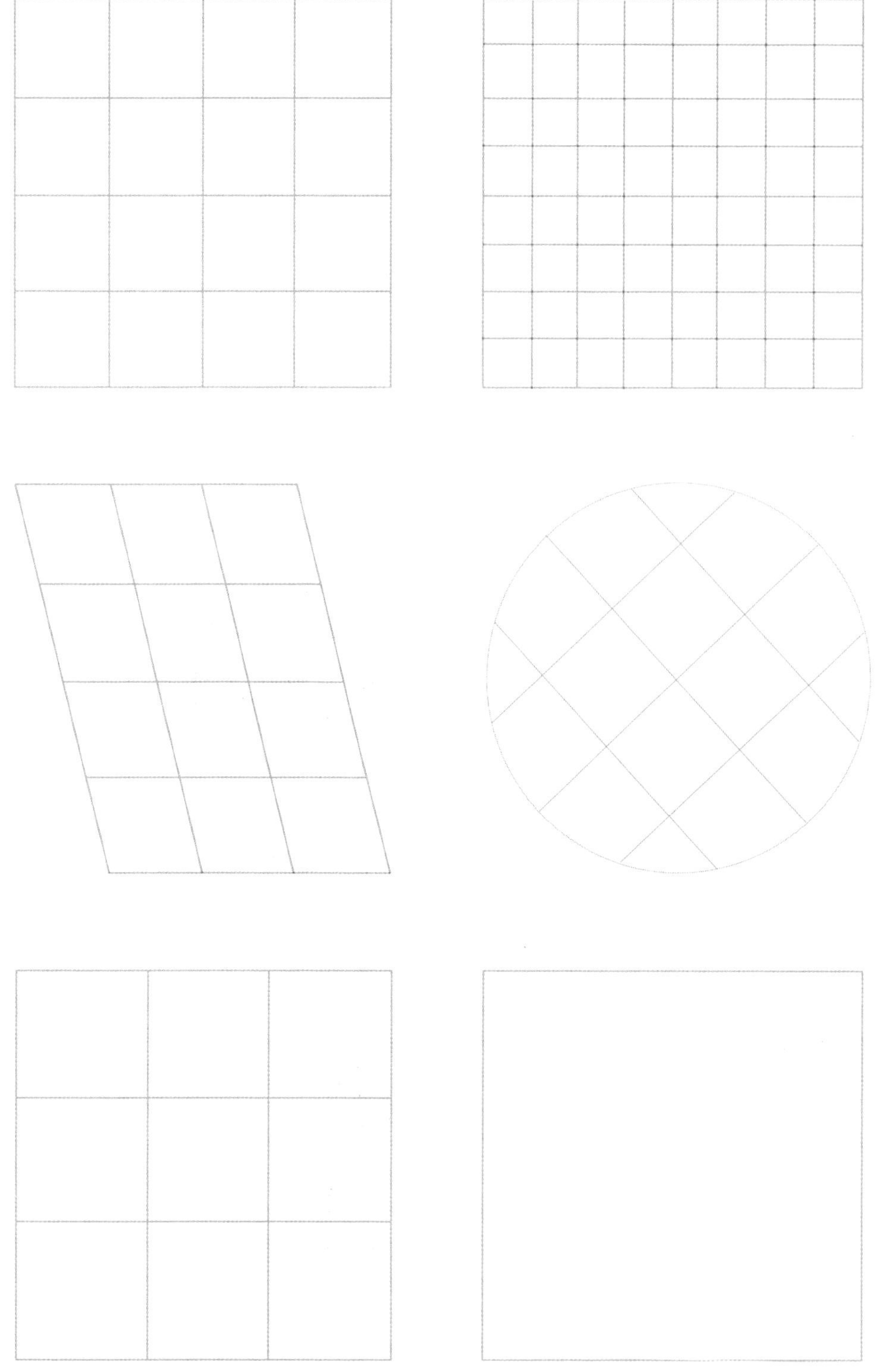

exercise

Add shapes using pencils, markers, or pens. Feel free to explore using other shapes from the examples below. Also, feel free to add cutouts using color or black and white paper. Options are limitless!

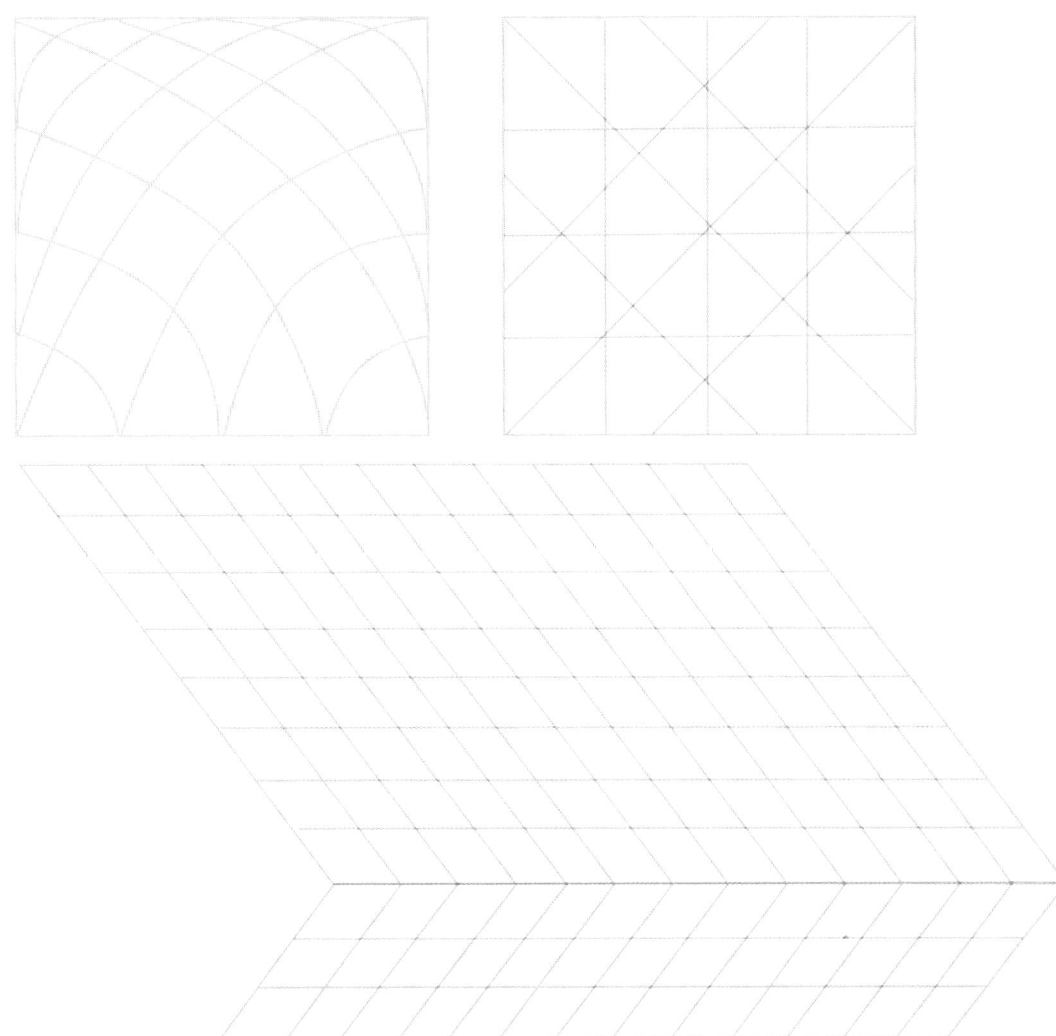

sketch, fold or cut here

3. spontaneity

The type of exercises in this chapter are usually undetermined, and it is only until when the creation starts that the form comes alive. This method of creation can have a message in or out of context. Also, there are moments with suddenly or unexpected results that create personal and emotional reactions, but they are still usable for structure. It is important to save ideas for future usage. Sometimes we do not know when we will be able to apply them. Overall, creating your own visual library of your work is important.

Structure sometimes does not give so much room for spontaneity, because of rules and specific ways of thinking that are set. Breaking out of mindsets and embracing other ways of interpretations and creation can be achieved with feedback from others.

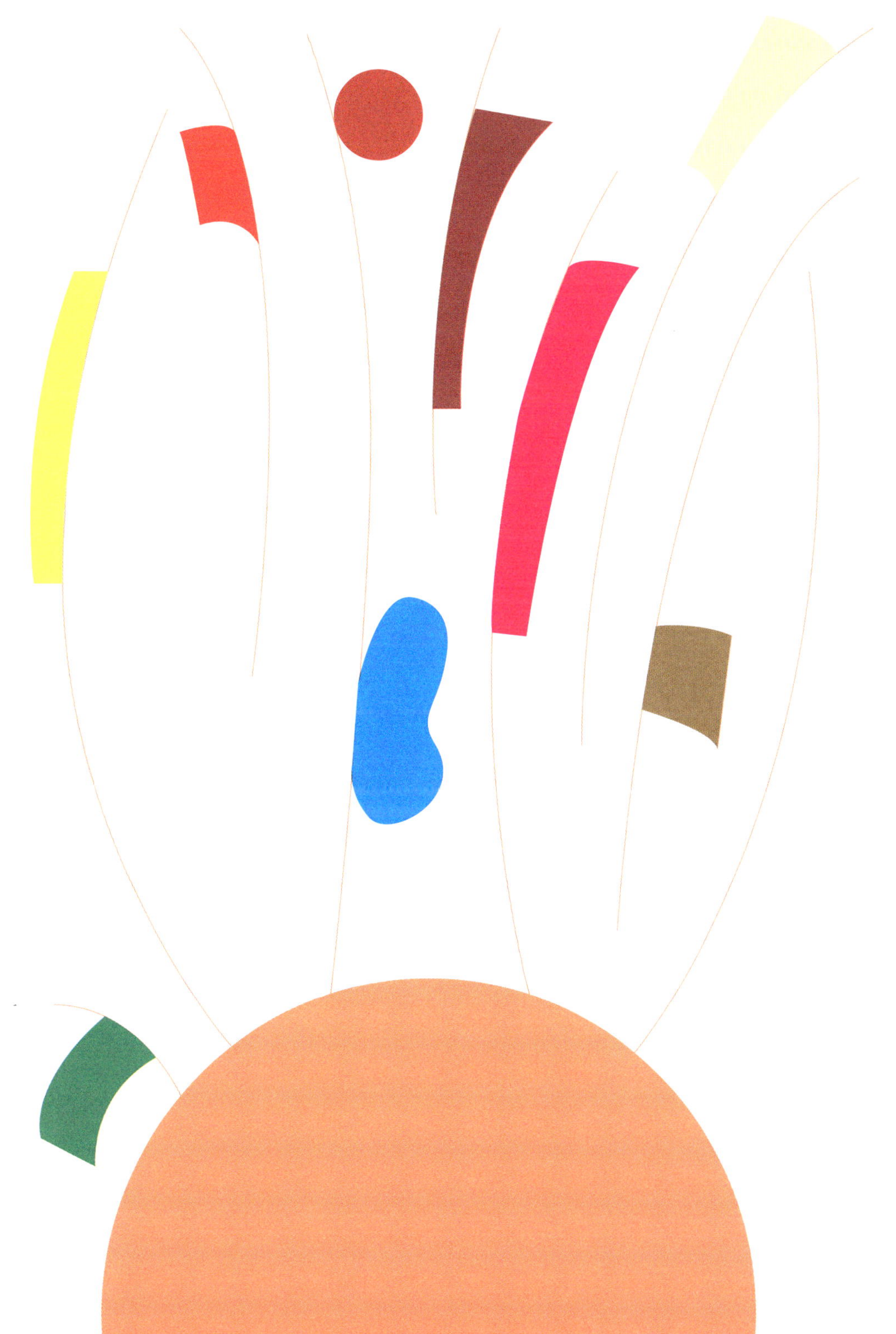

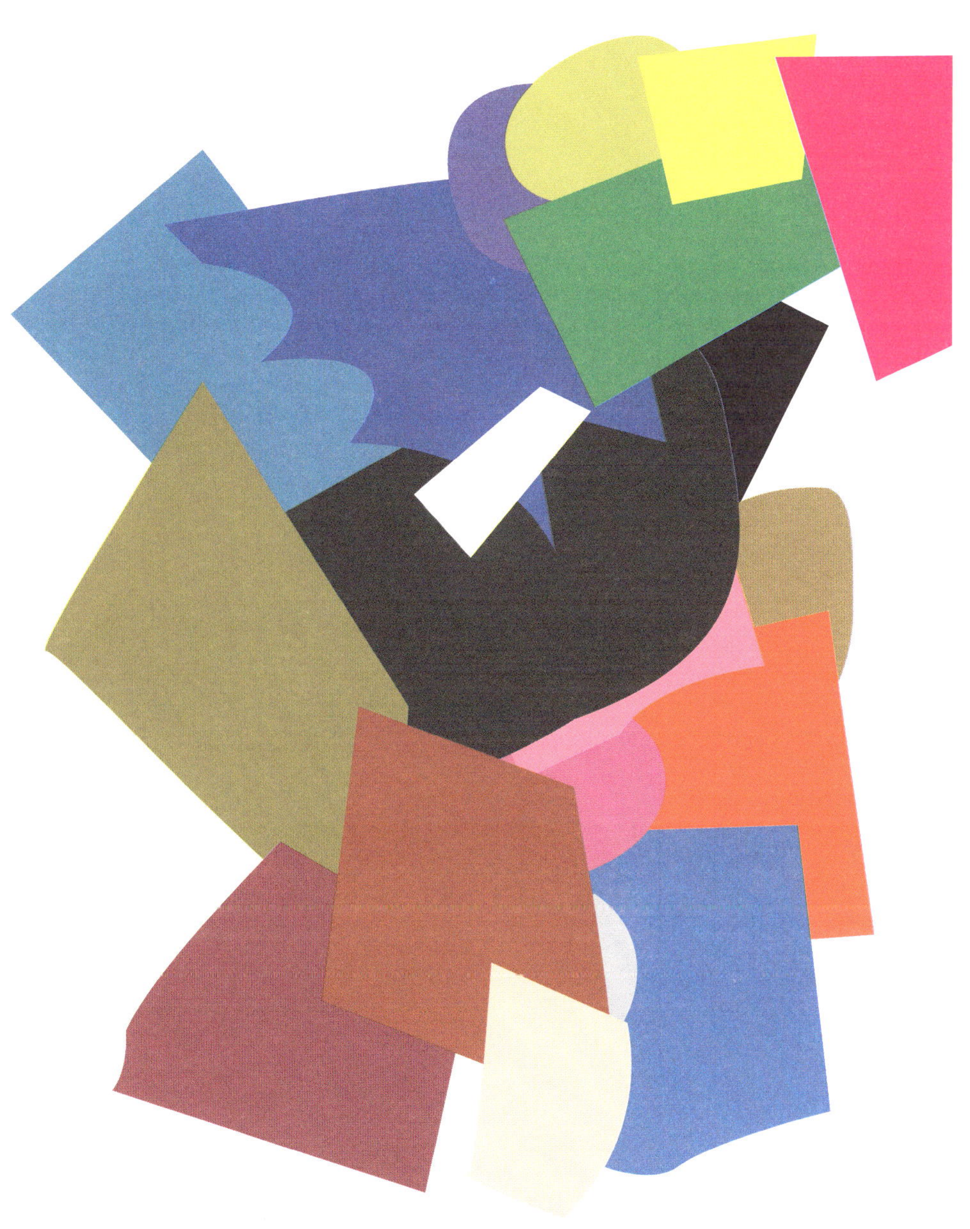

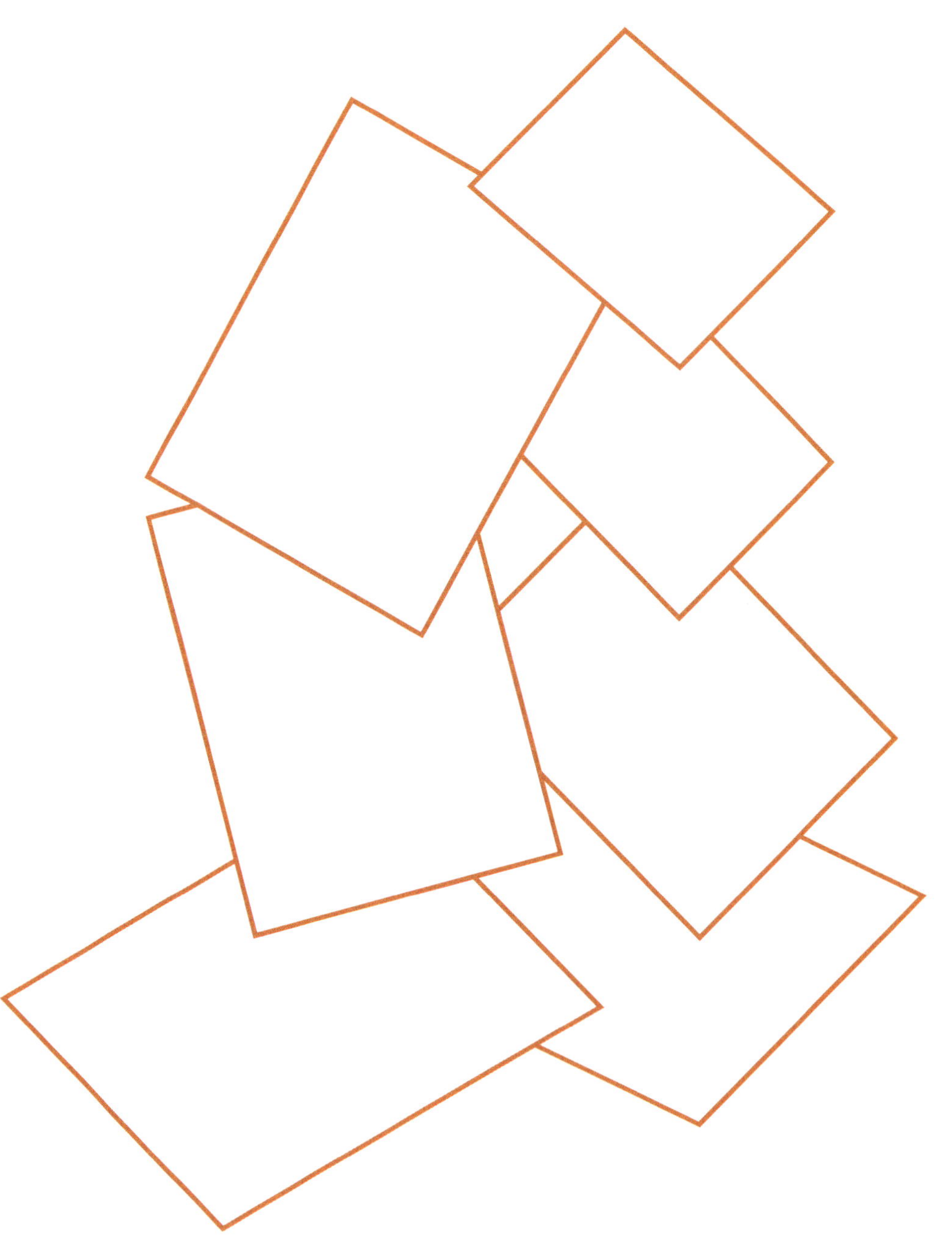

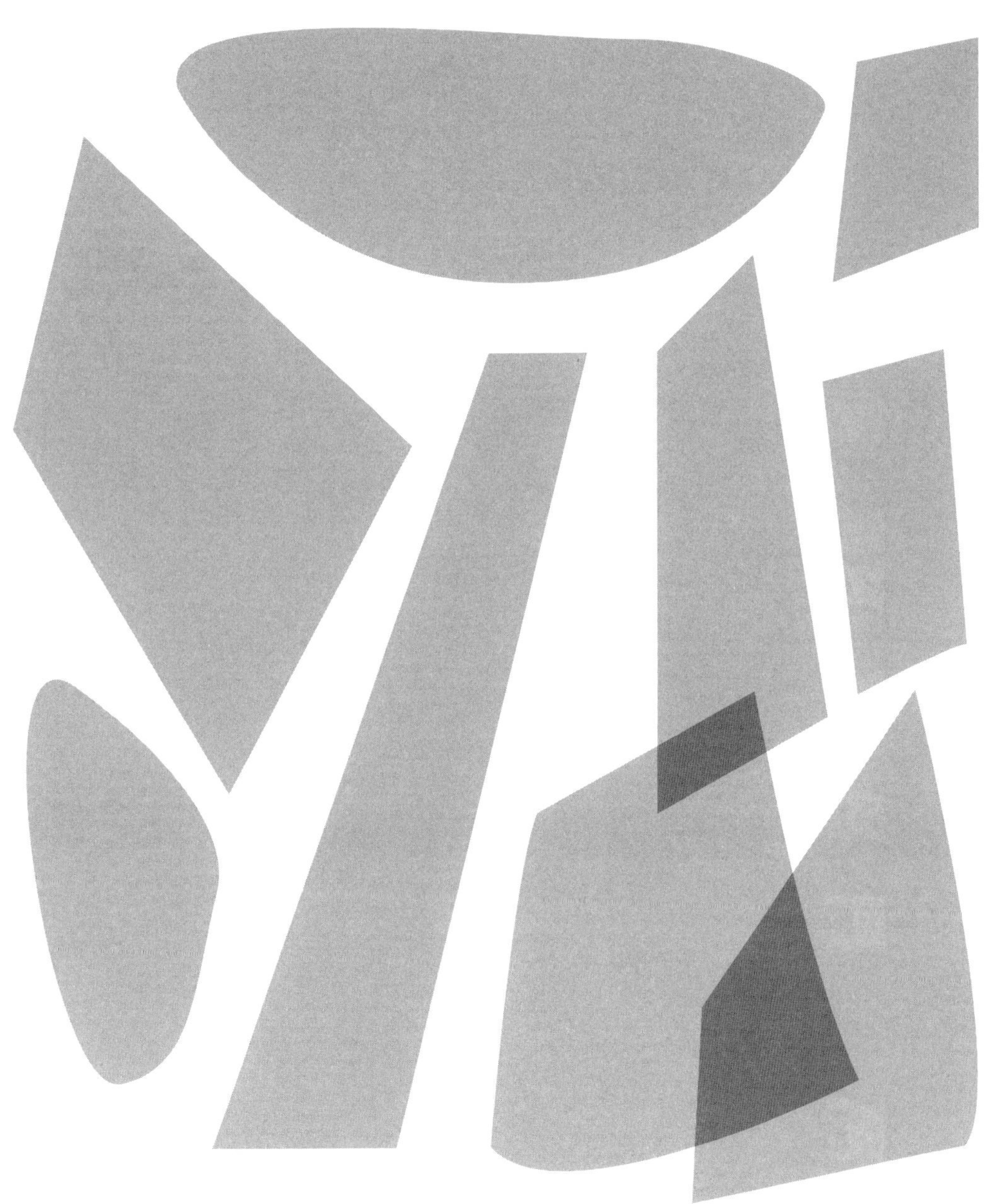

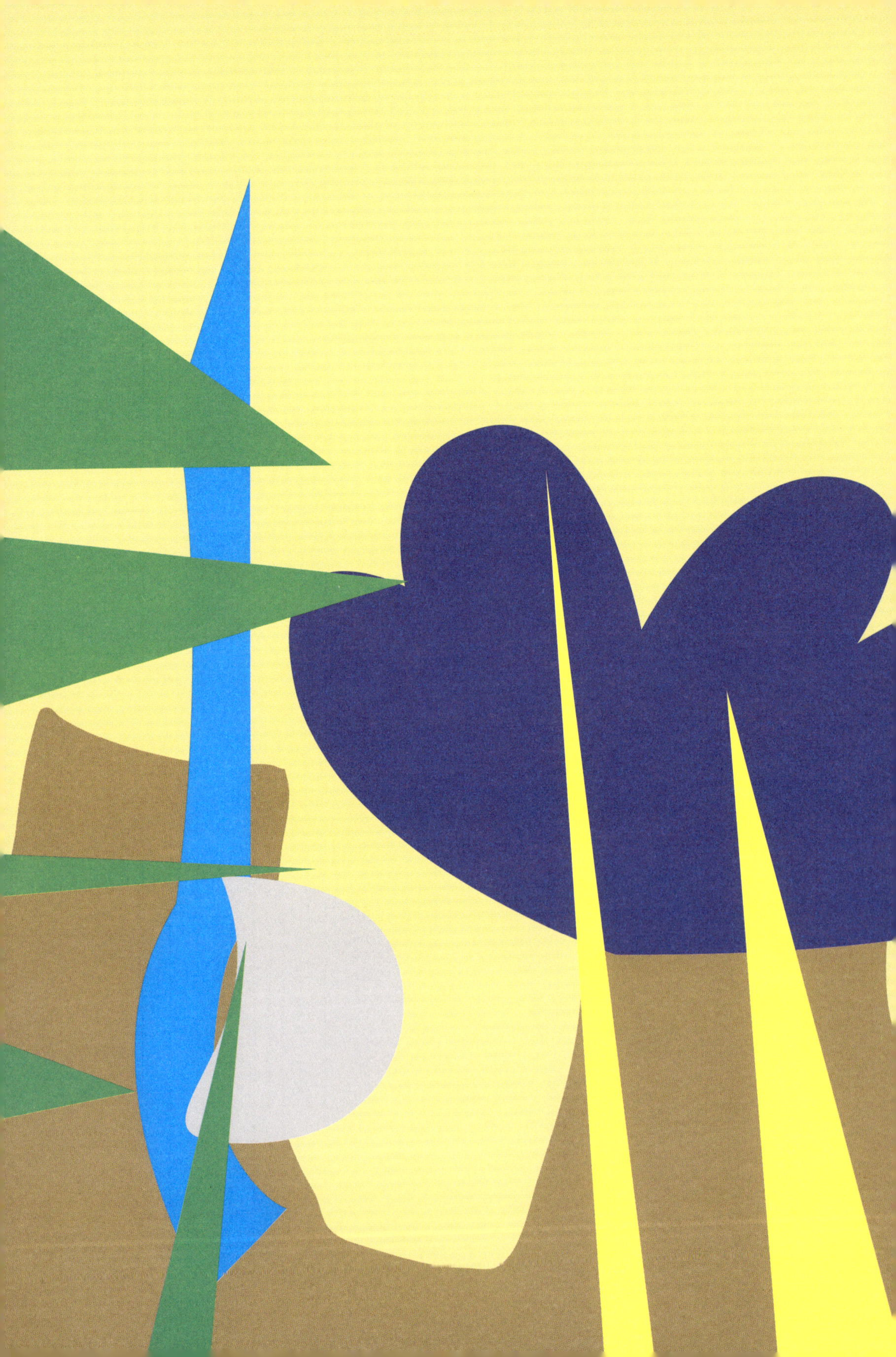

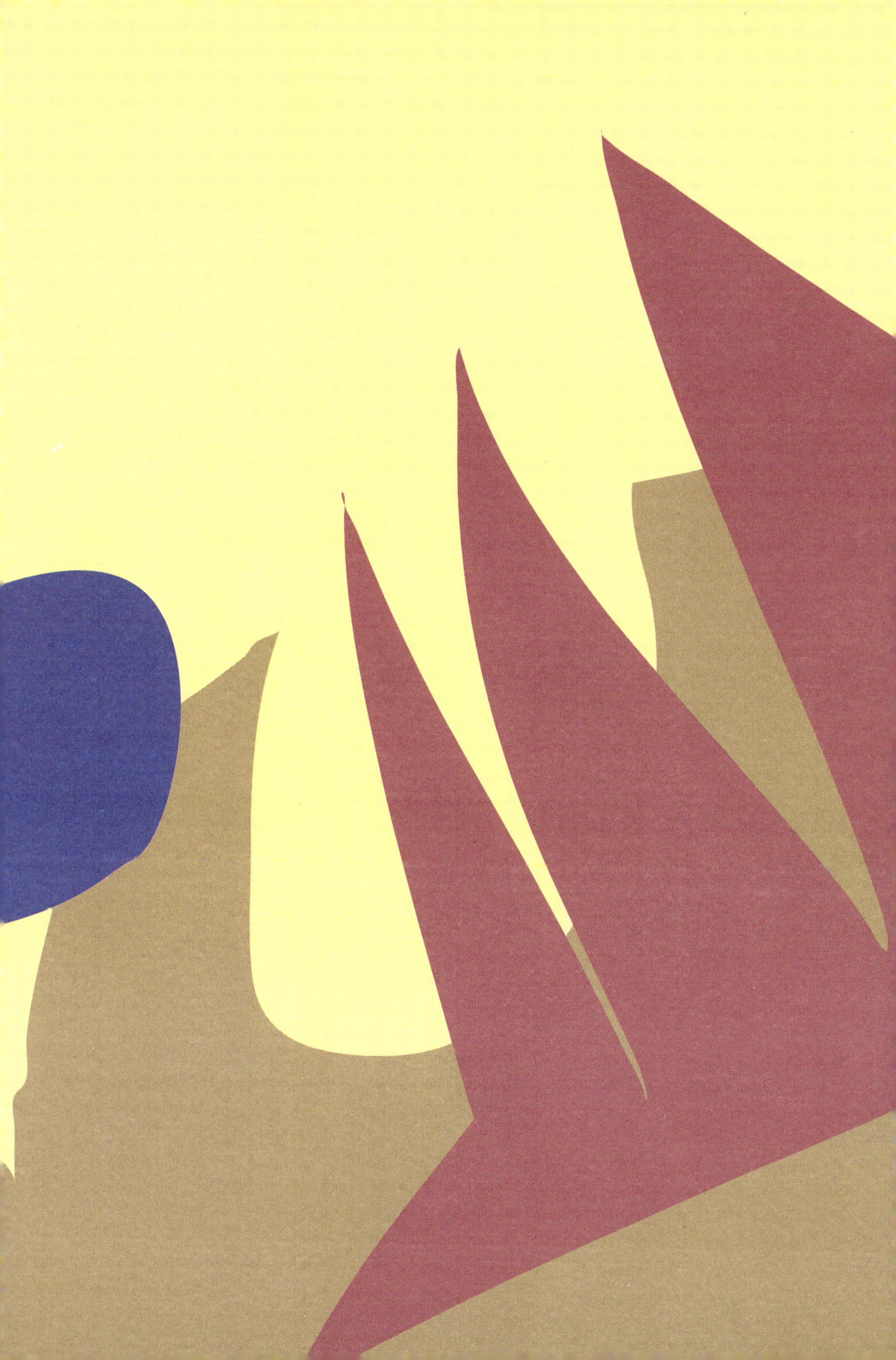

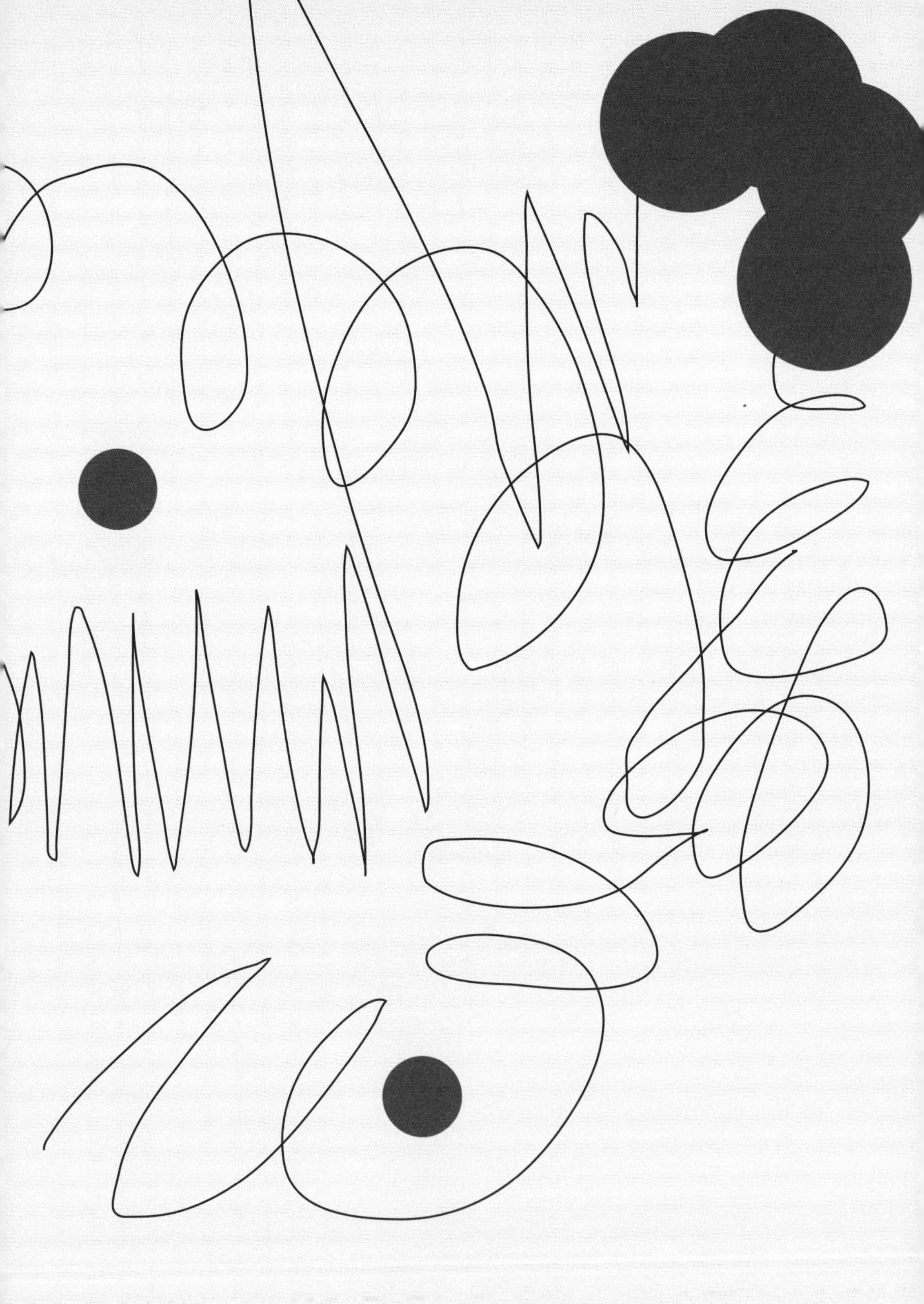

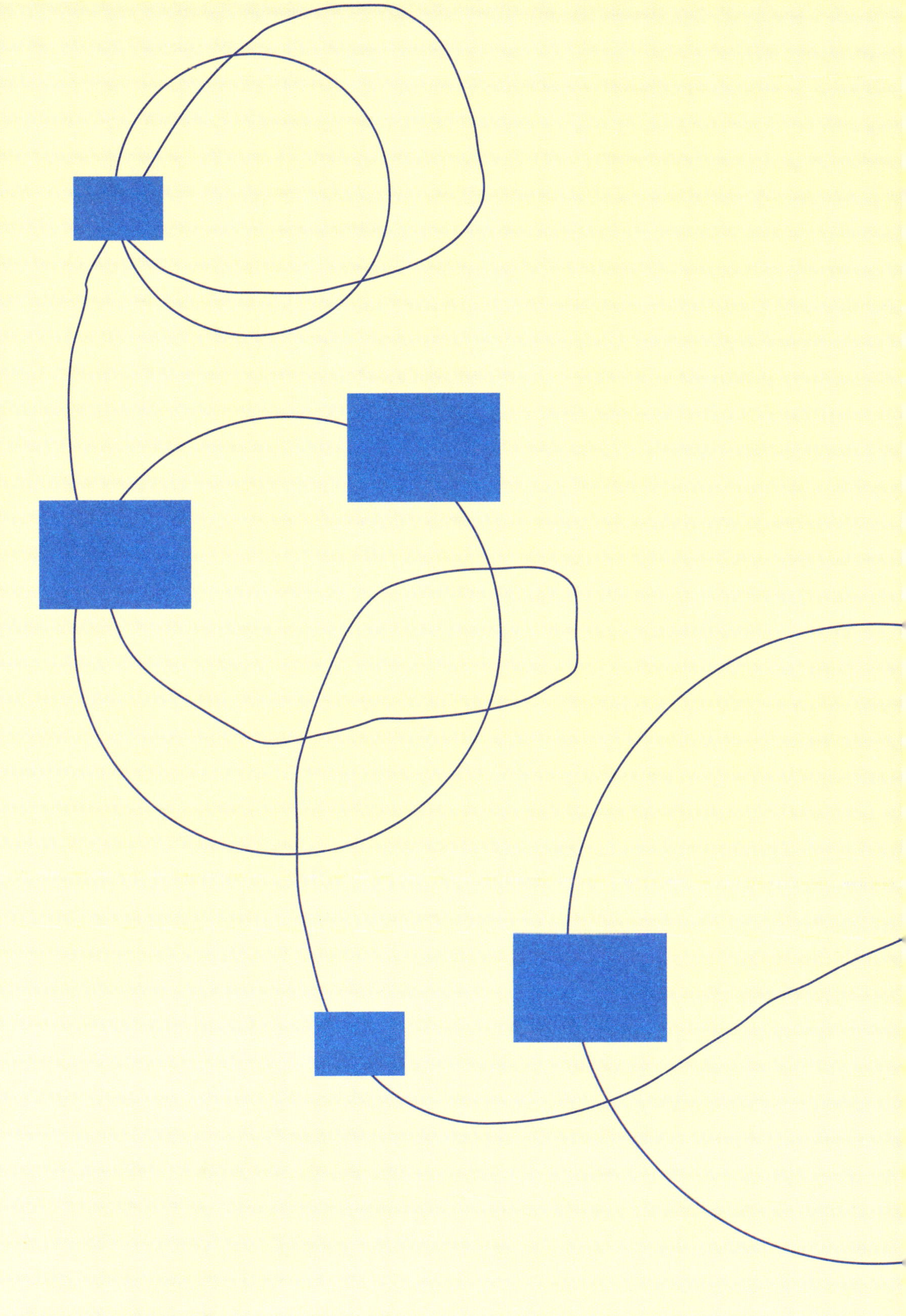

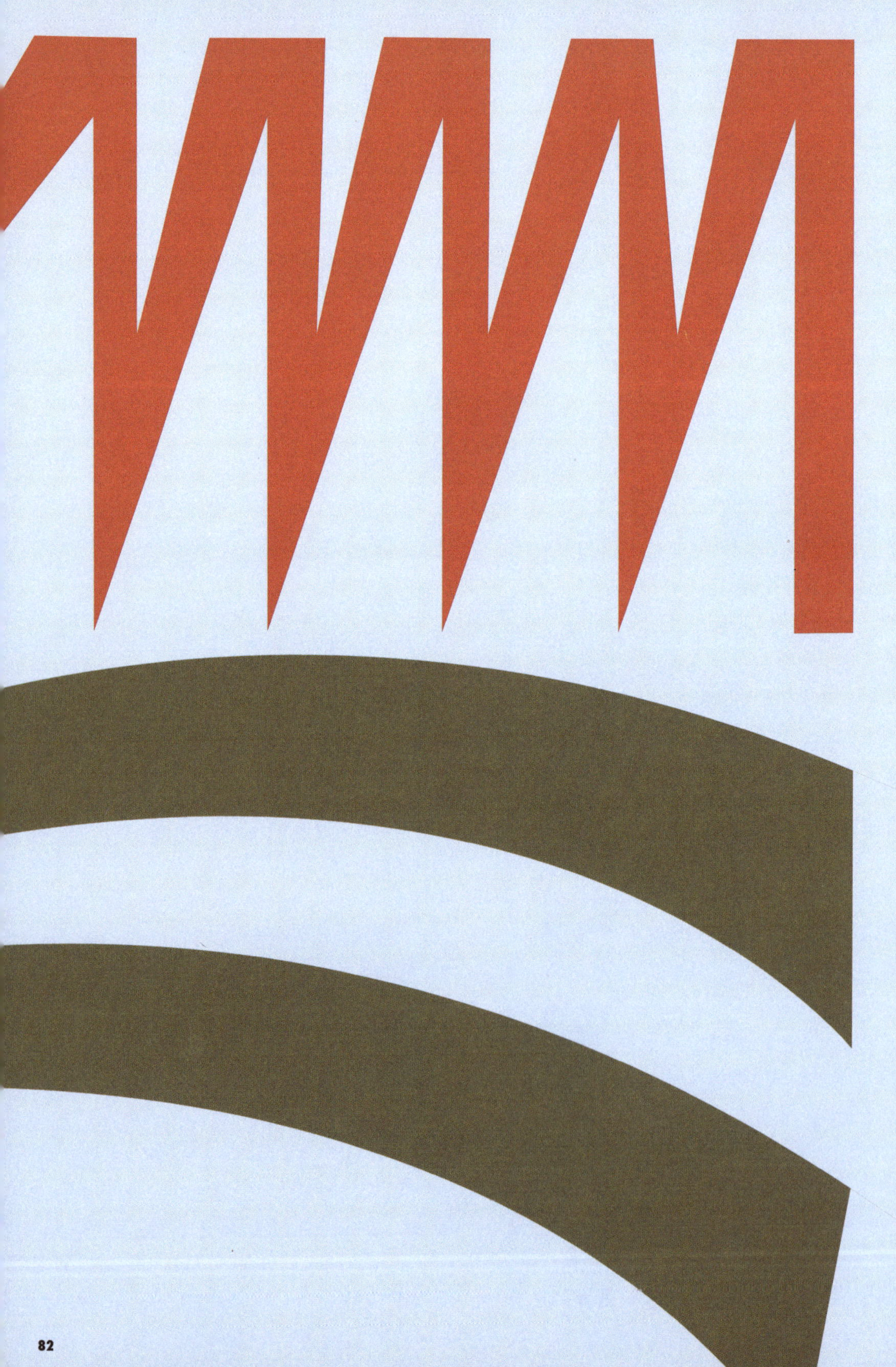

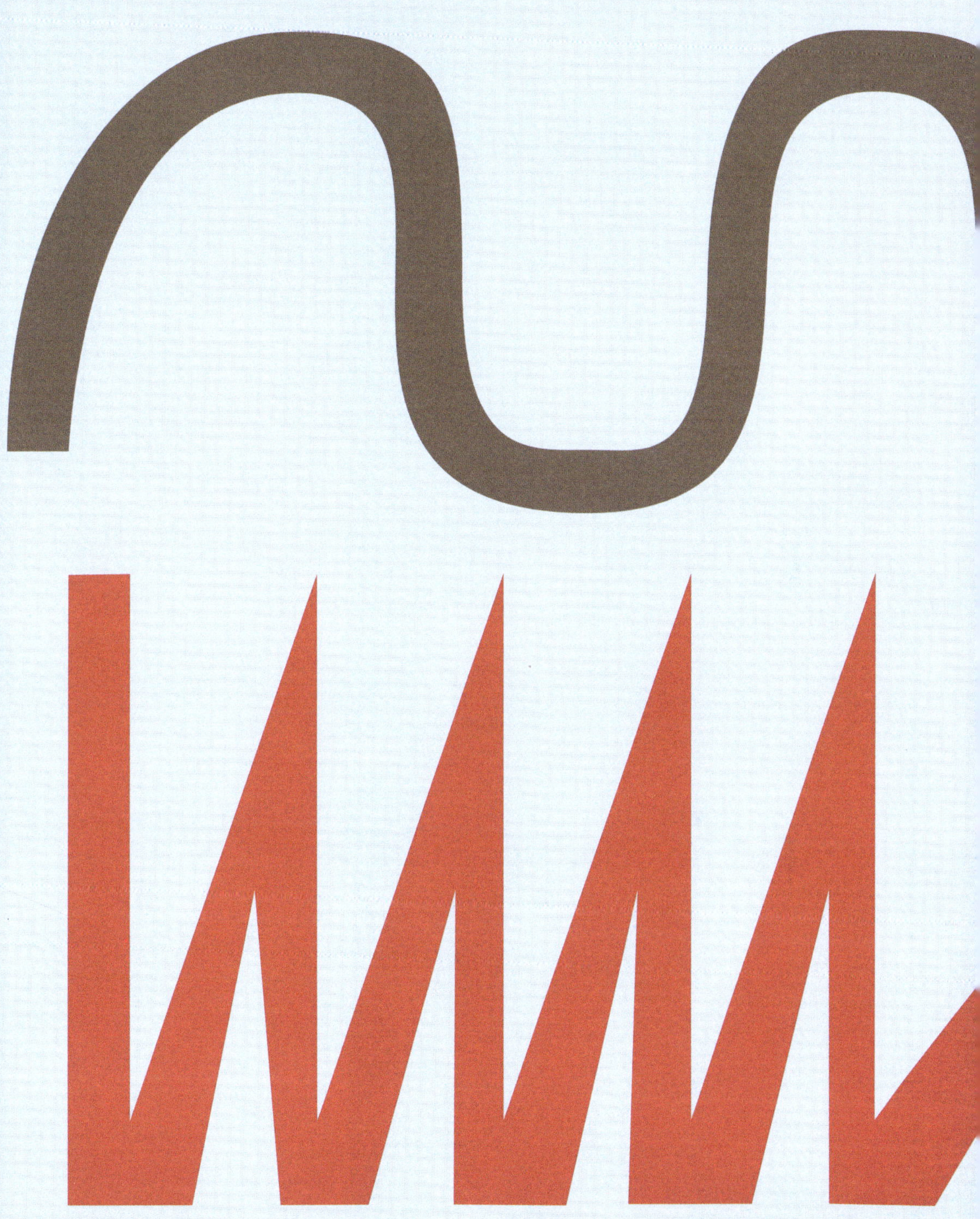

exercise

Add shapes using pencils, markers, or pens. Feel free to explore using other shapes from the examples below. Also, feel free to add cutouts using color or black and white paper. Options are limitless!

4. order and disorder

Order has a voice that ranges from a soft to a loud voice that is delivered through a visual message, which not only brings the content together through organization but also creates hierarchy in the content. It is almost like a perfect line or a building structure. Meanwhile, disorder can be like a paint spill, black hole in space, or a tornado.

Making the choice of designing using order can be the safest option and also the most successful one. But not all messages of content speak order to viewers, therefore disorder can be very useful when the meaning is coming together. Overall, some people may dislike disorder but if it is validating its significance and giving itself a purpose, then its function is following form or its form follows its function.

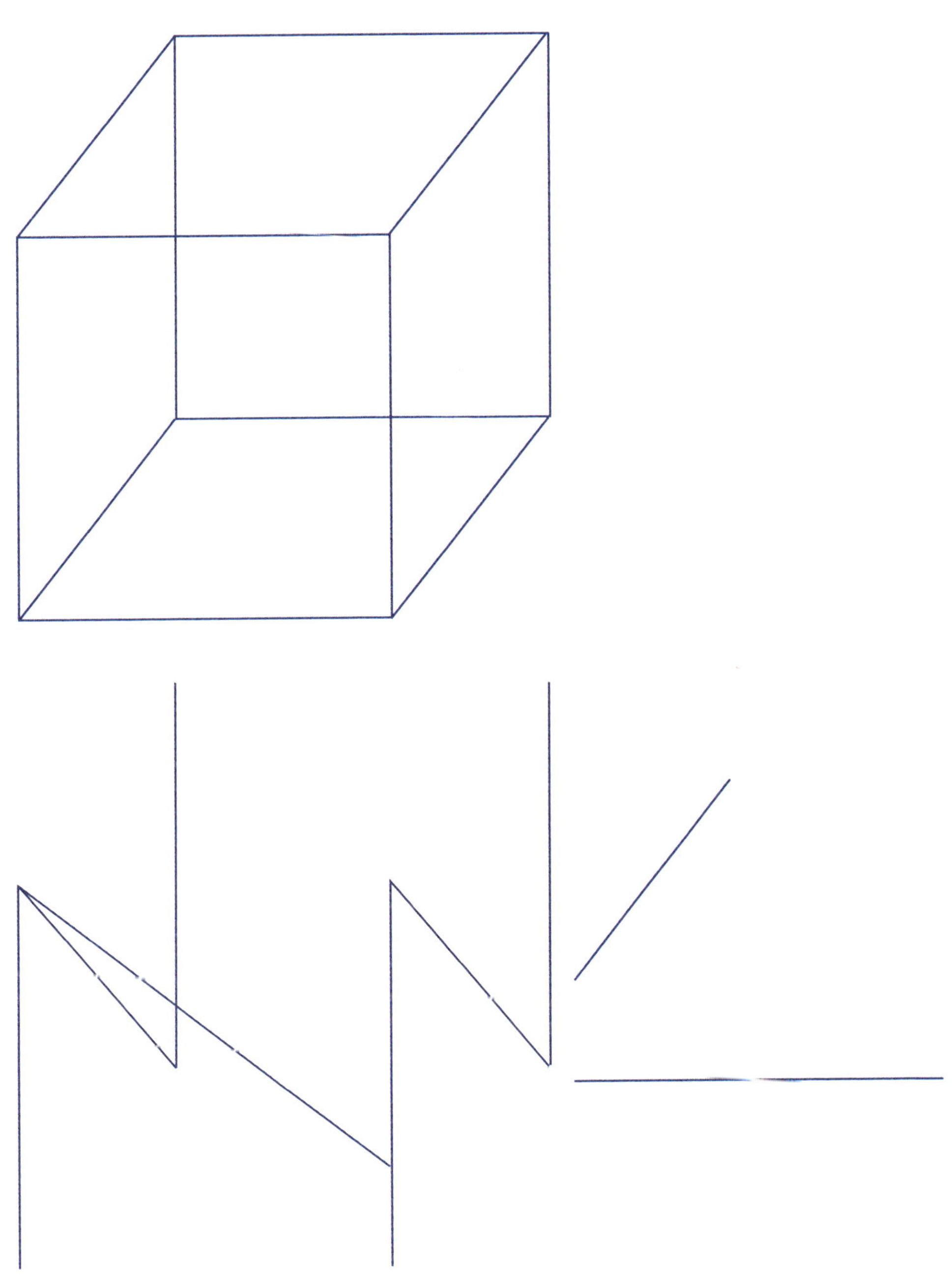

cube and brokeness

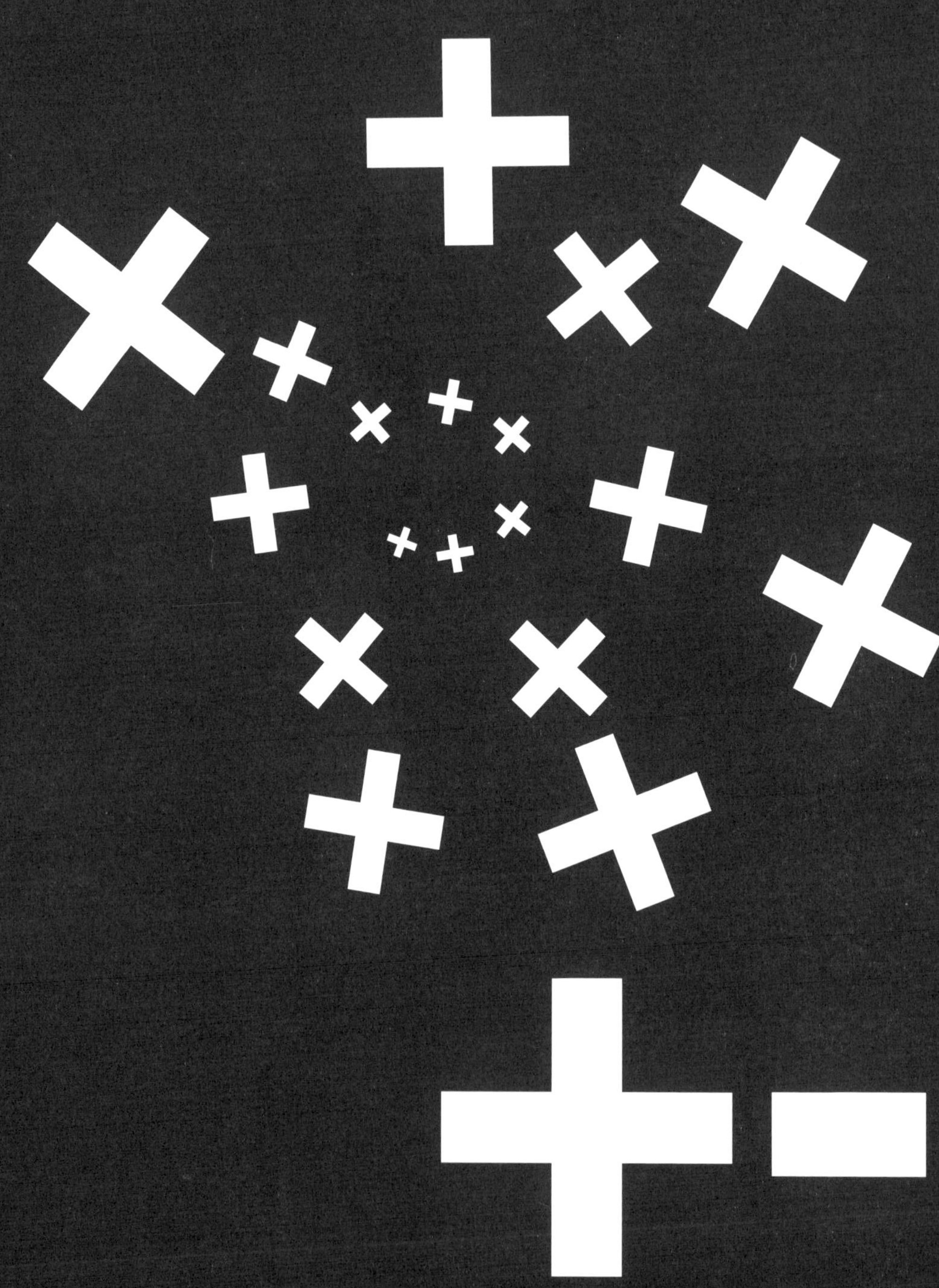

positive and negative energies

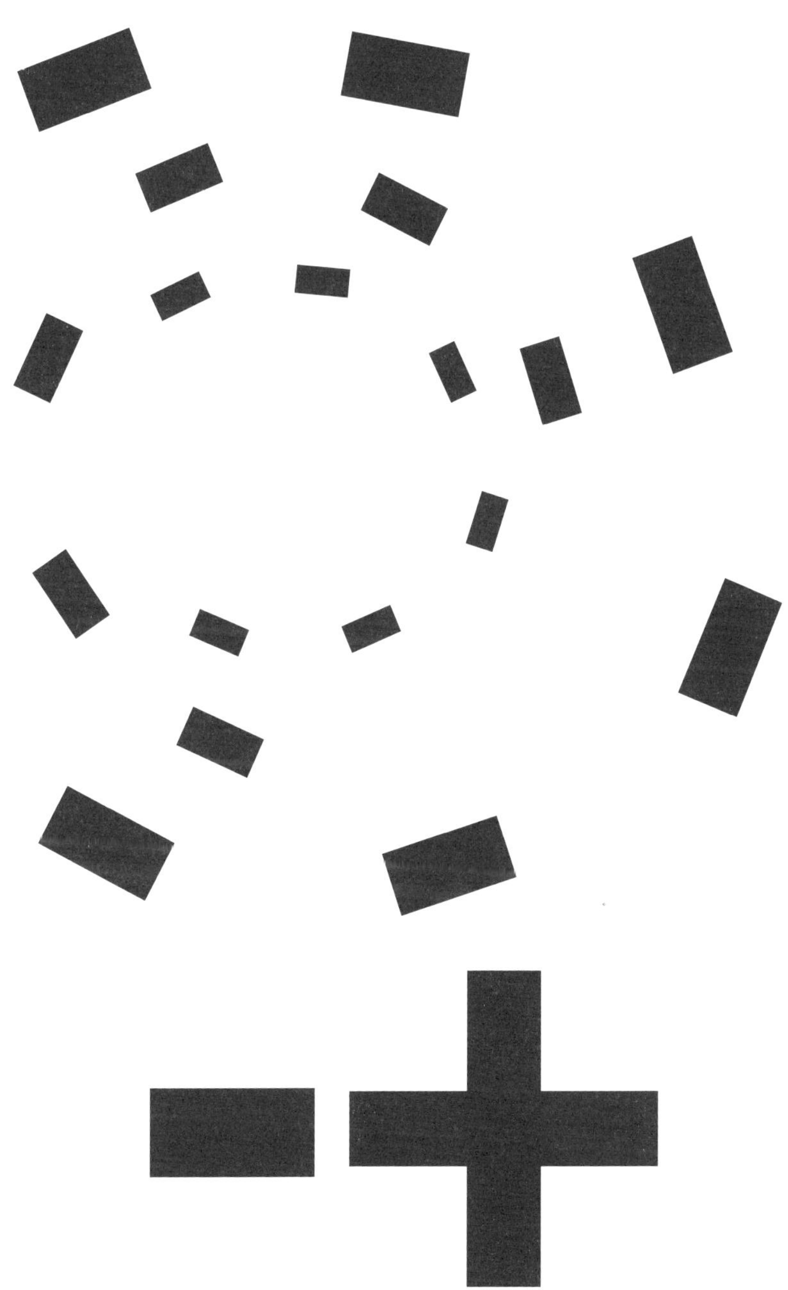

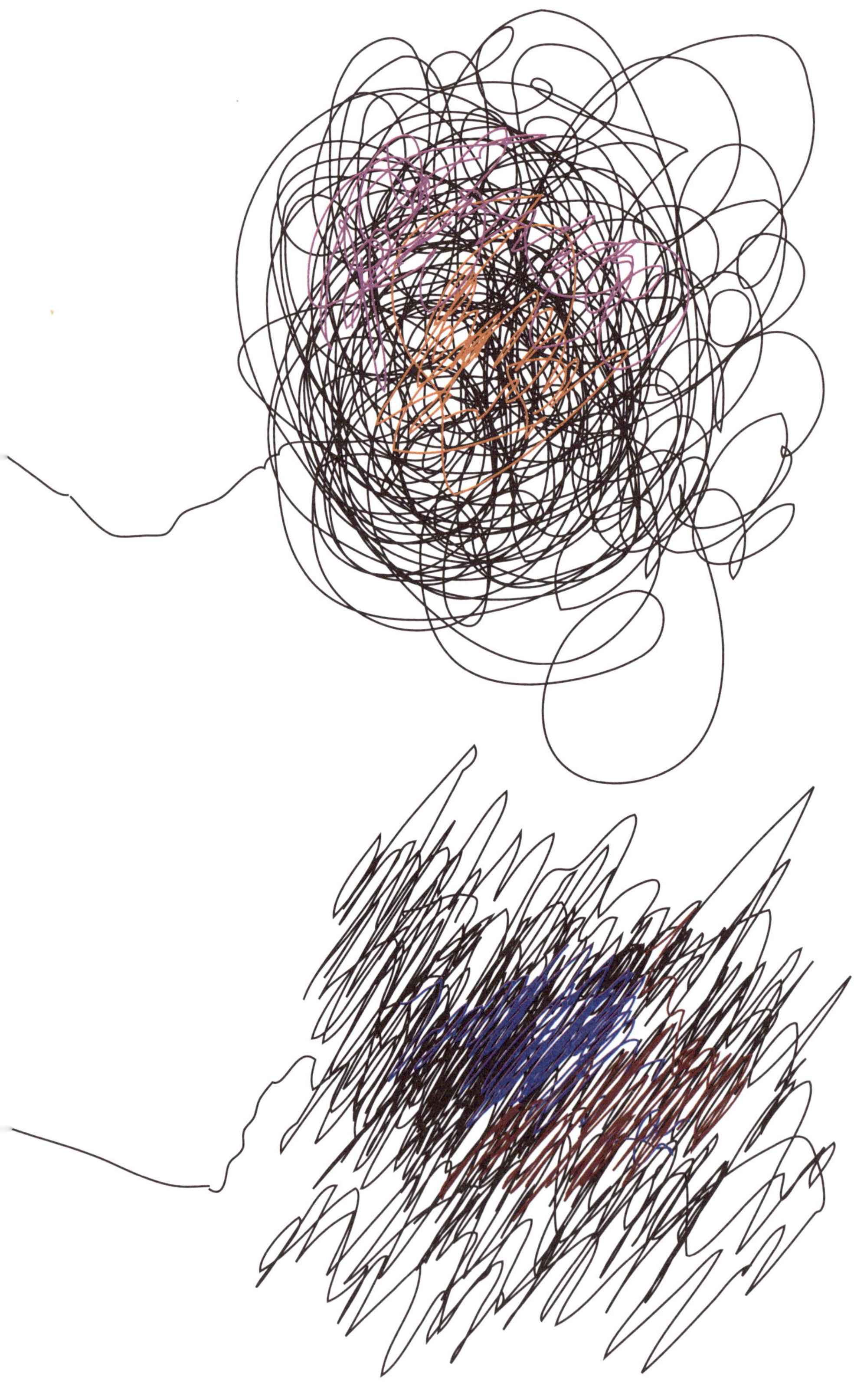

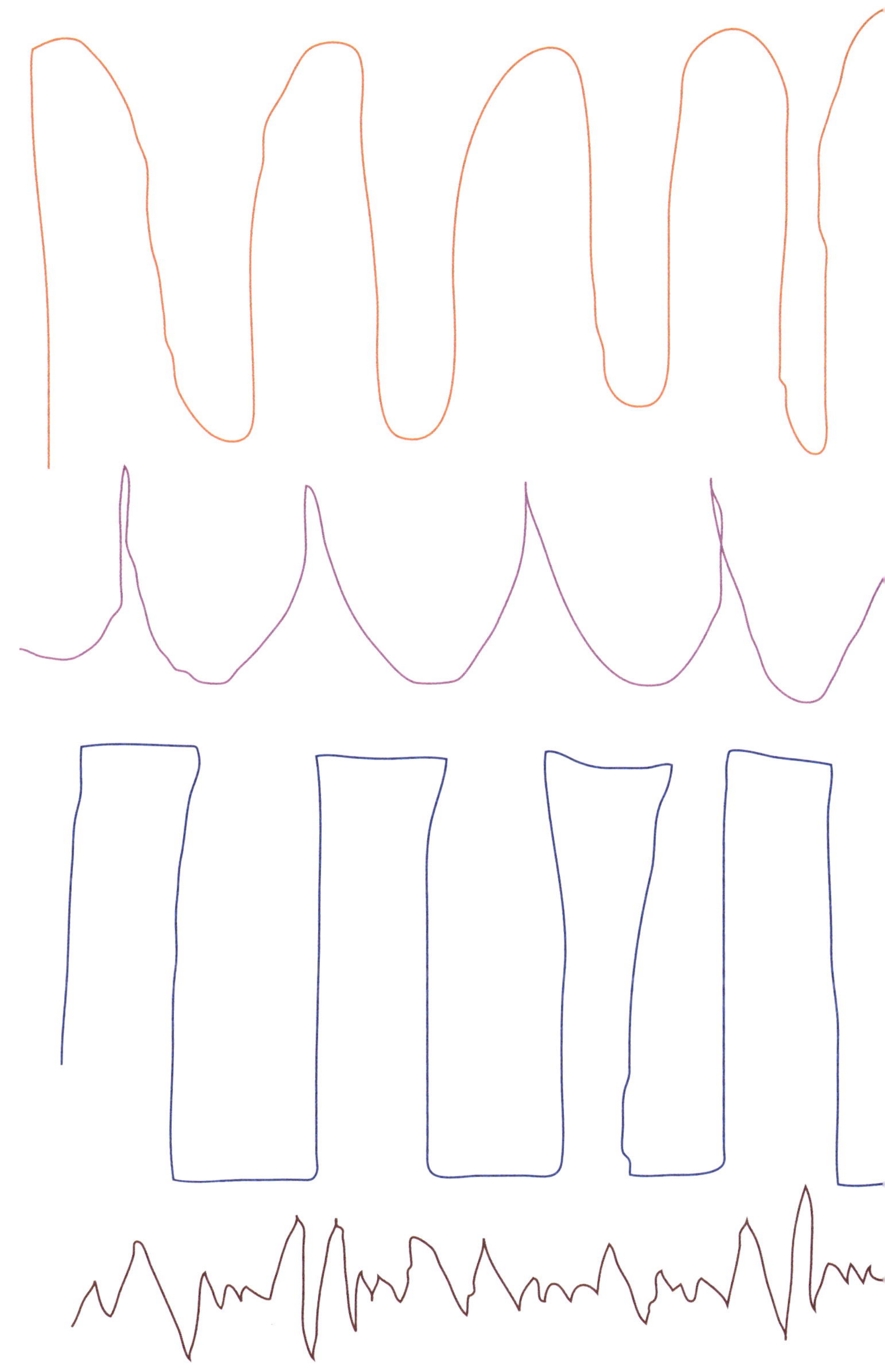

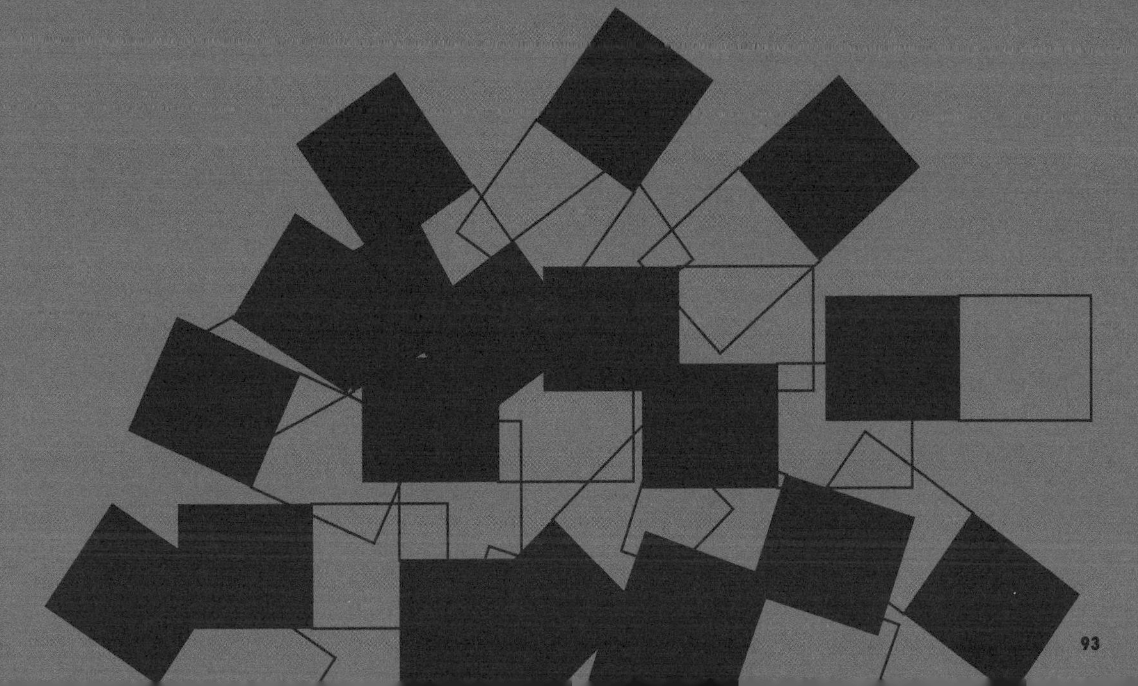

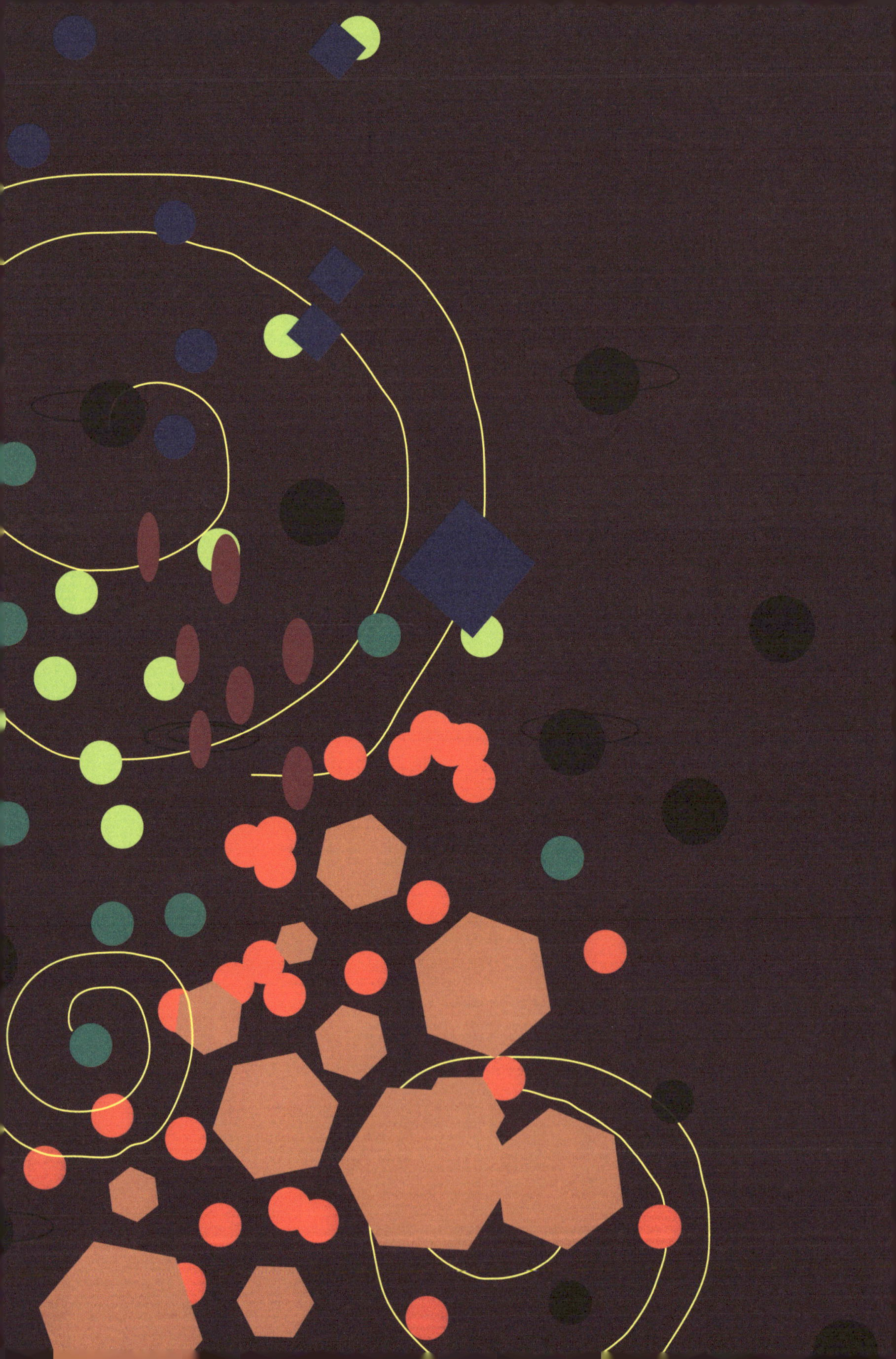

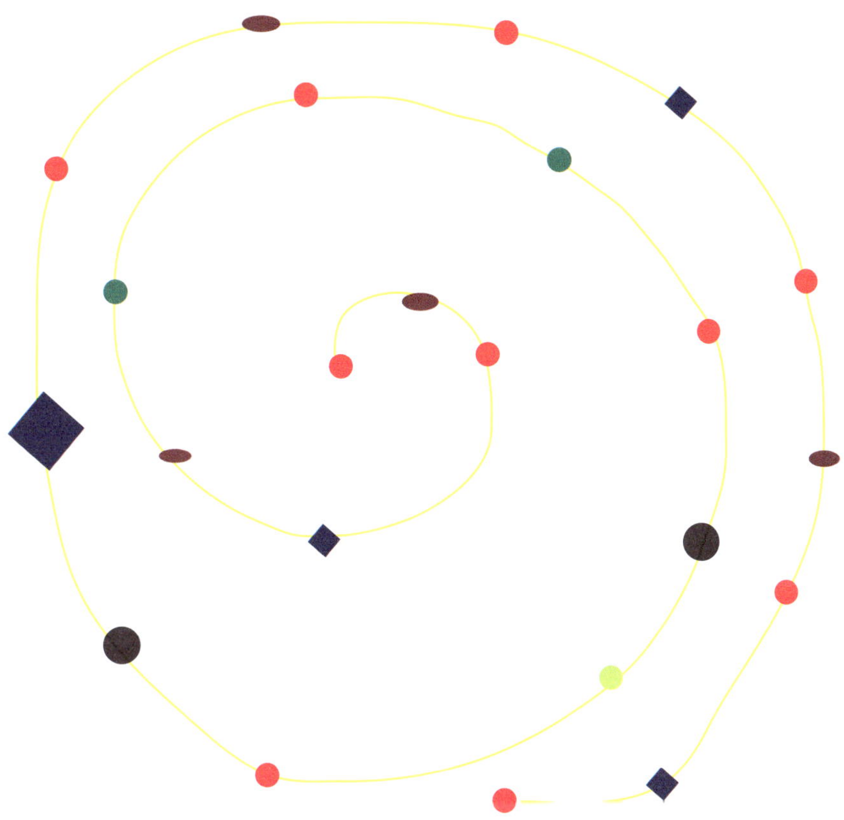

sketch, fold or cut

exercise

Create various examples that bring order and chaos. Also, feel free to add cutouts using color or black and white paper. Options are limitless!

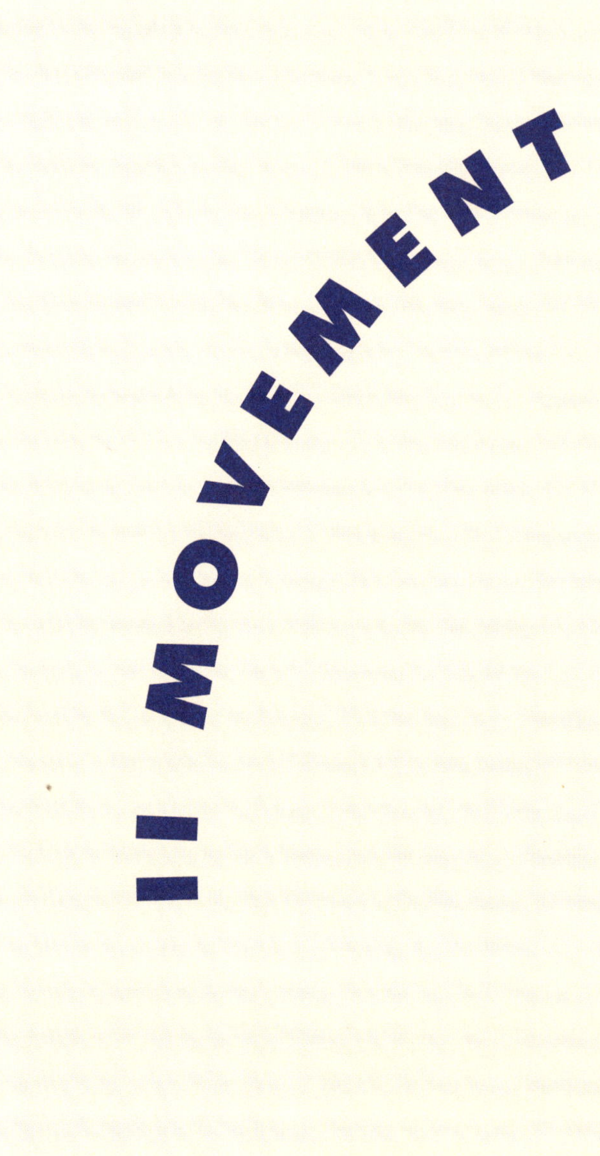
III MOVEMENT

5. paradigmatic

Being able to create a great example that can be applied to other designs has to be successful and easy to understand. The implementation of already great work can become monotonous if it is applied over and over again, and the repetition has no incentive to the eye anymore. That can become overdone, and it has reached the possibilities or capacity of its function. This can be caused because it has been overworked or overused and is no longer what the author of the design intended and what the audience is meant to receive.

Innovation and change is important when it comes to resolving the organization of content and that varies. Many of us create, but the re–evaluation and re–thinking of work has done so much and it will always help us become better designers for the next project.

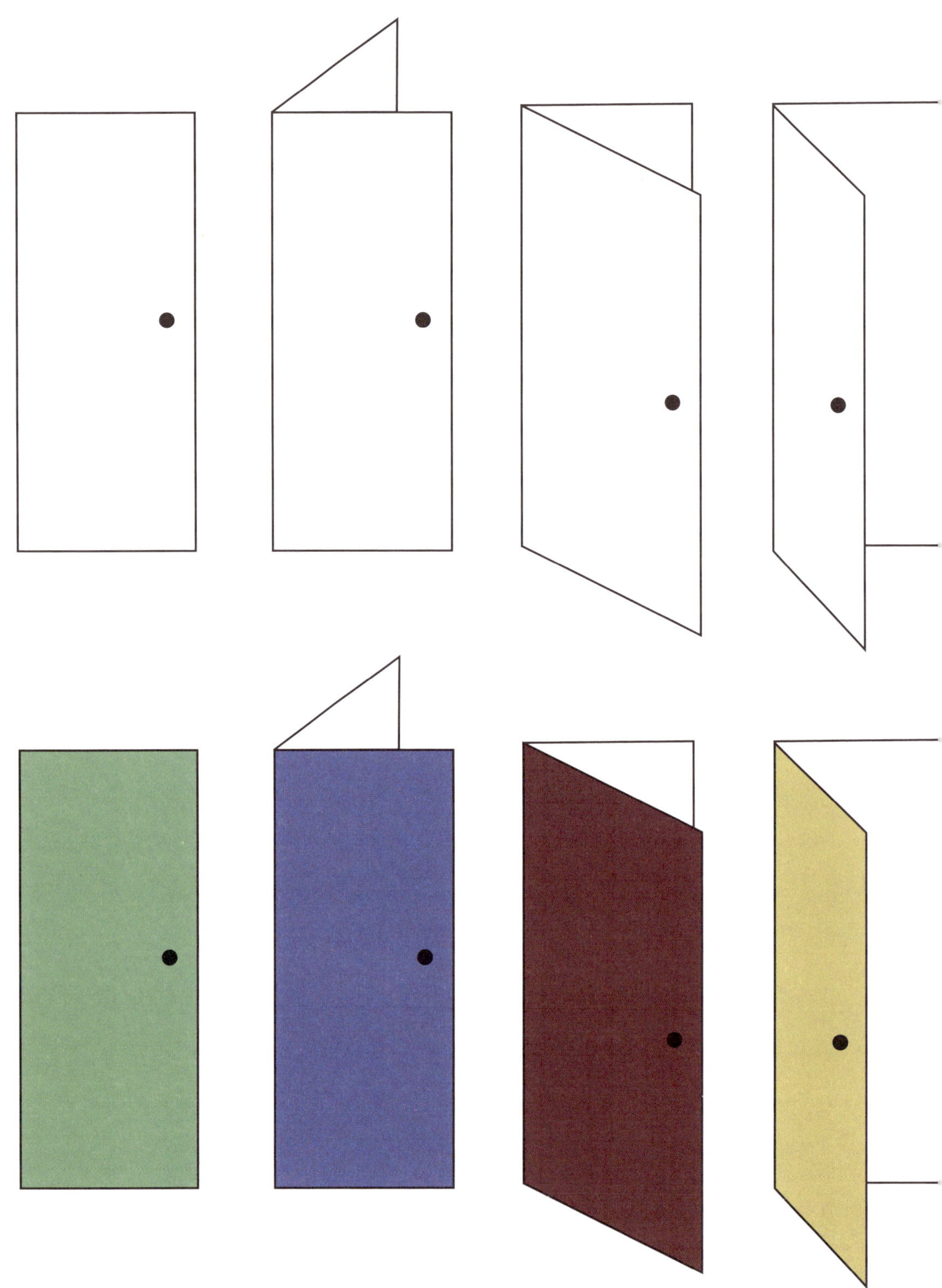

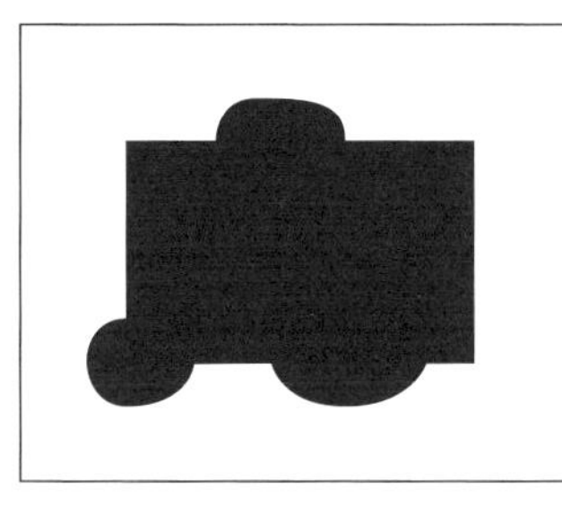
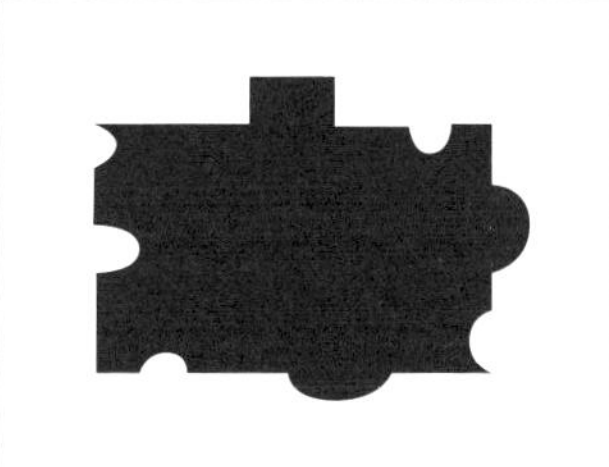
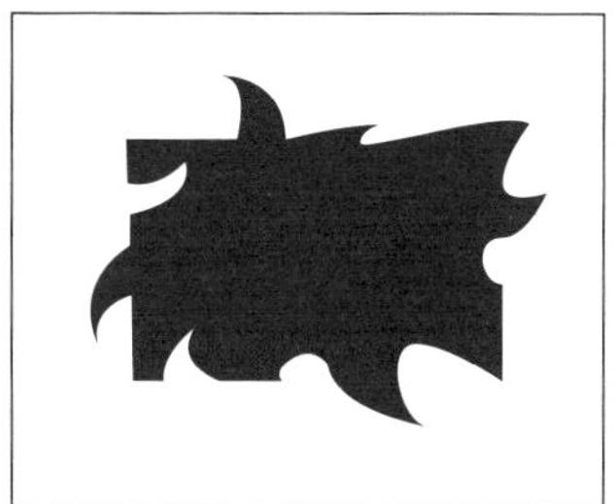
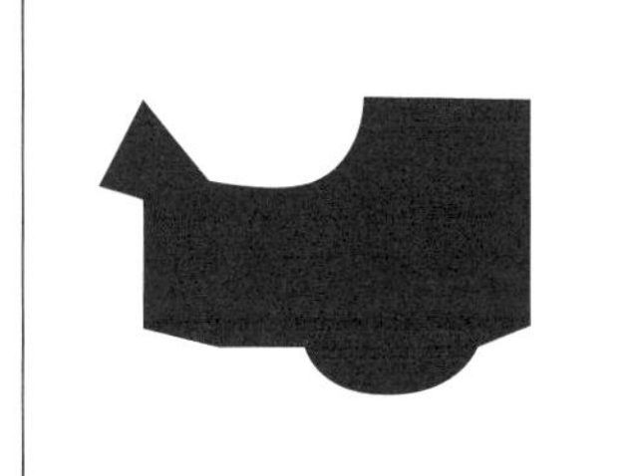

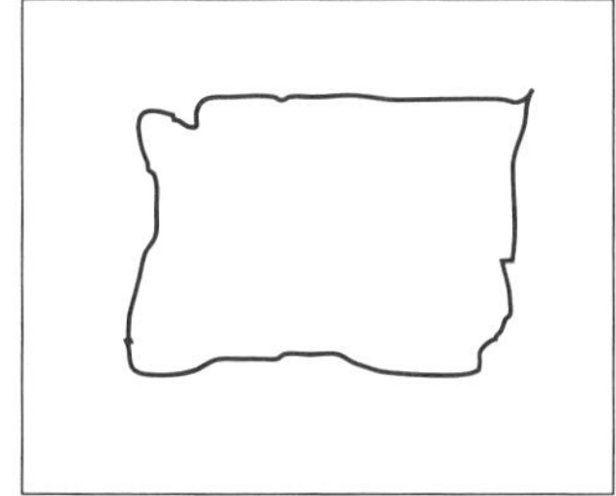
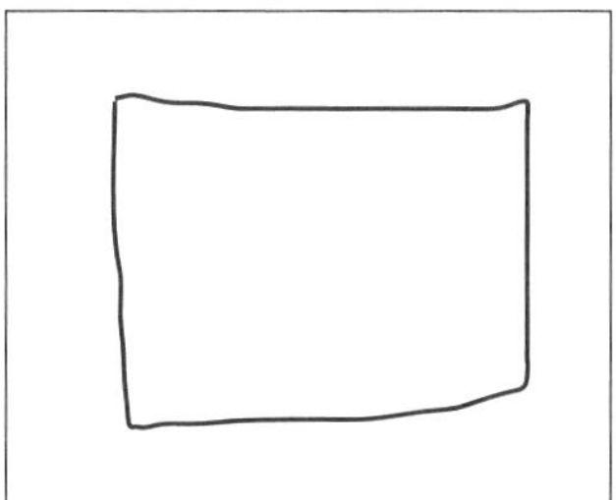
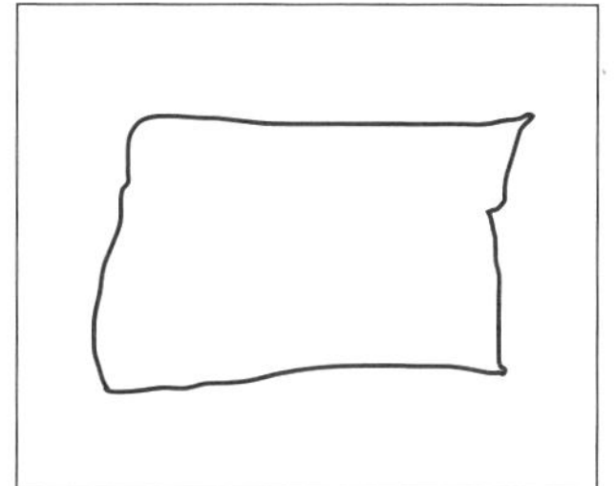

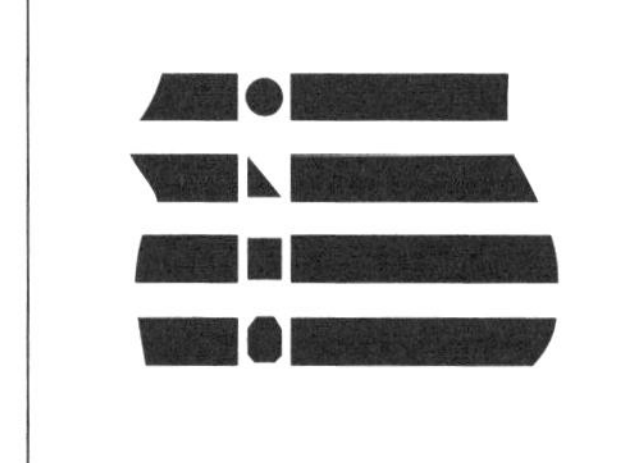
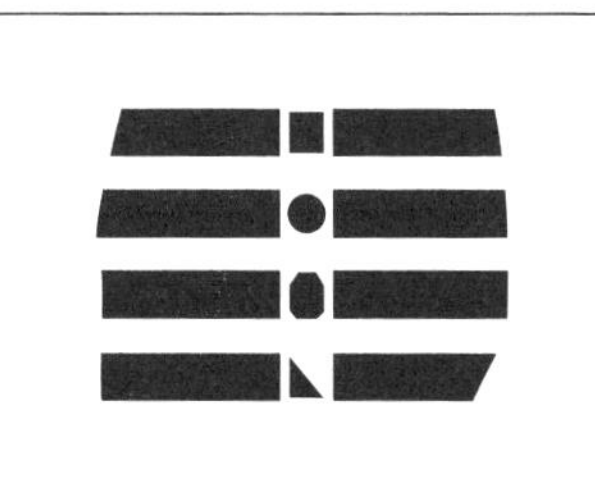
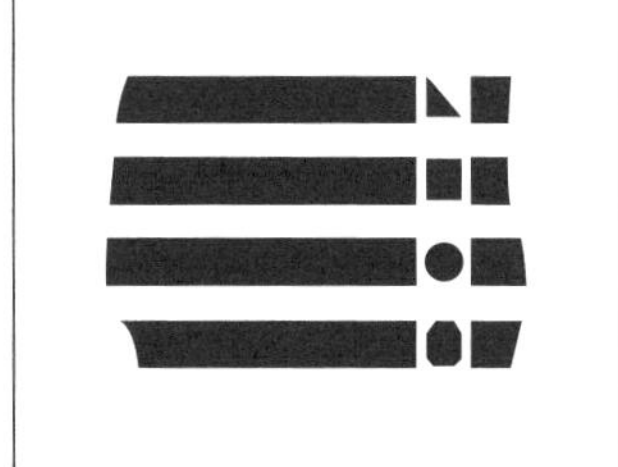

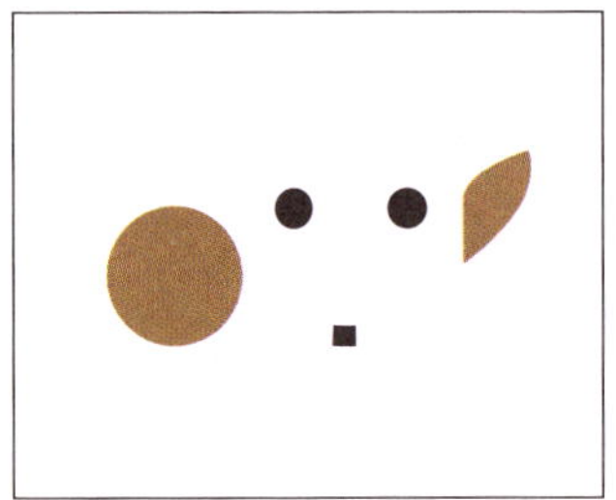
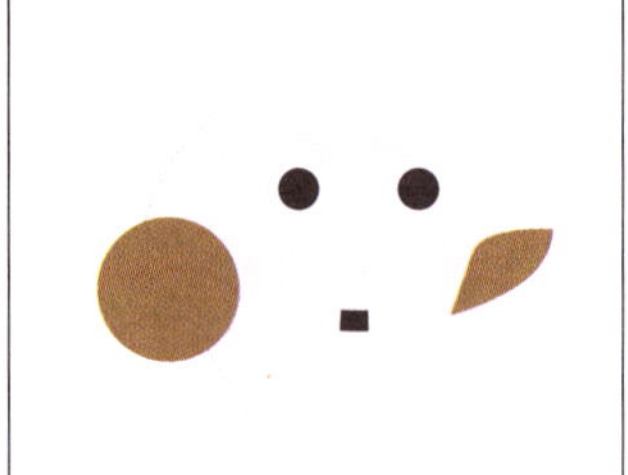
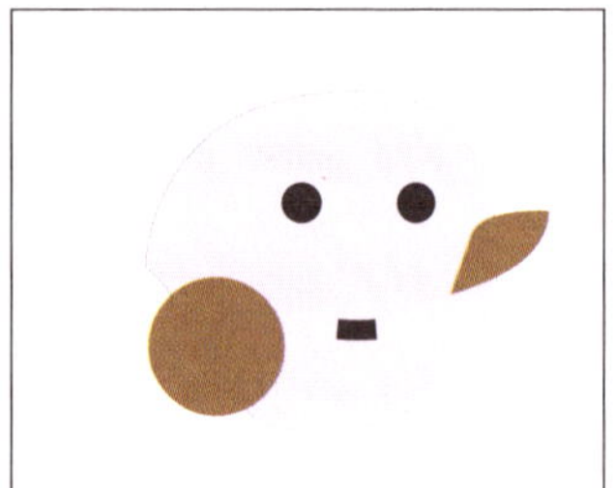
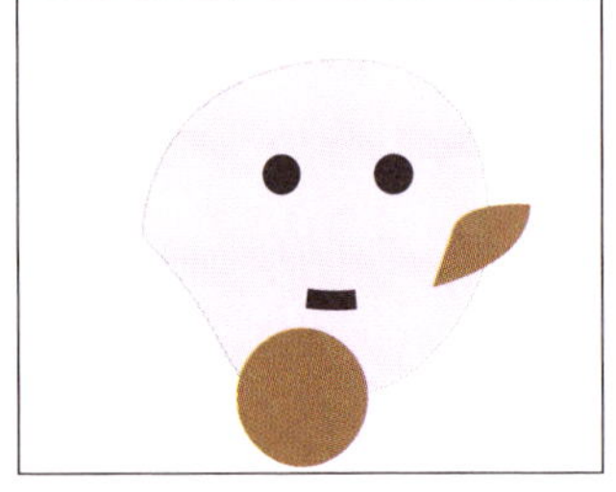
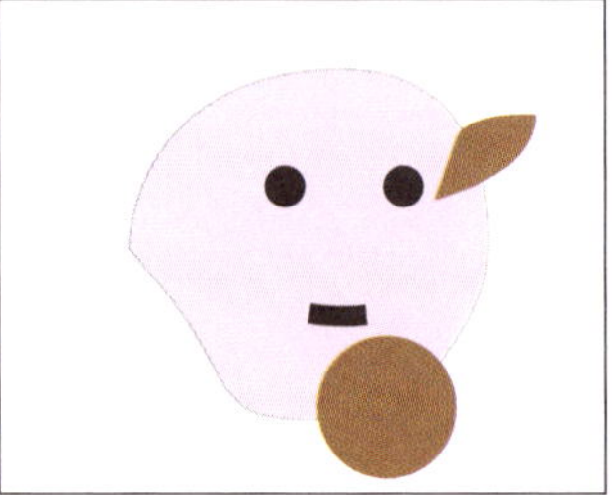
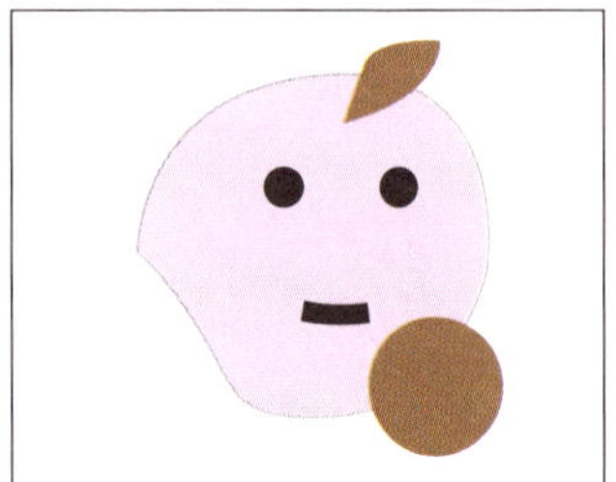
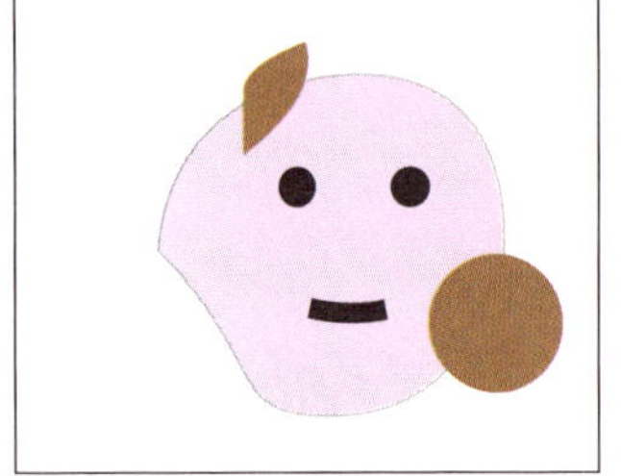
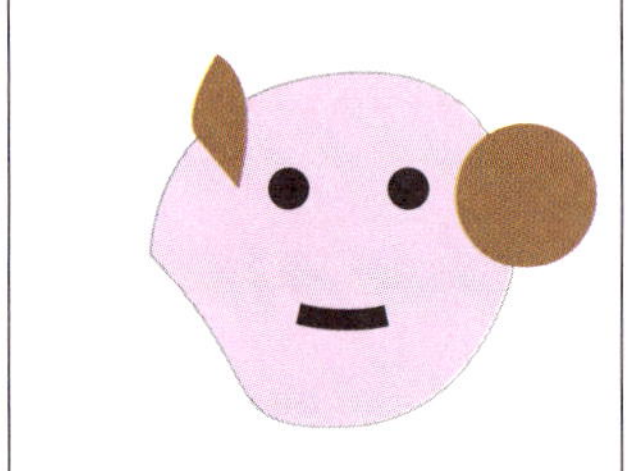
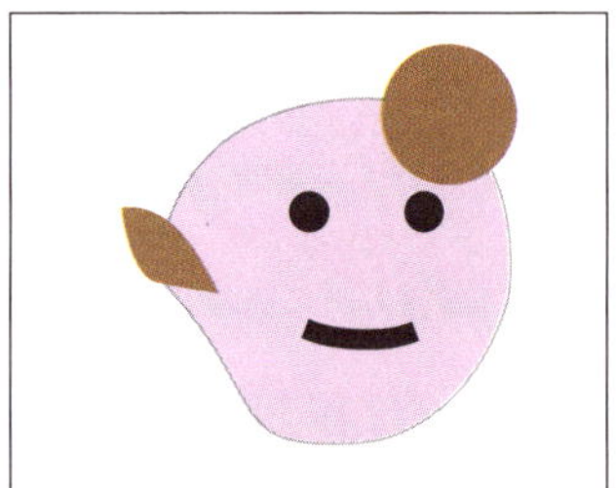
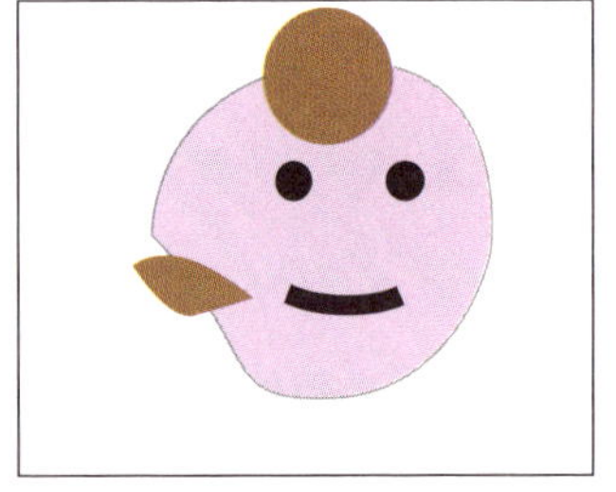
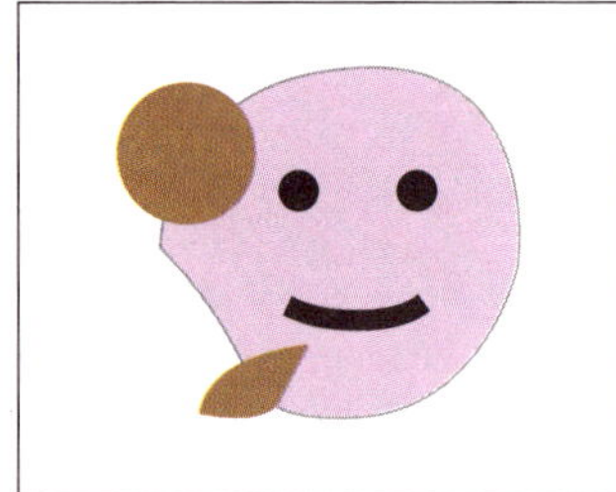
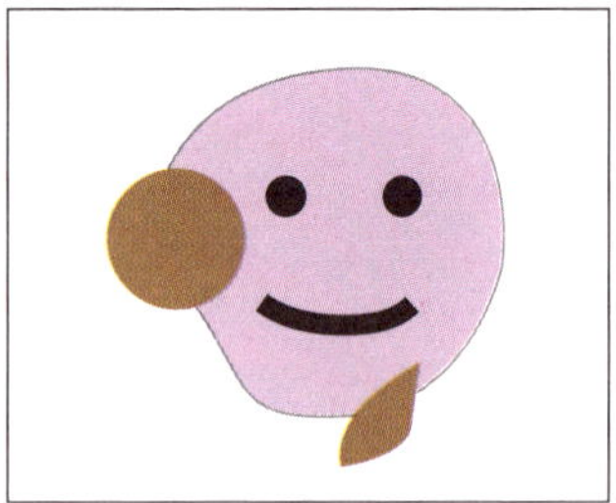
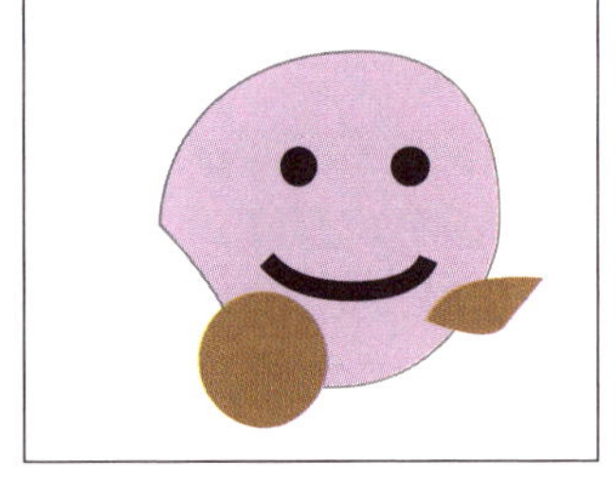
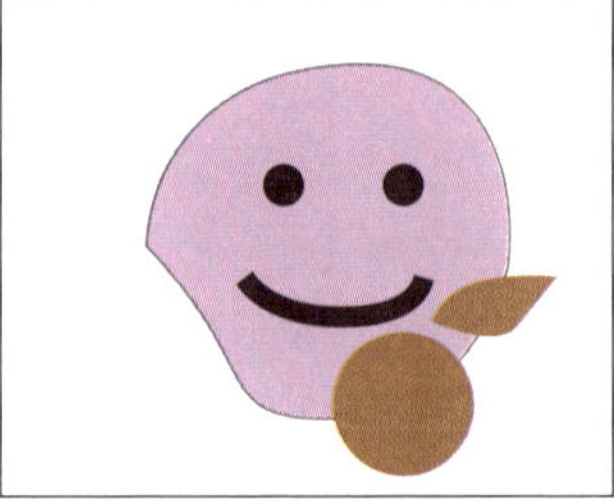
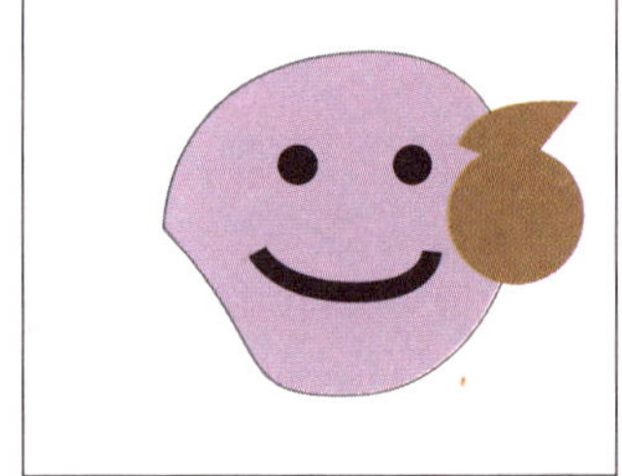

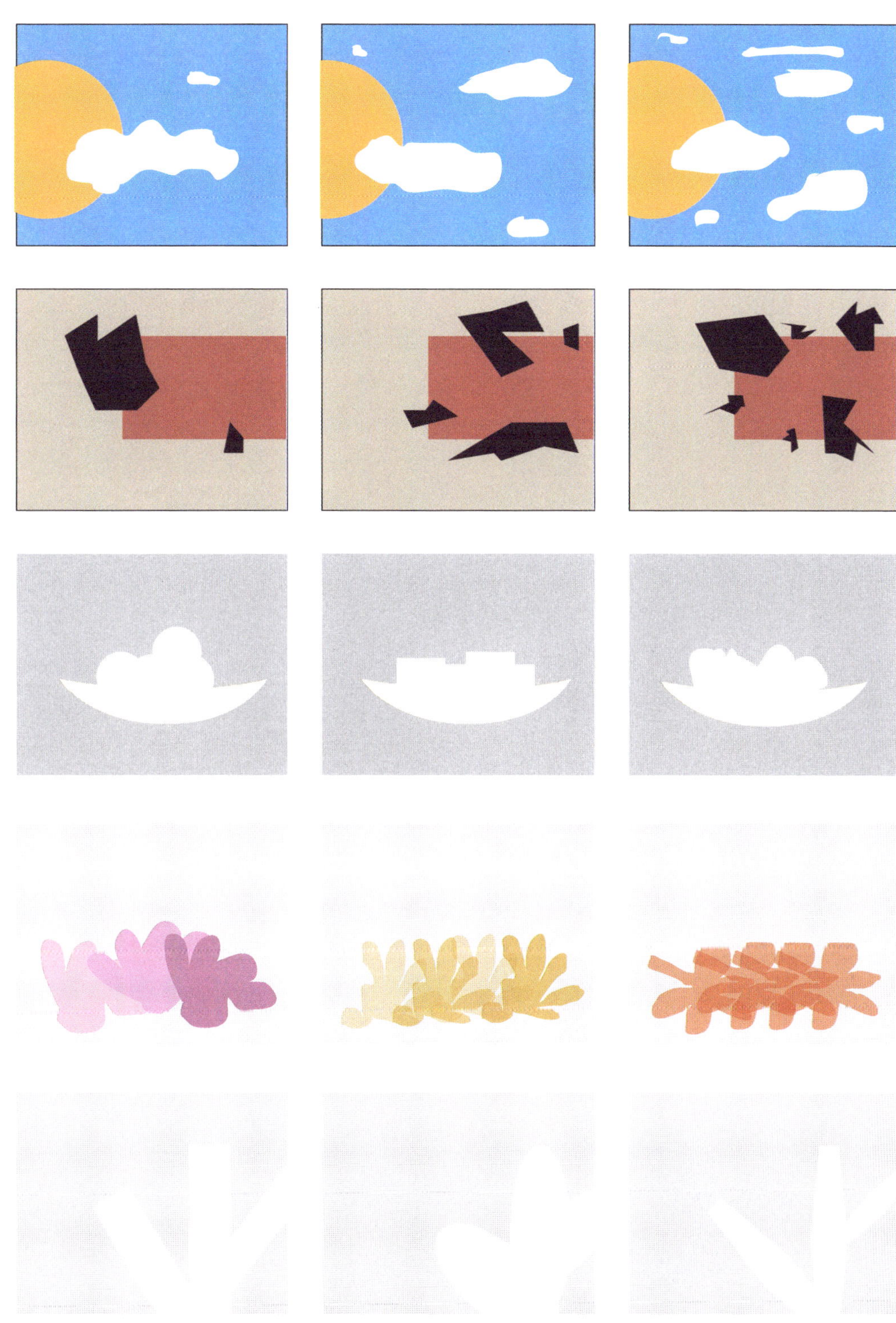

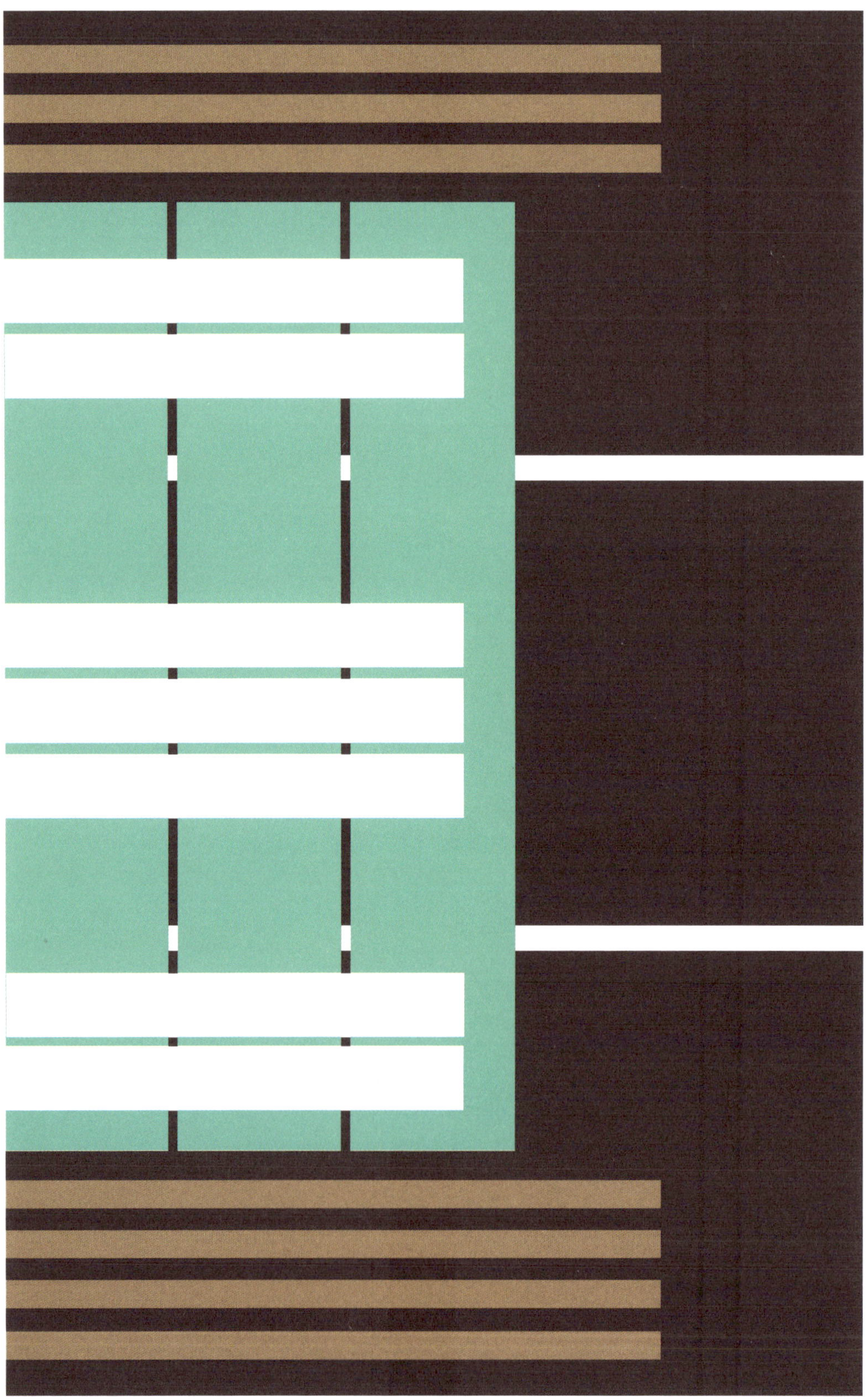

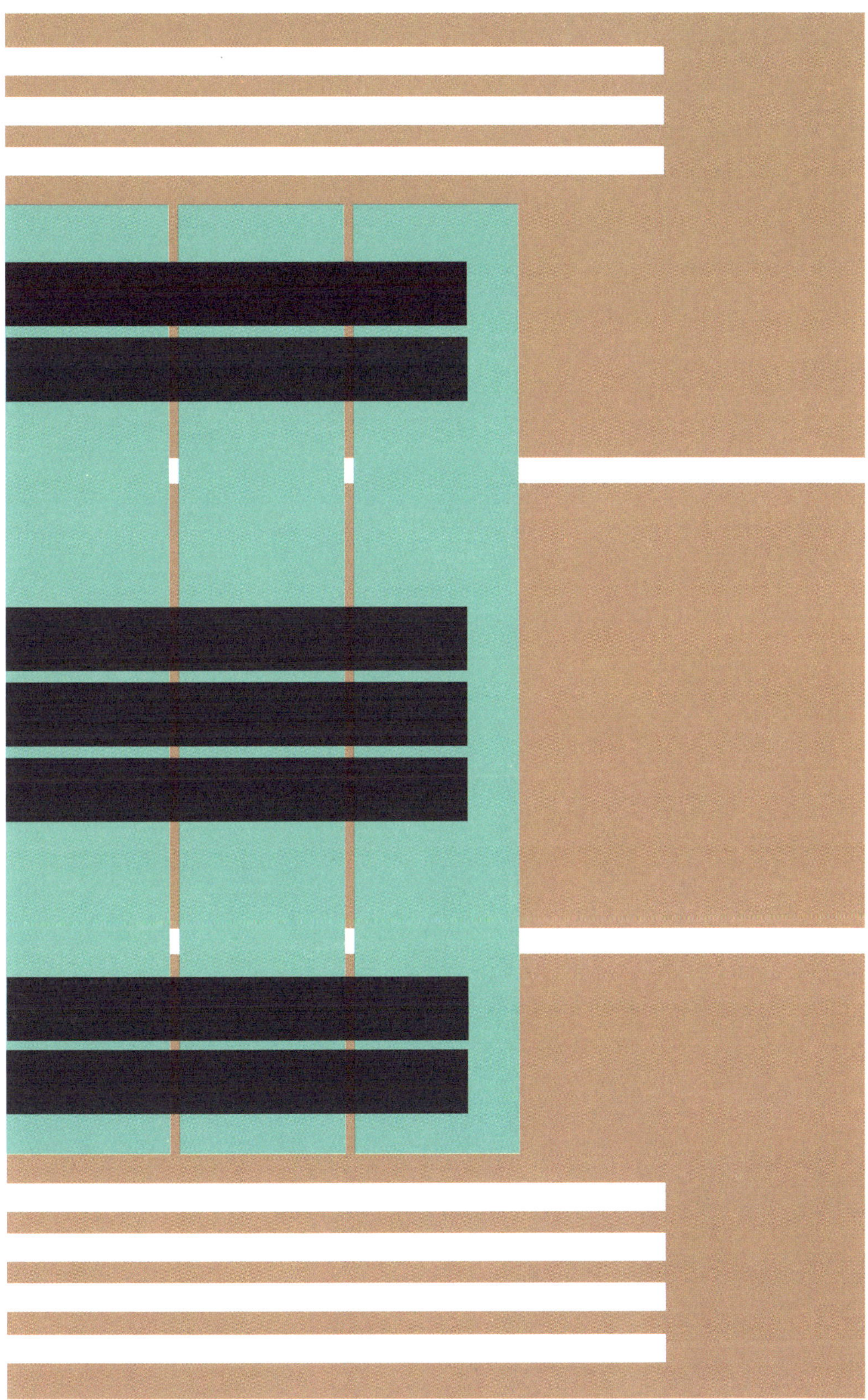

exercise

Add shapes using pencils, markers, or pens. Feel free to explore using storyboards below. Also, feel free to add cutouts using color or black and white paper. Options are limitless!

fold or cut here

fold or cut here

fold or cut here

fold or cut here

6. experimental

Adding freedom to structure is the greatest formula never resolved but it has great outcomes that can be of great application to new designs. Thinking on experimenting and always looking for brand new outcomes is what thrives experimentation, sometimes combining things that go together and sometimes not, but it works.

Also, there is no perfect formula or research that should be counted as irrelevant to help explore further and getting ideas. Content can be vessels with no form but as they take shape and are placed in a way that the message comes across the shape or shapes are already successfully formed.

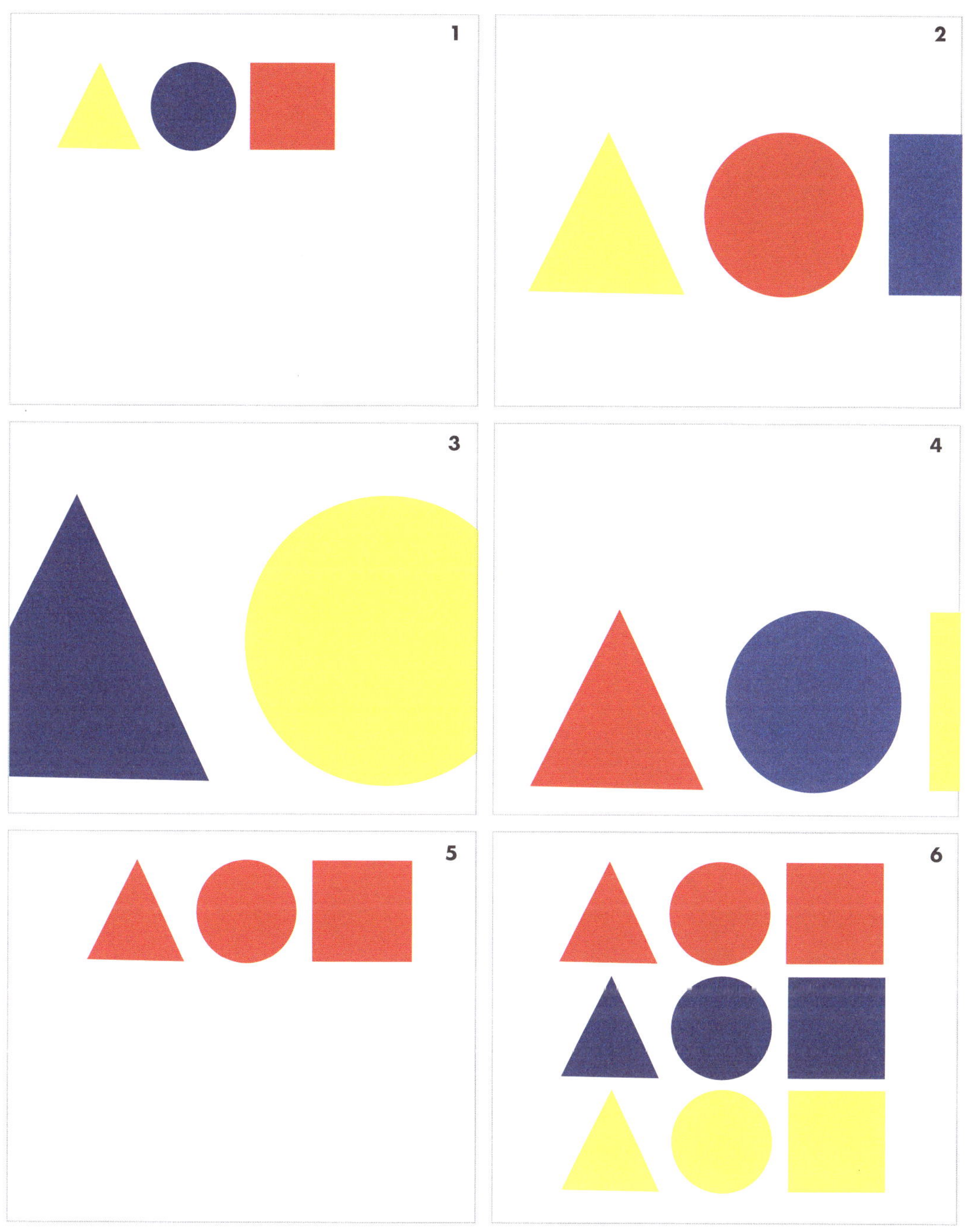

movement of shapes

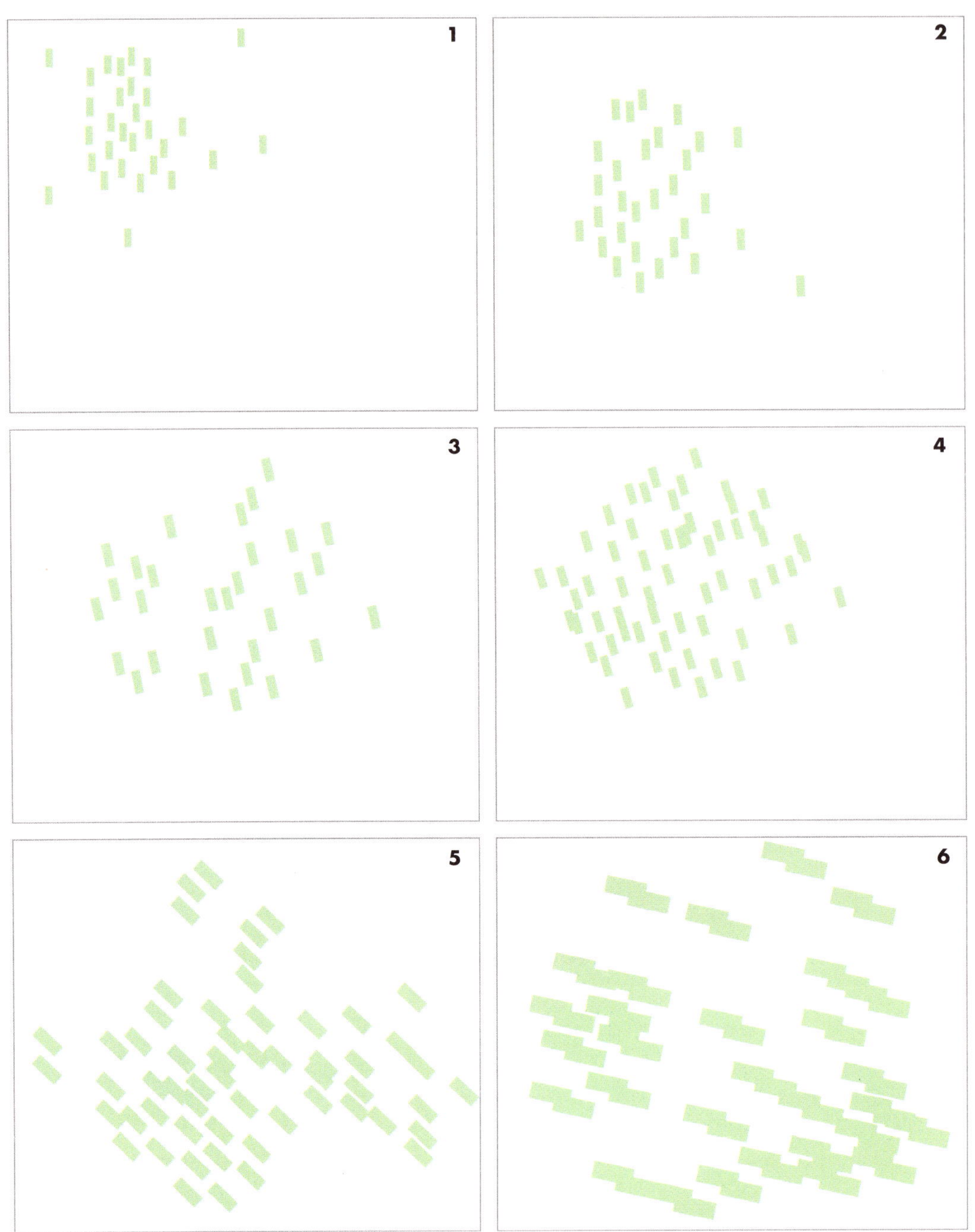

movement of basic shapes

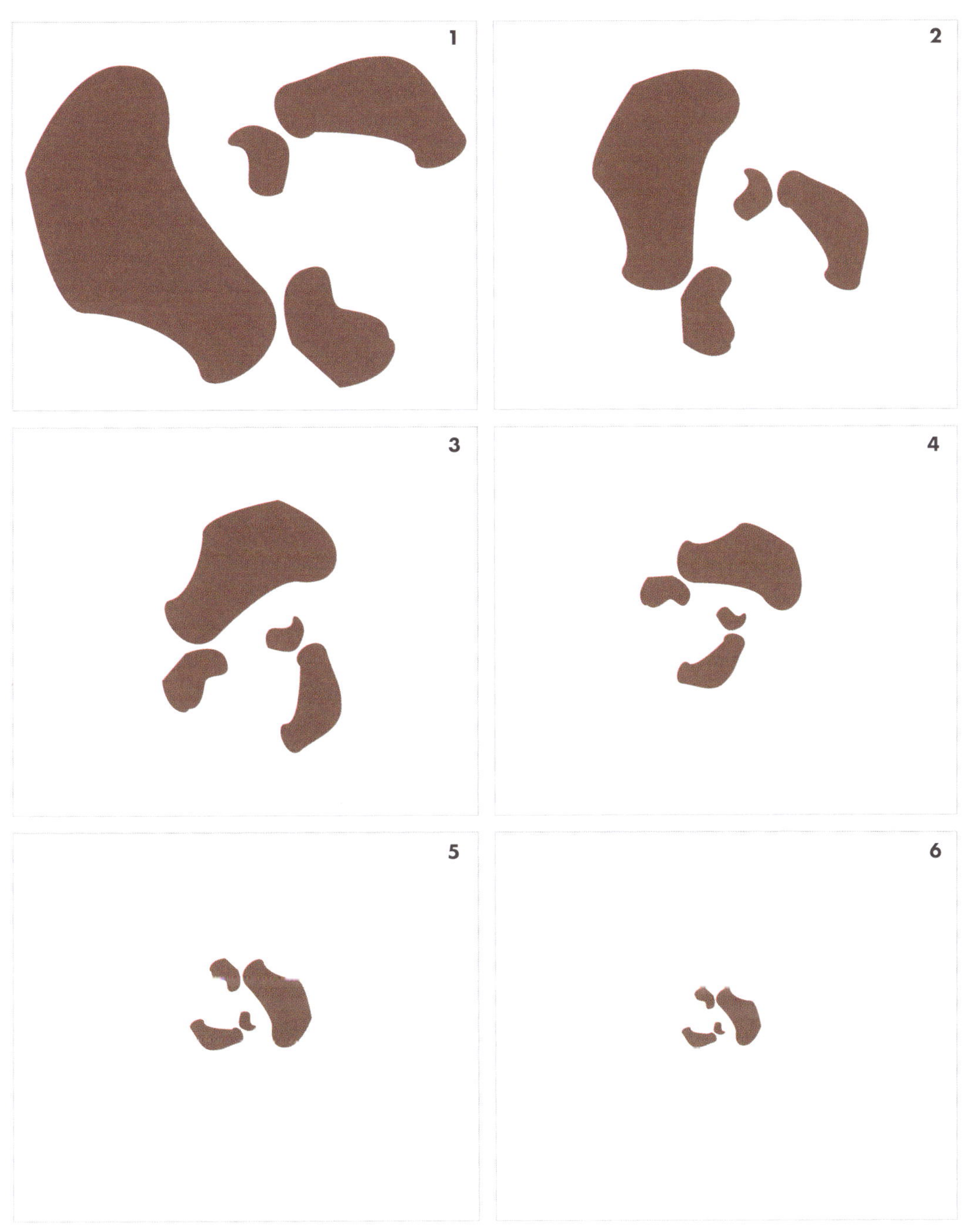

movement of organic shapes

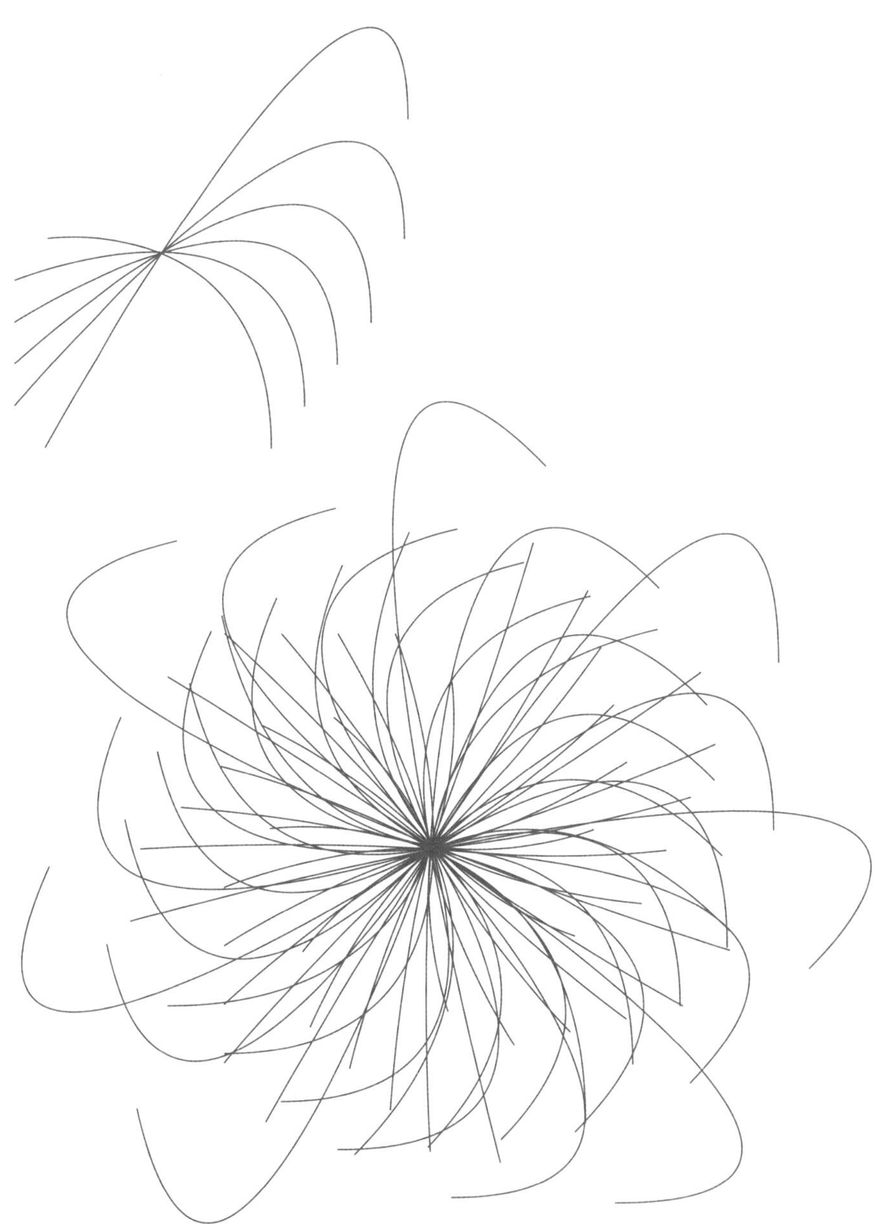

arcs creating depth

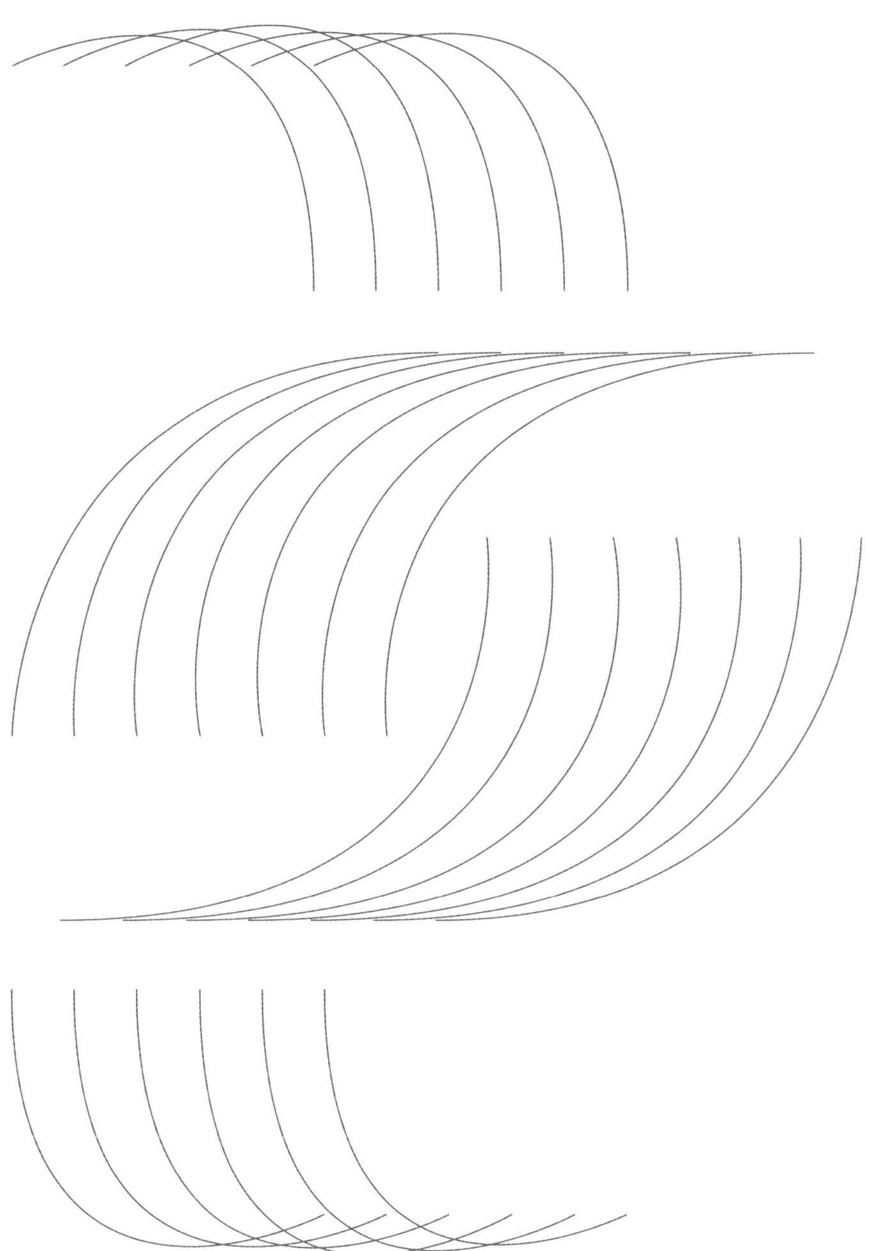

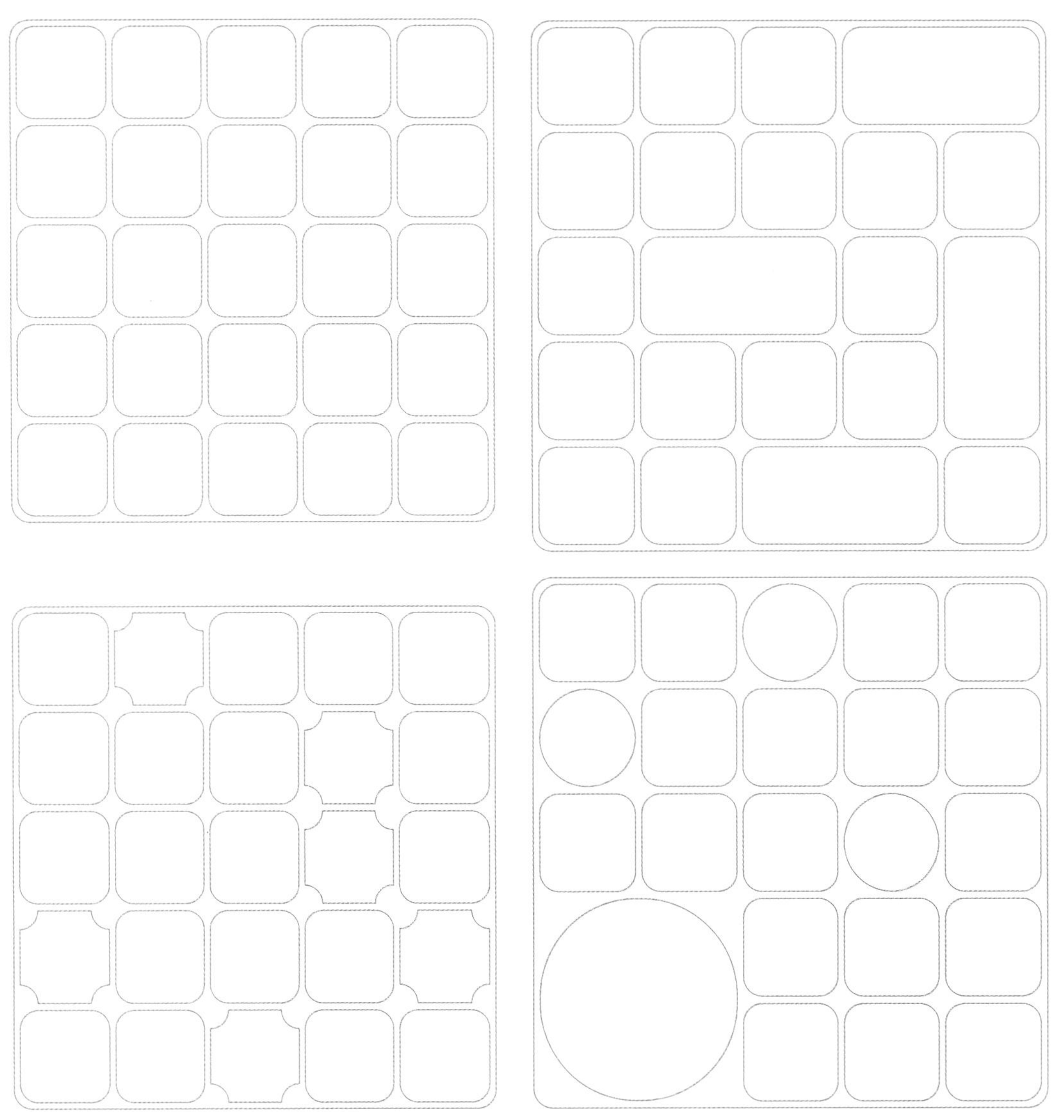

grids that are creating explorative subdivisions

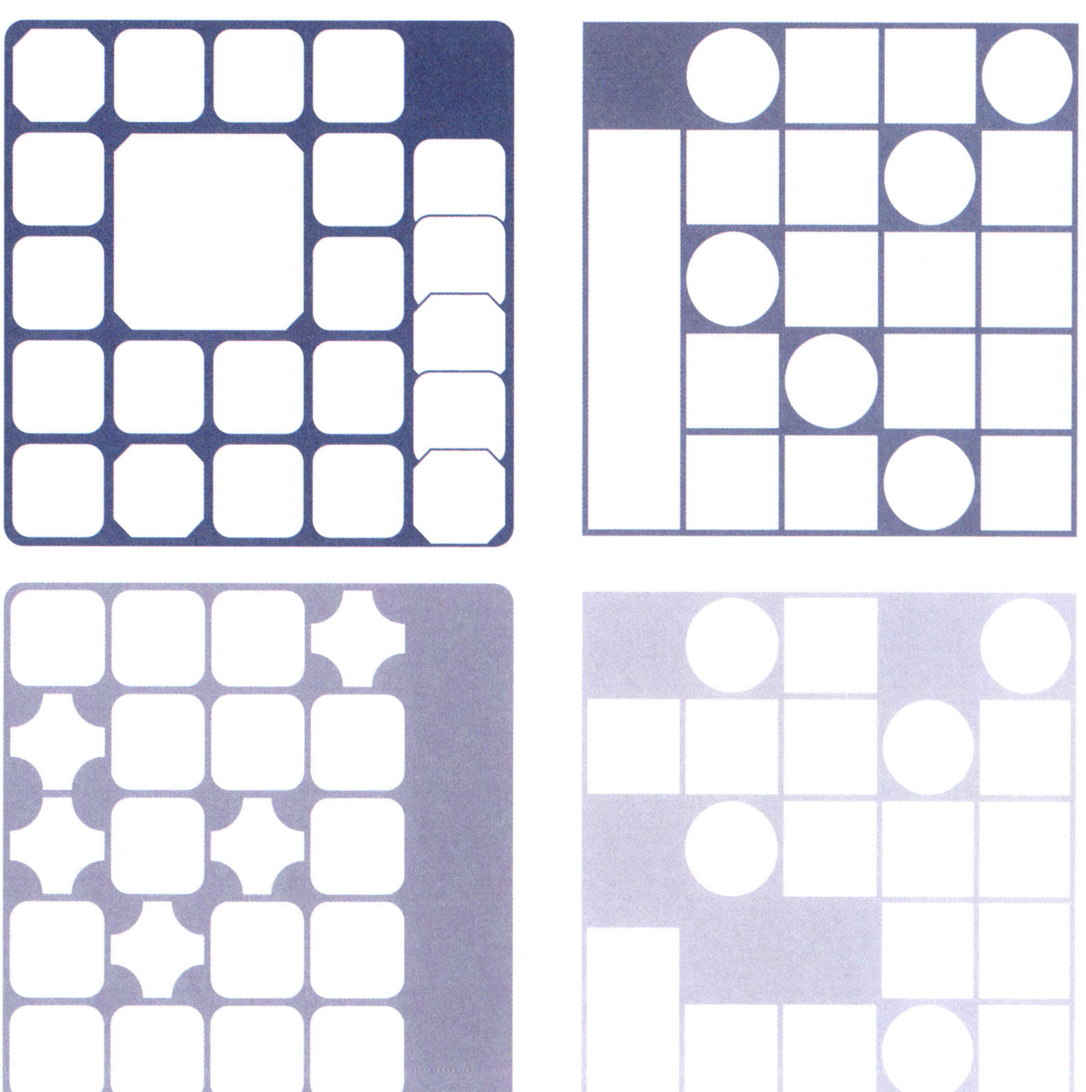

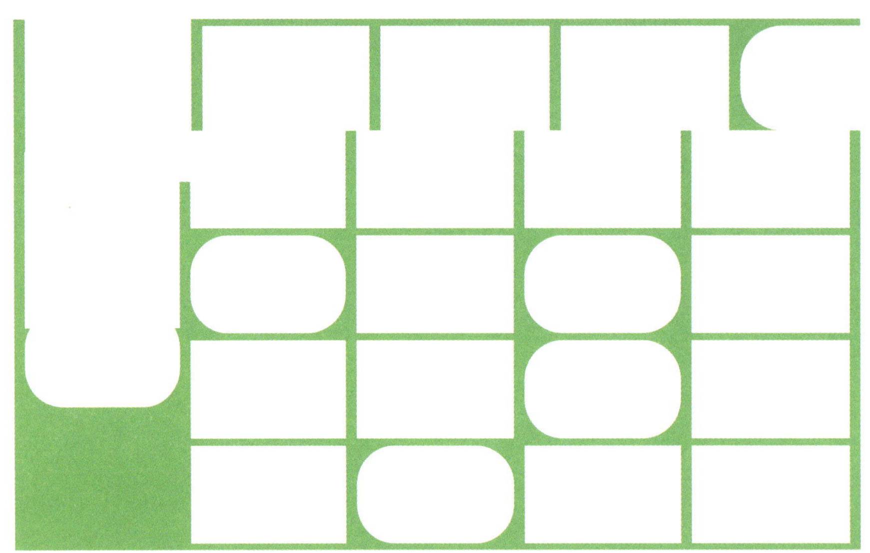

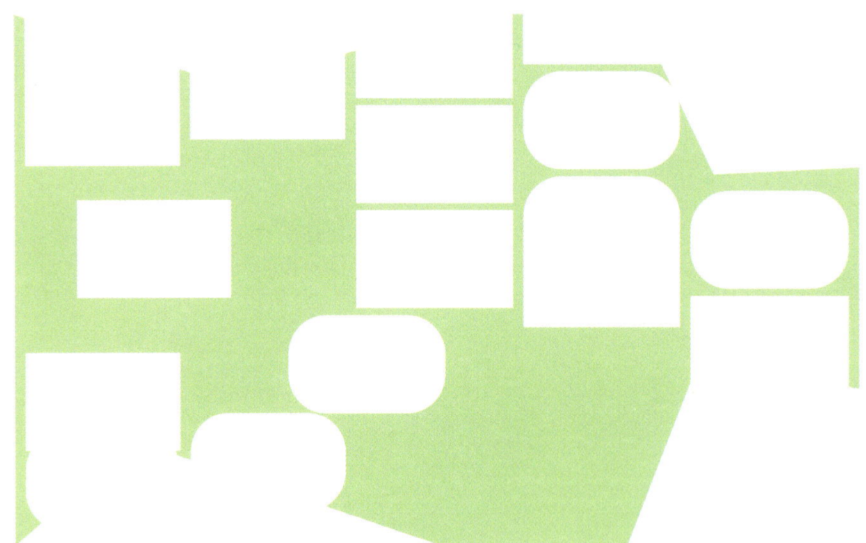

grids that are creating explorative backgrounds

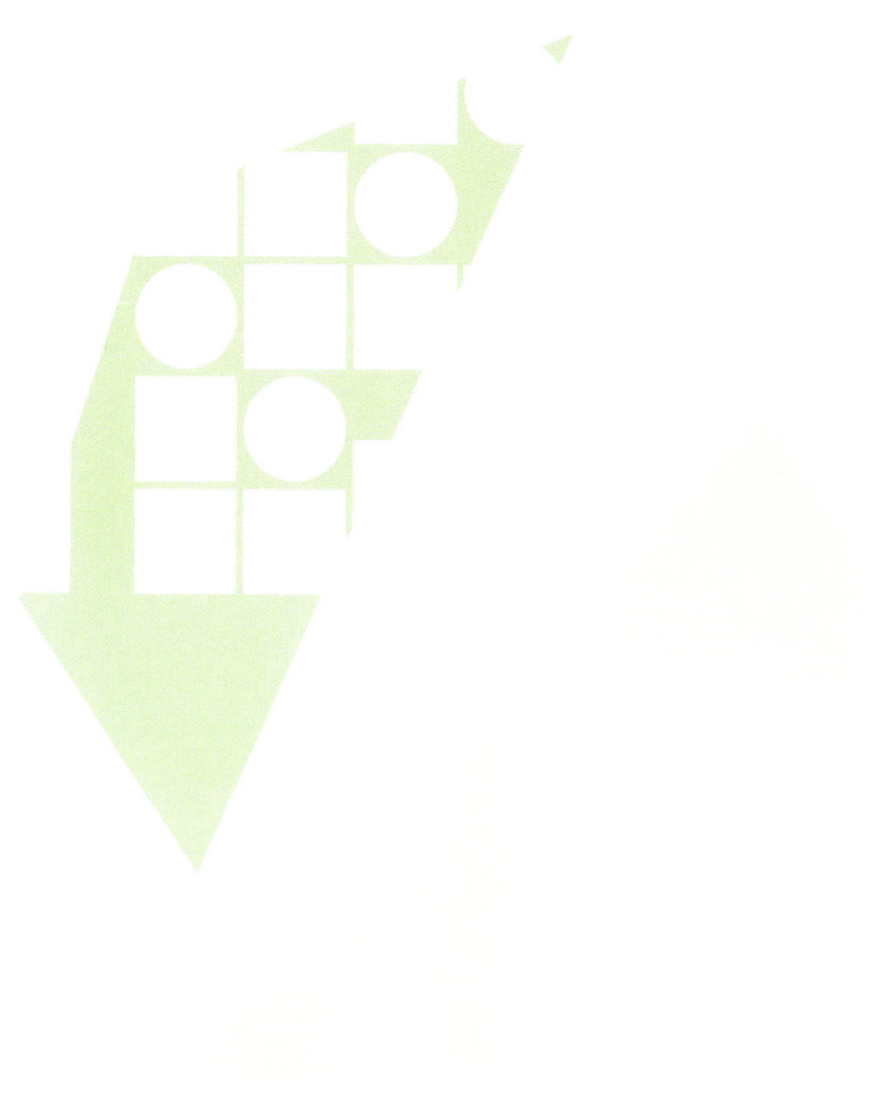

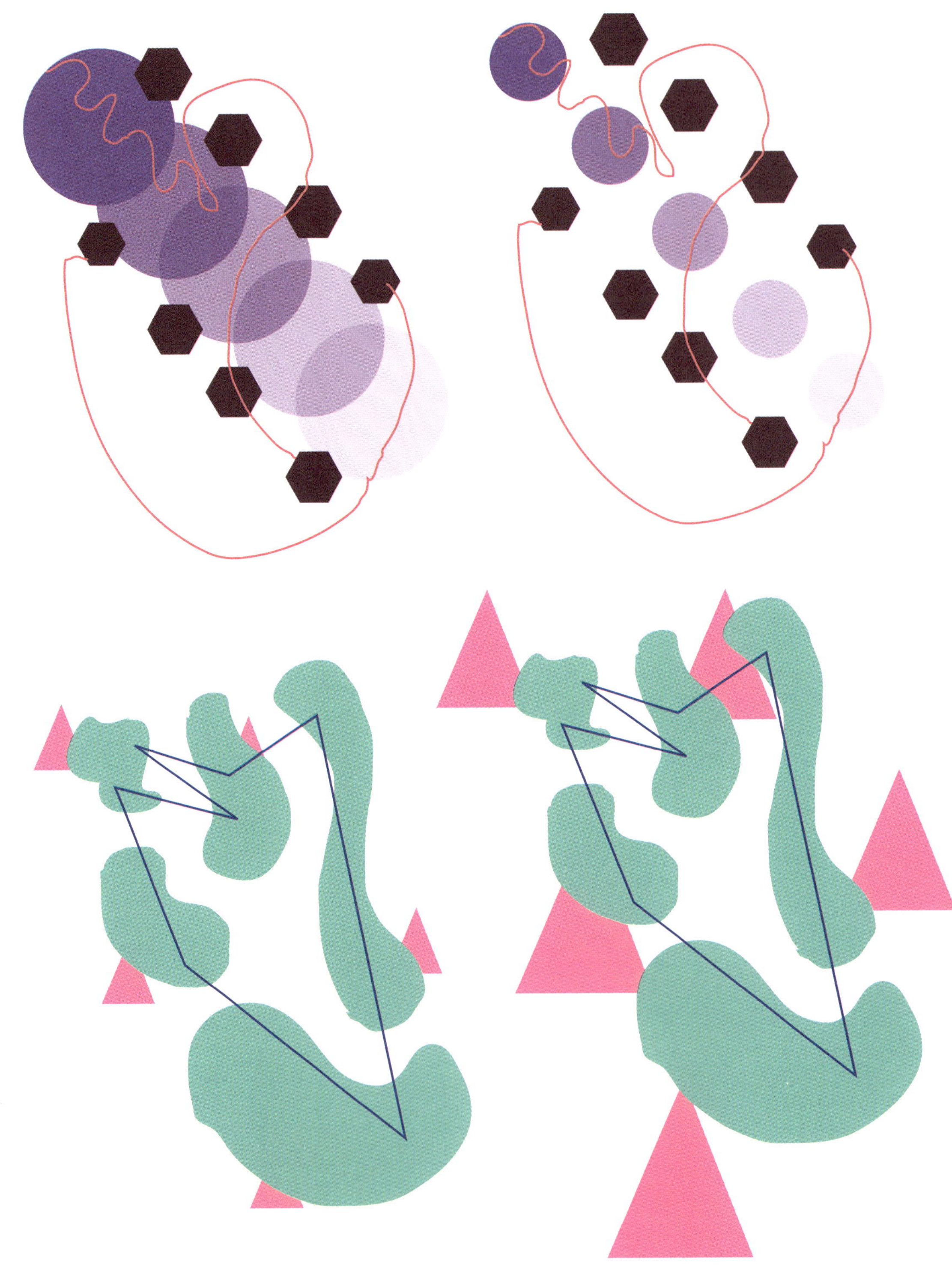

organic grids with explorative shapes

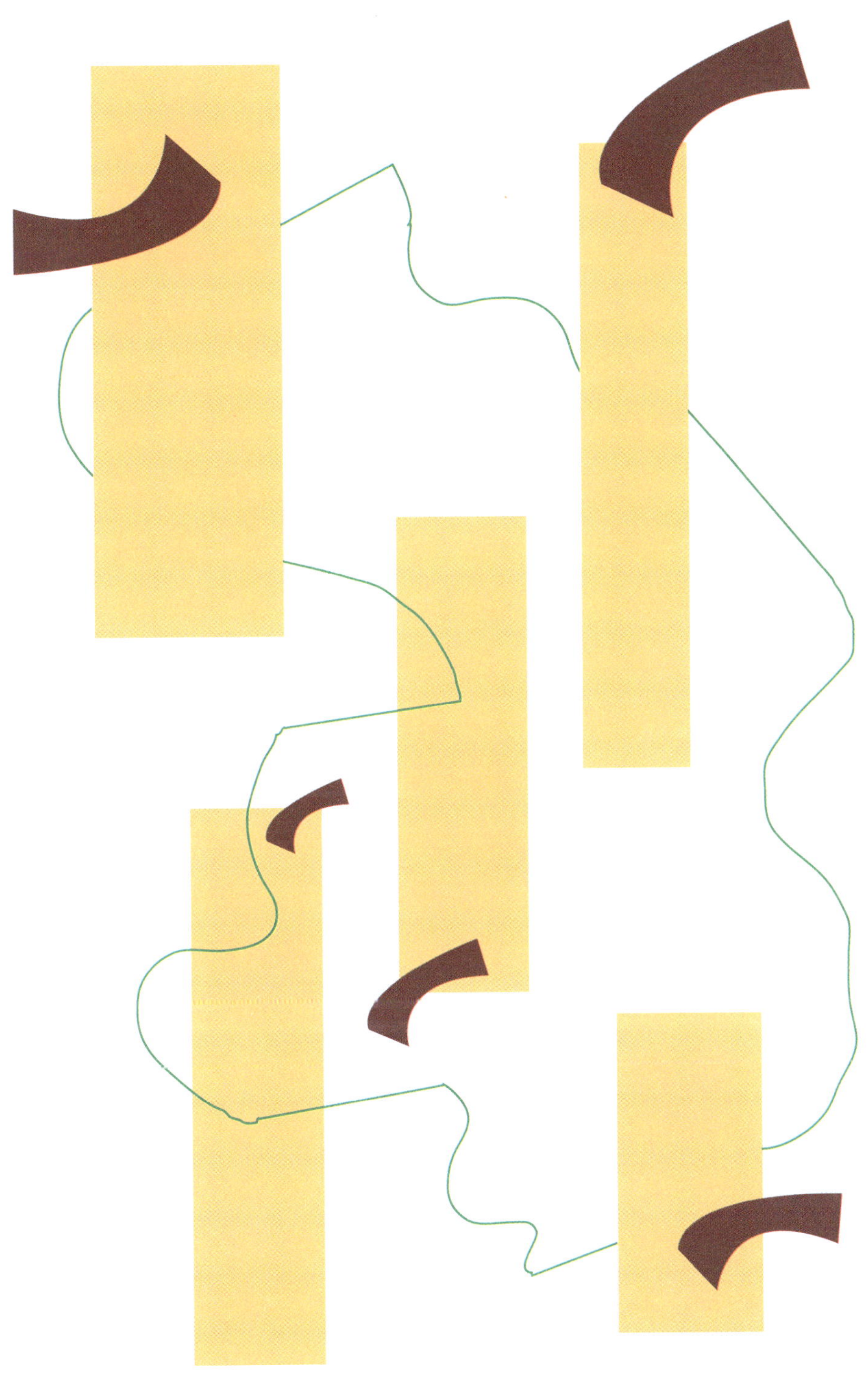

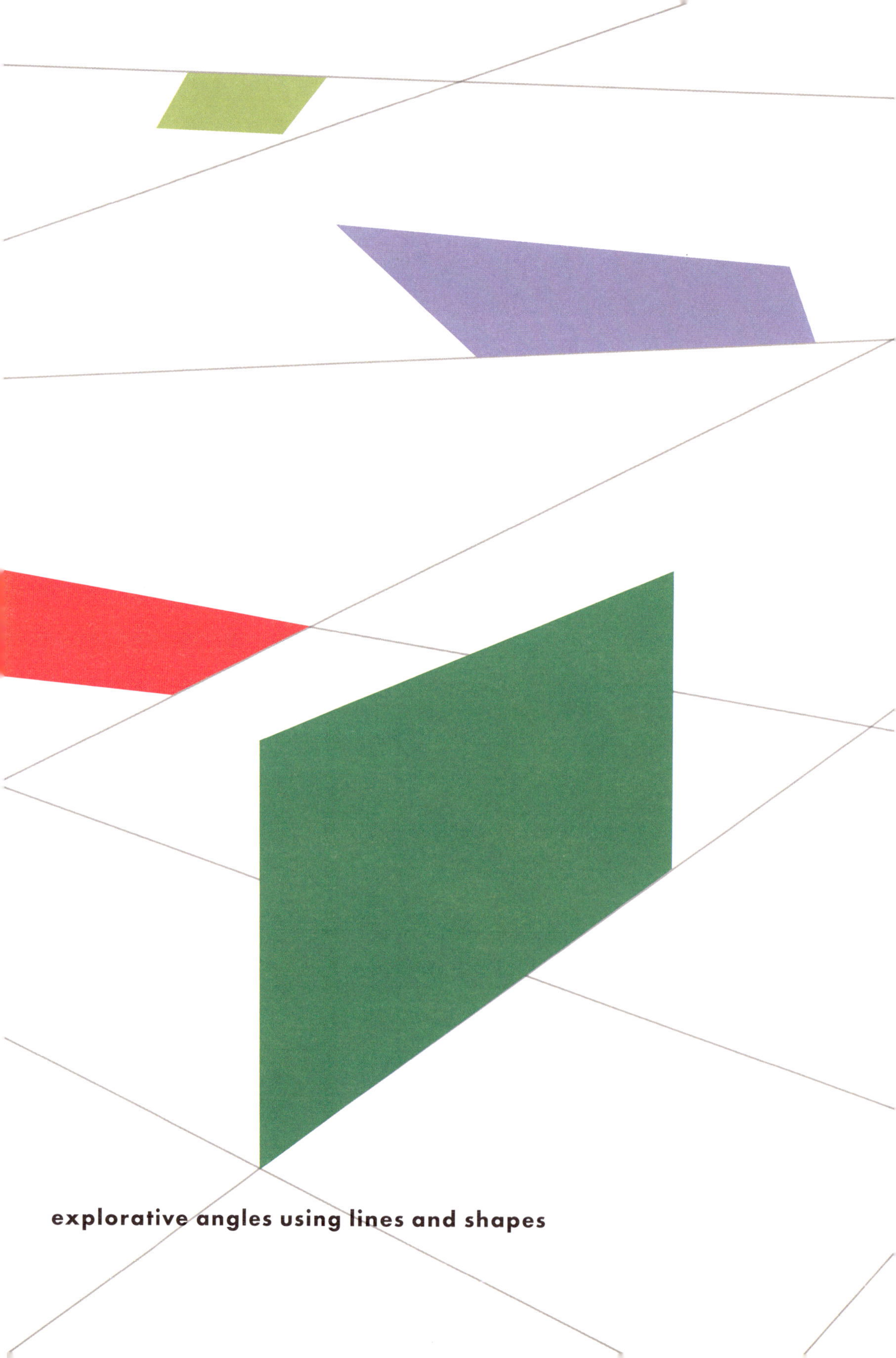
explorative angles using lines and shapes

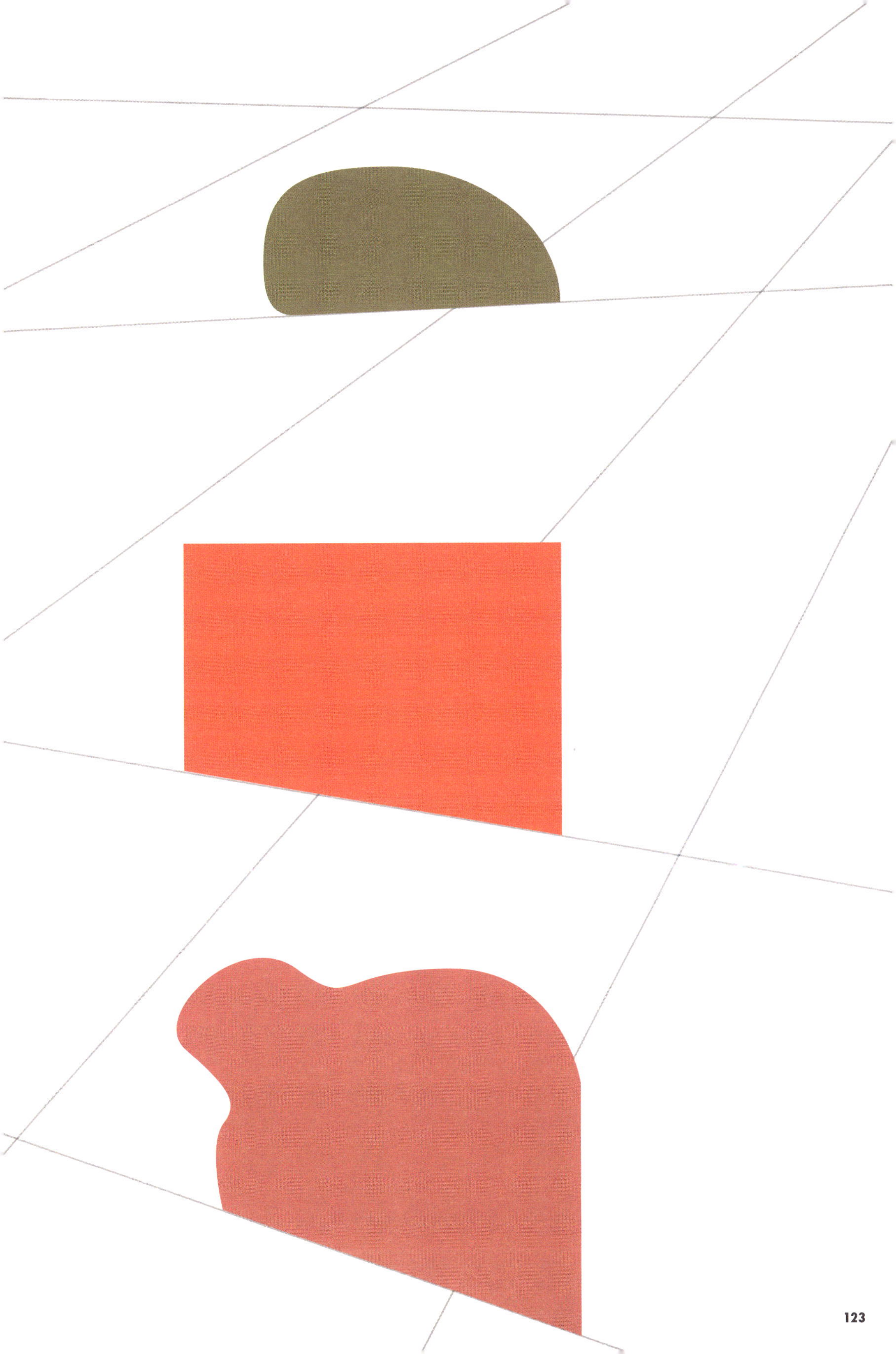

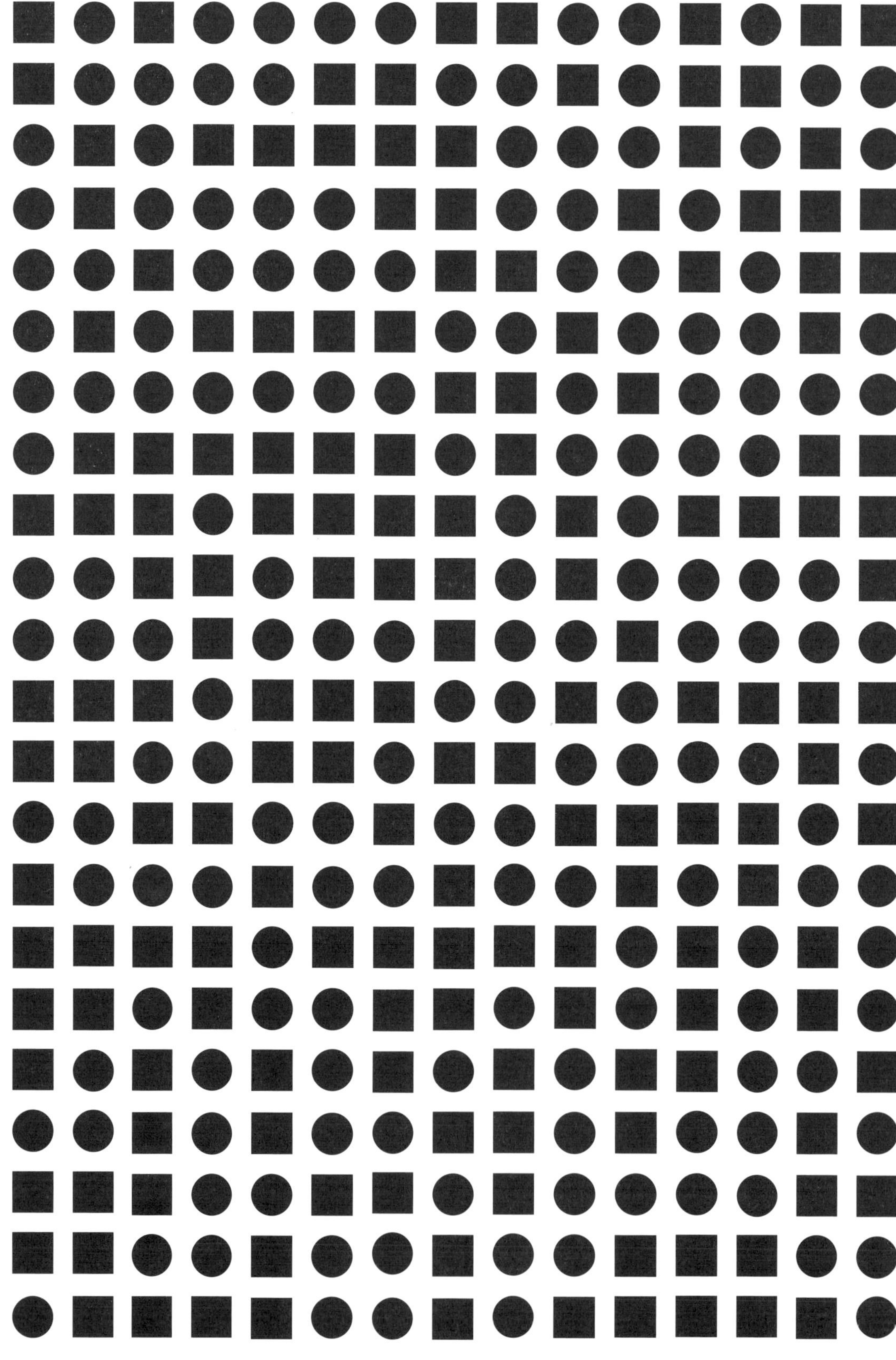

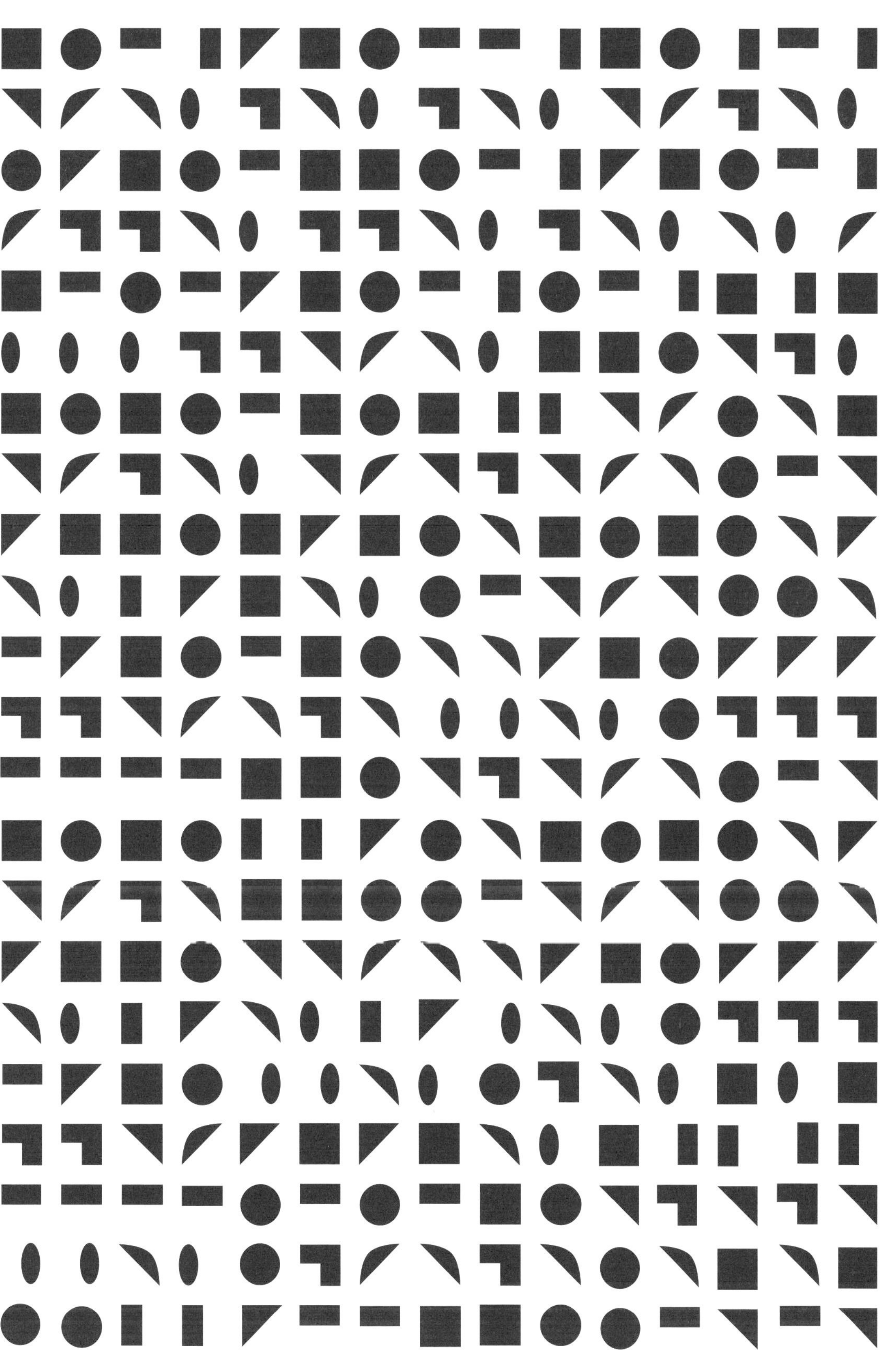

exercise

Add shapes using pencils, markers or pens.

fold or cut here

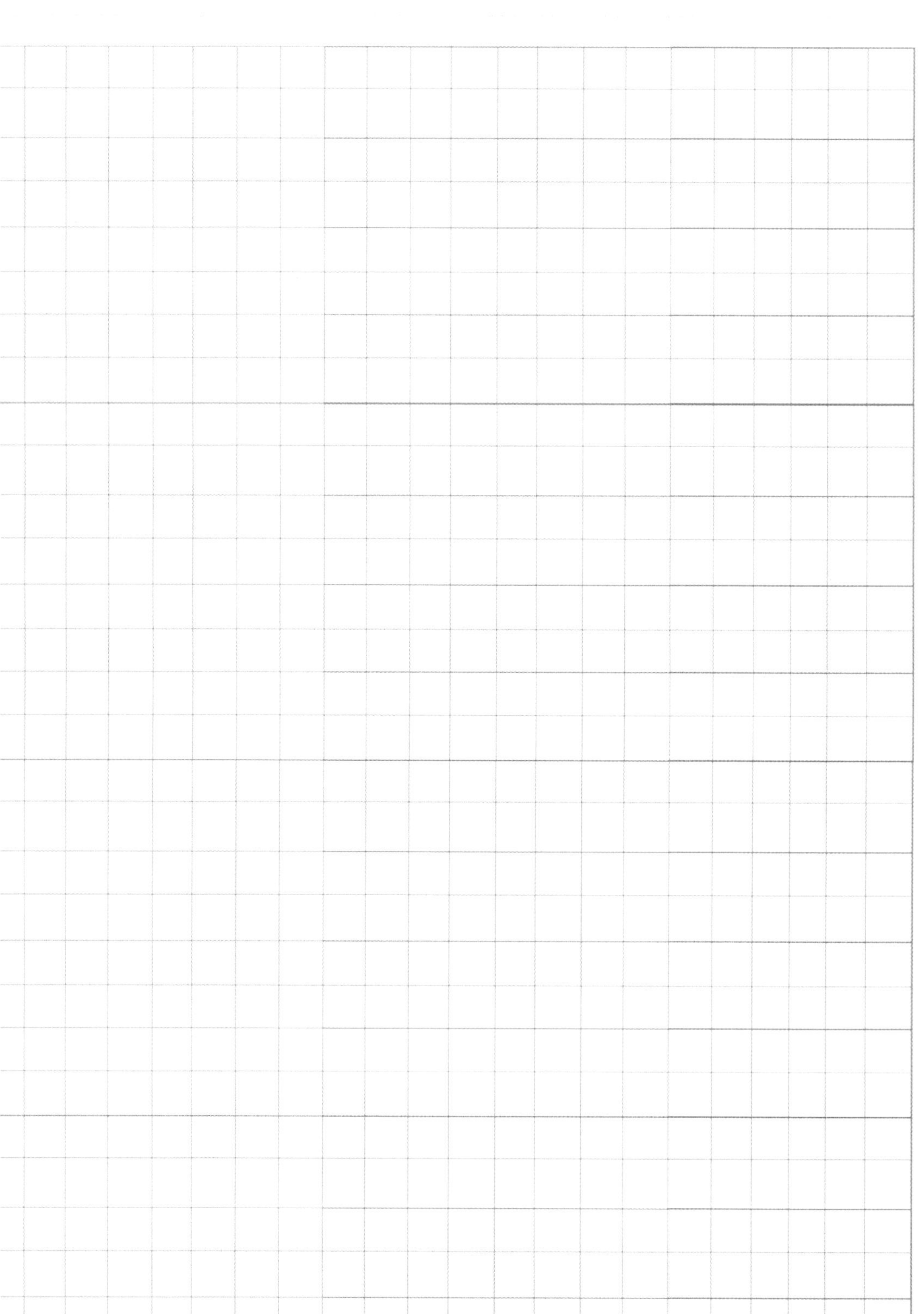

fold or cut here

fold or cut here

fold or cut here

7. directional

According to our eyes and the direction we see, directions can help us understand, for example wayfinding which allows us to move from one space to another. Signals can give us information on what direction to follow such as arrows. Understanding color through the street lights, green, yellow and red, which is a universal way to understand go, warning and stop. Also, through reading a map it will be directing the person where to go or give information that allows to choose a beginning and an end.

Other examples are reading through a menu, following any guided instructions, repairing an object, putting an object together that it takes directional information, and even interacting through an object that informs as well. Throughout this chapter there are going to be basic concepts of wayfinding and diagrams that are essential to brainstorm a successful level of understanding through directional design.

When some type of direction is give from only one symbol, hierarchy is already at work. As a viewer or designer we have access to many levels of hierarchy within directional design. It can get so complex and being able to manage simplicity and complexity can become and extra task resolving a visual design problem.

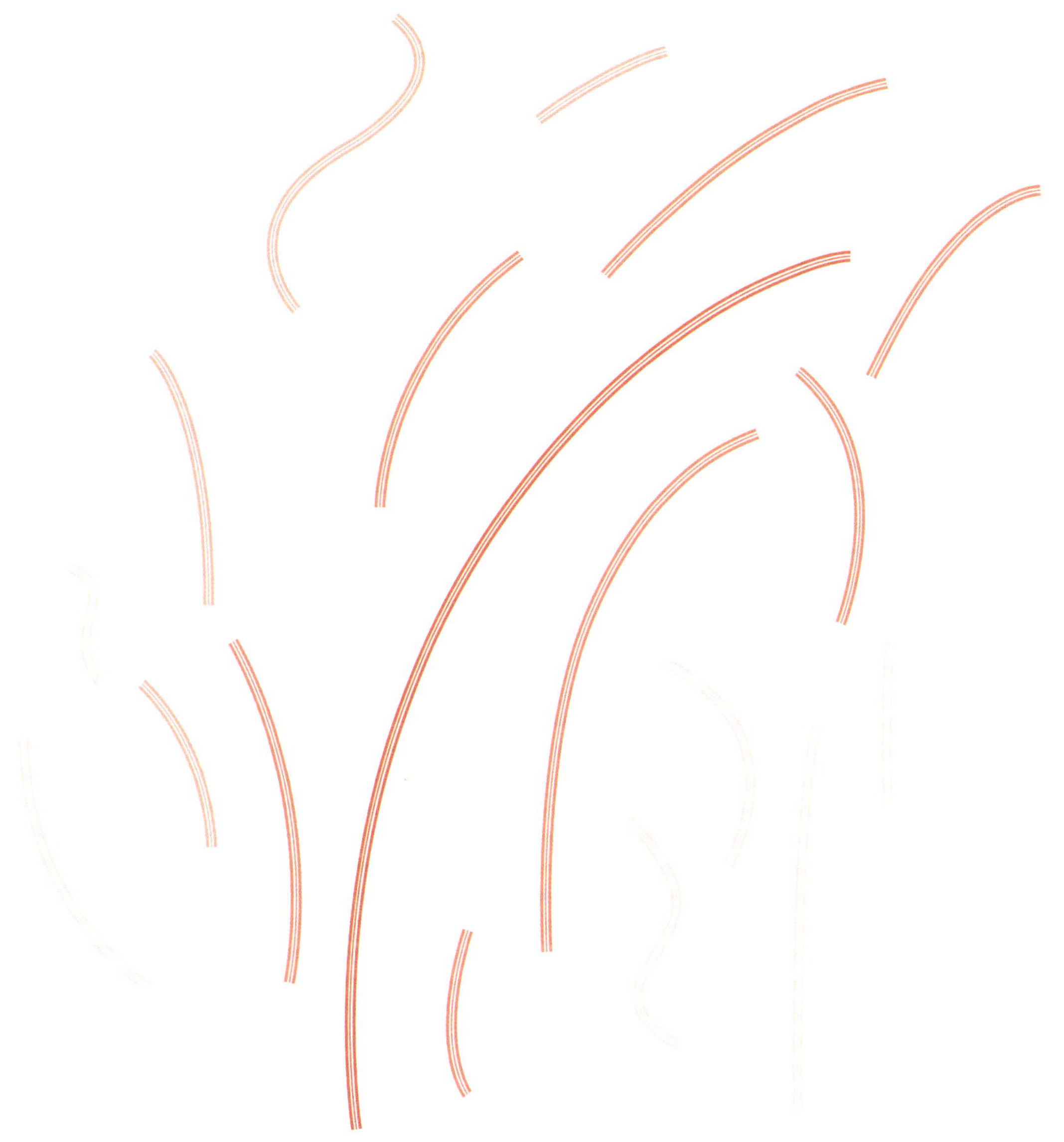

flow

Creating a sensation of movement brings a new level of activation of space as the viewer looks for the most important part of the image or diagram and follows the instructions or line work.

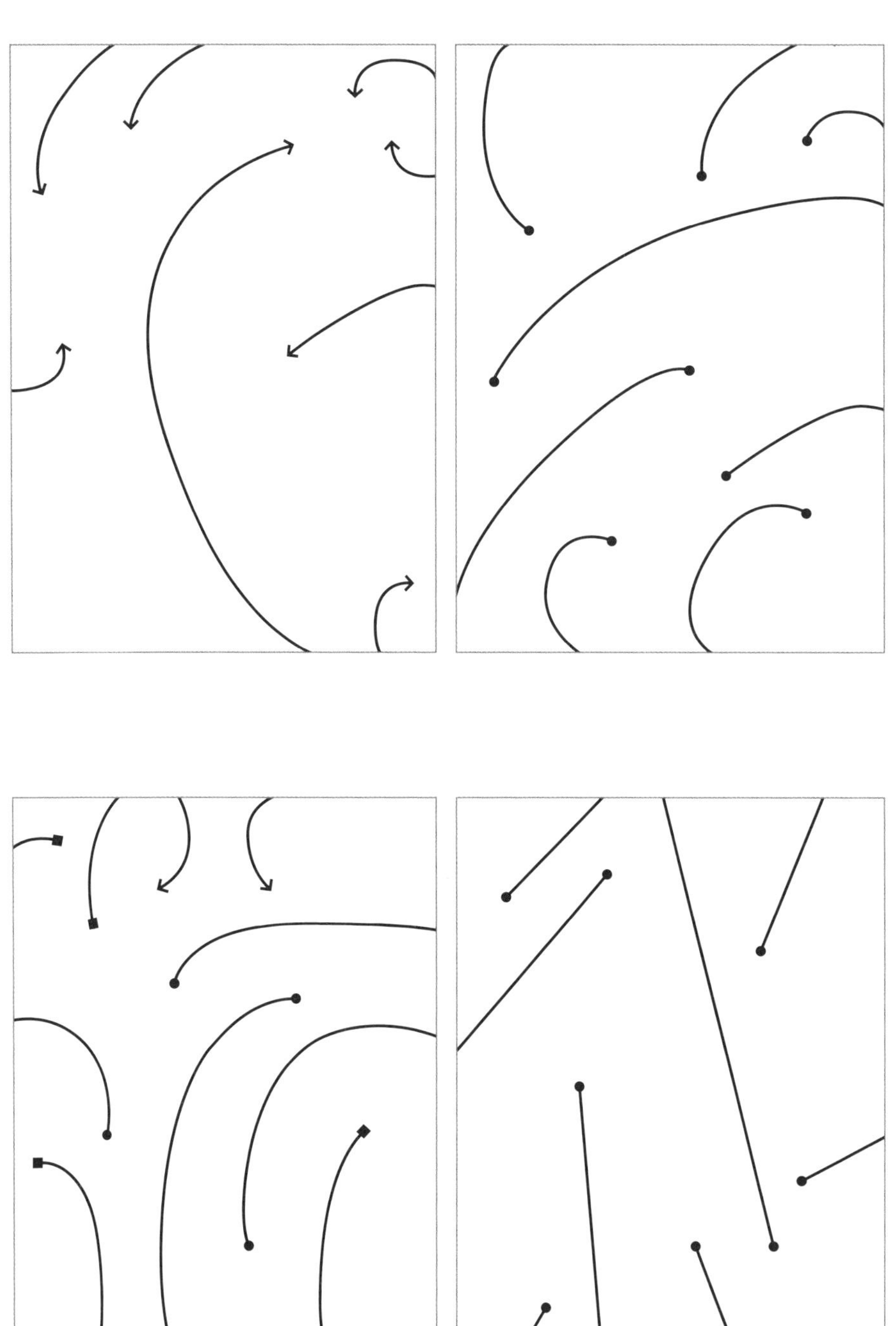

arrows

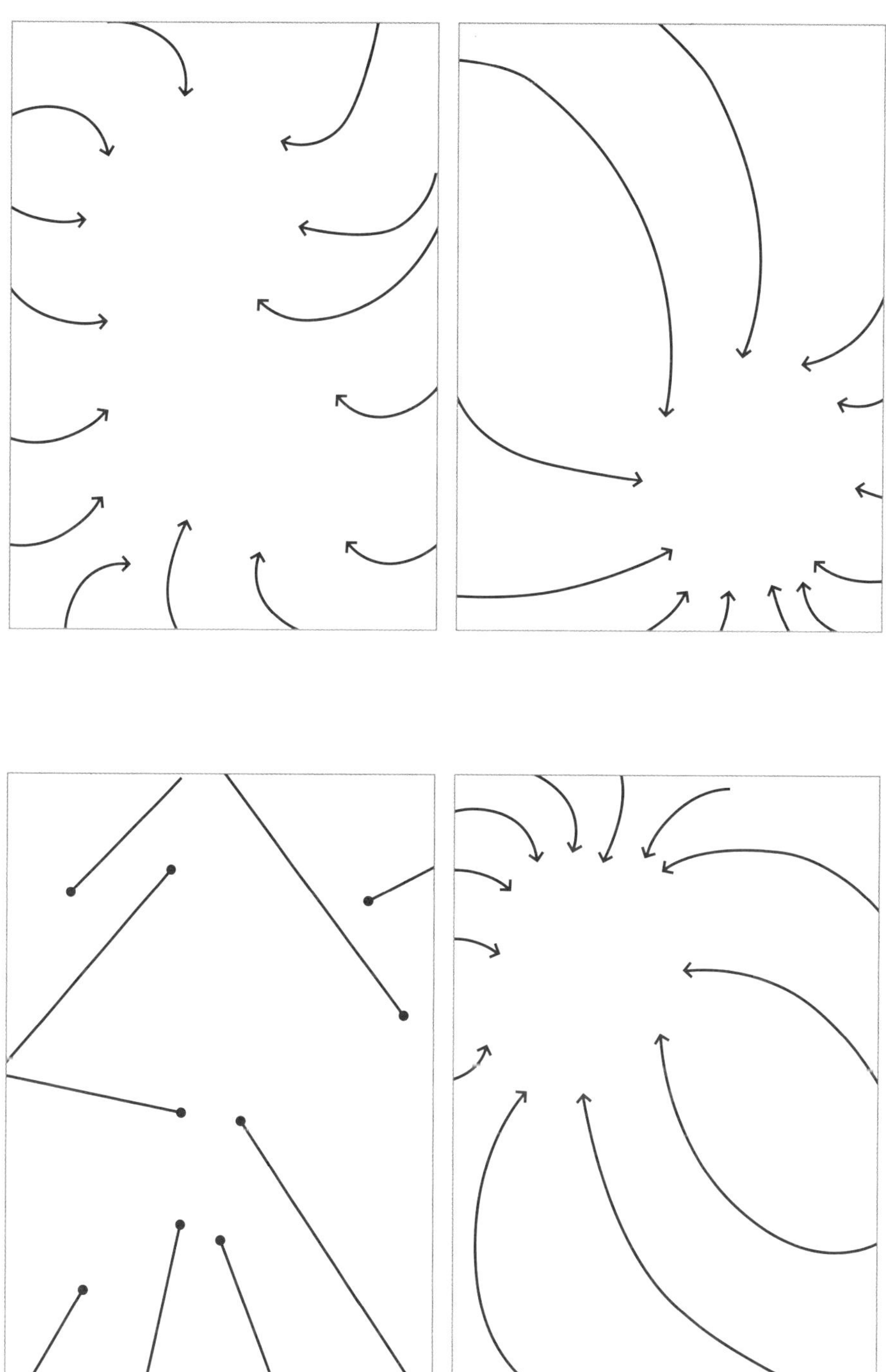

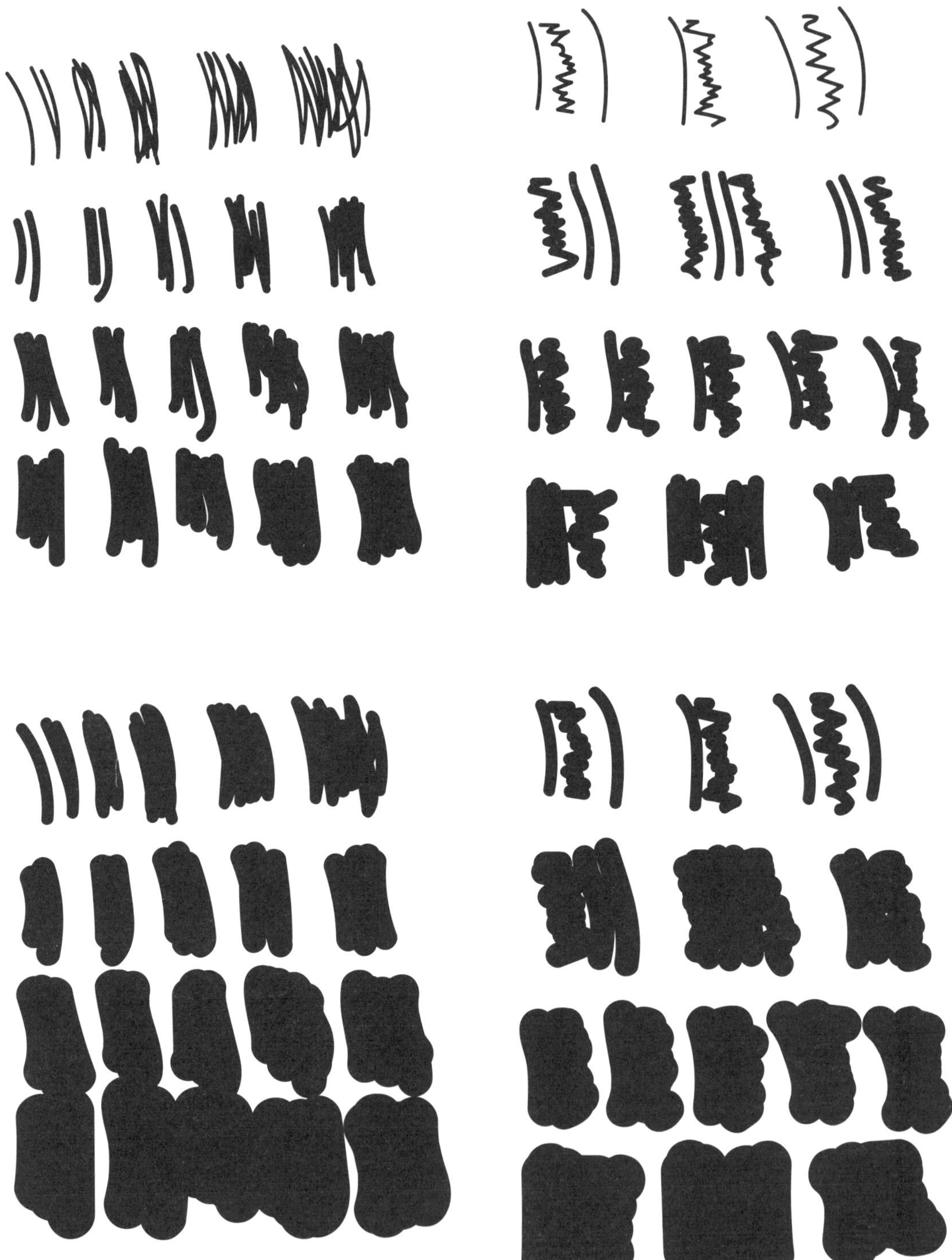

weights of lines

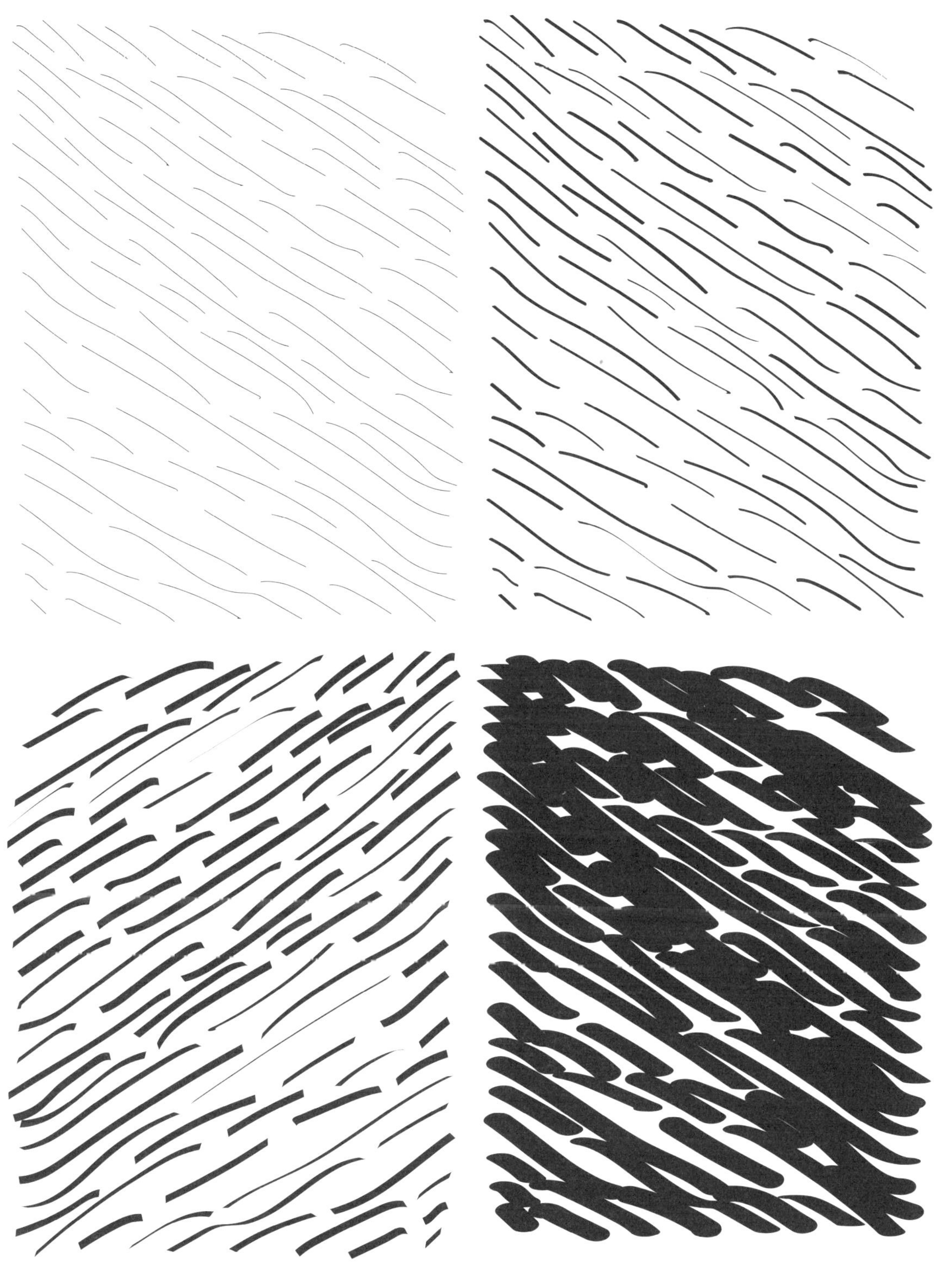

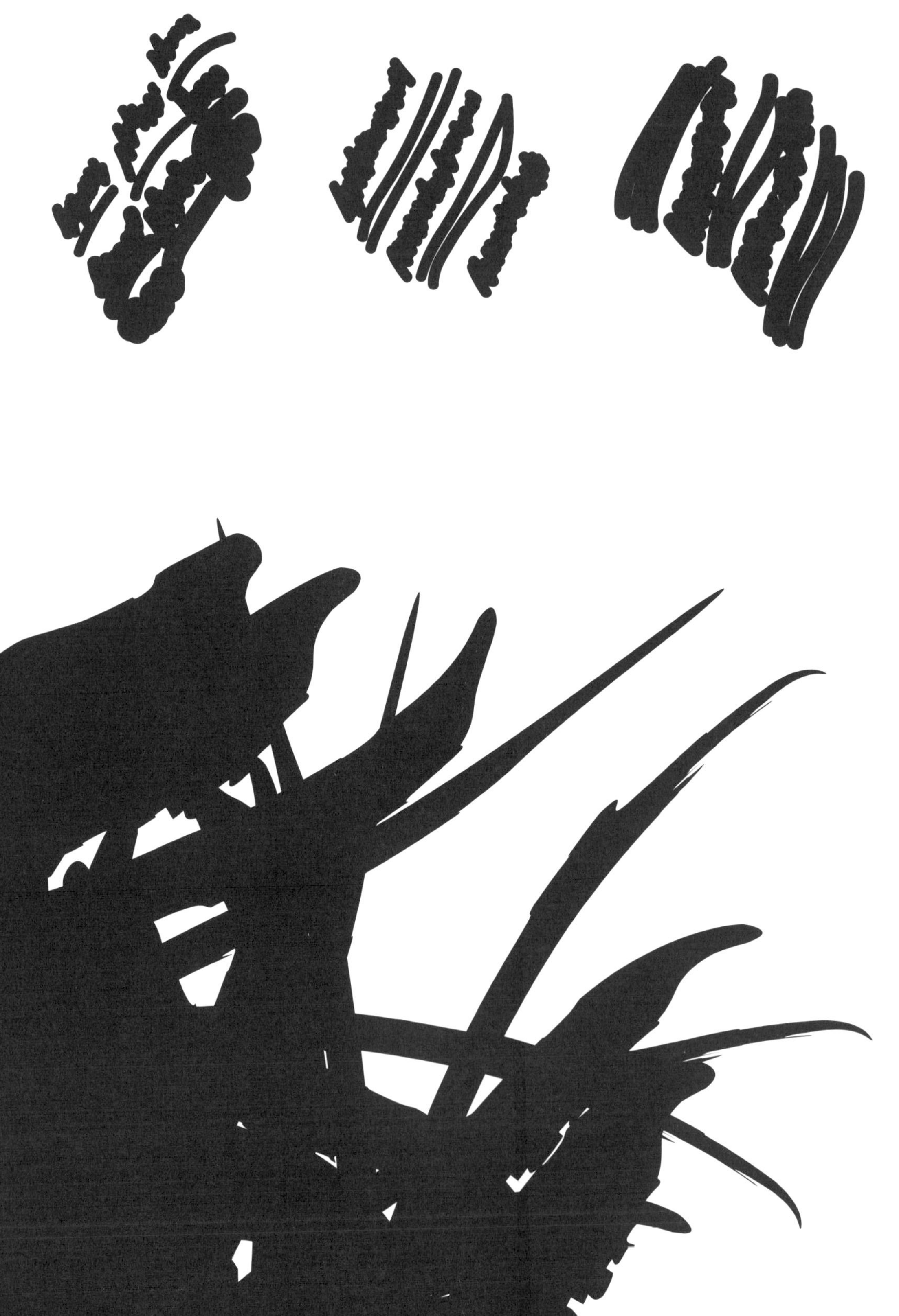

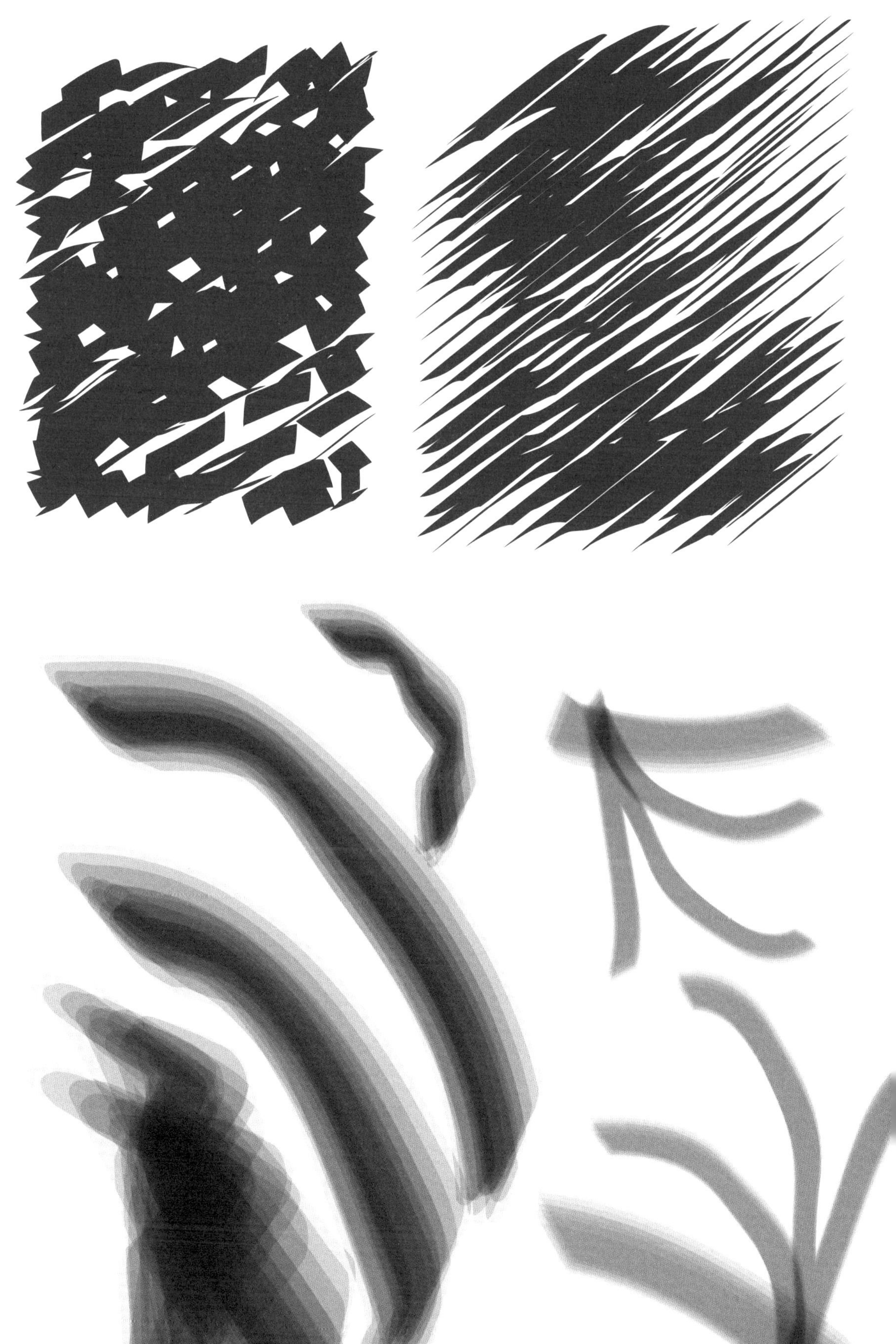

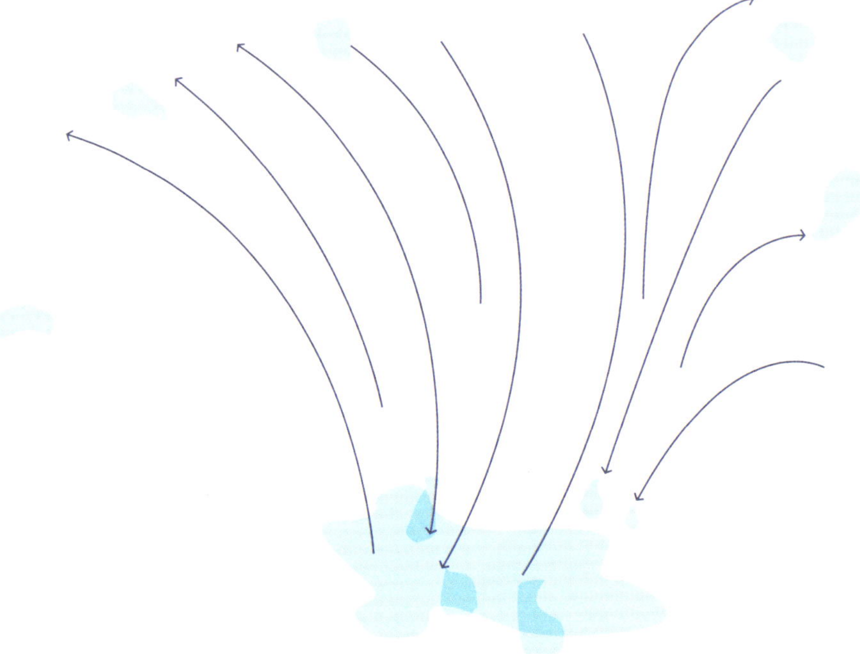

splash

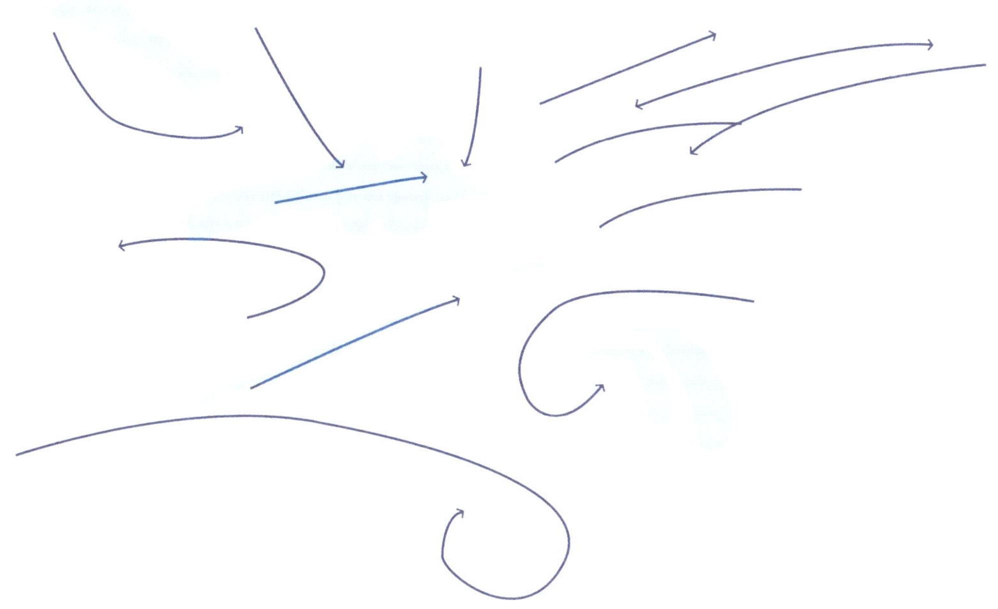

current winds

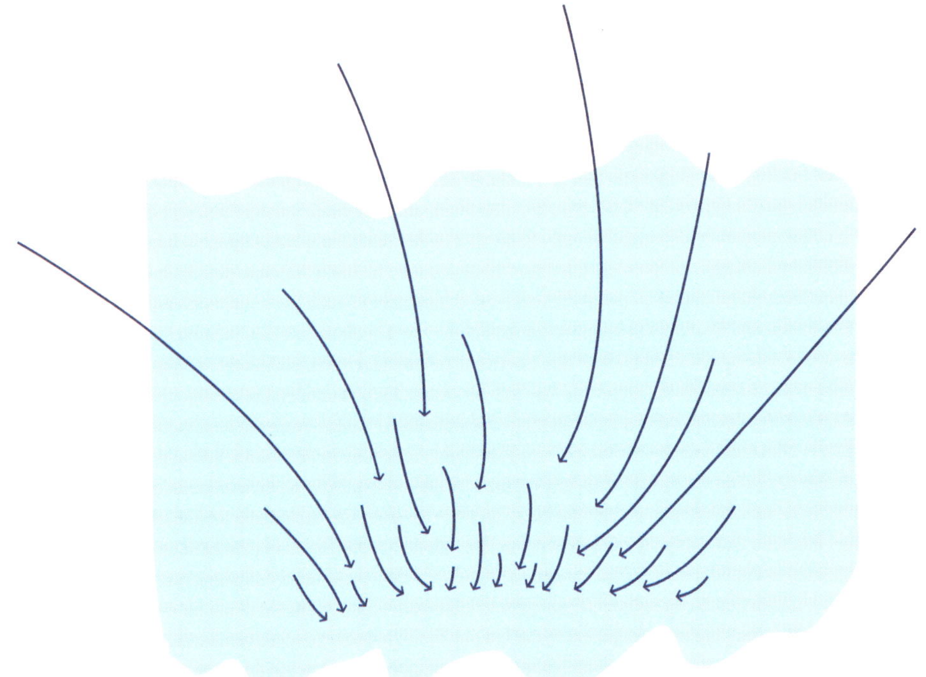

water depth

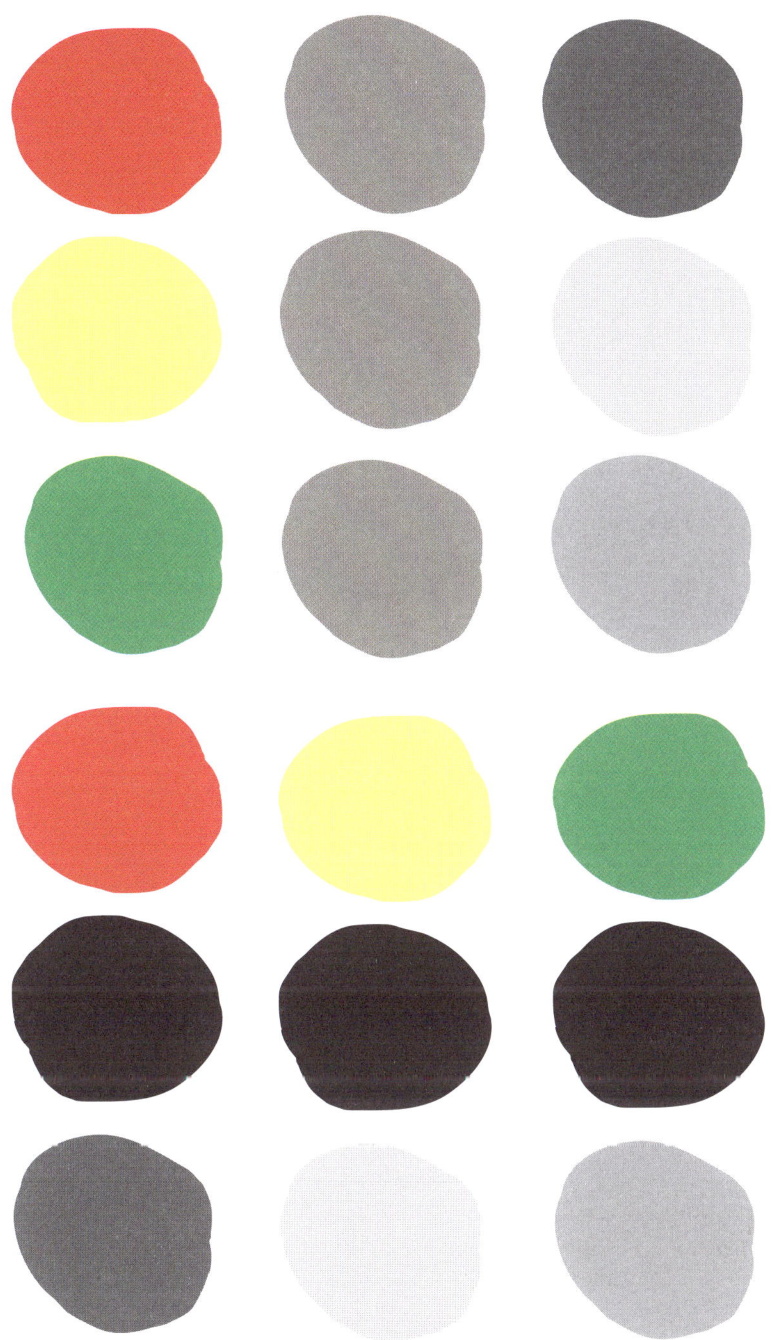

traffic lights

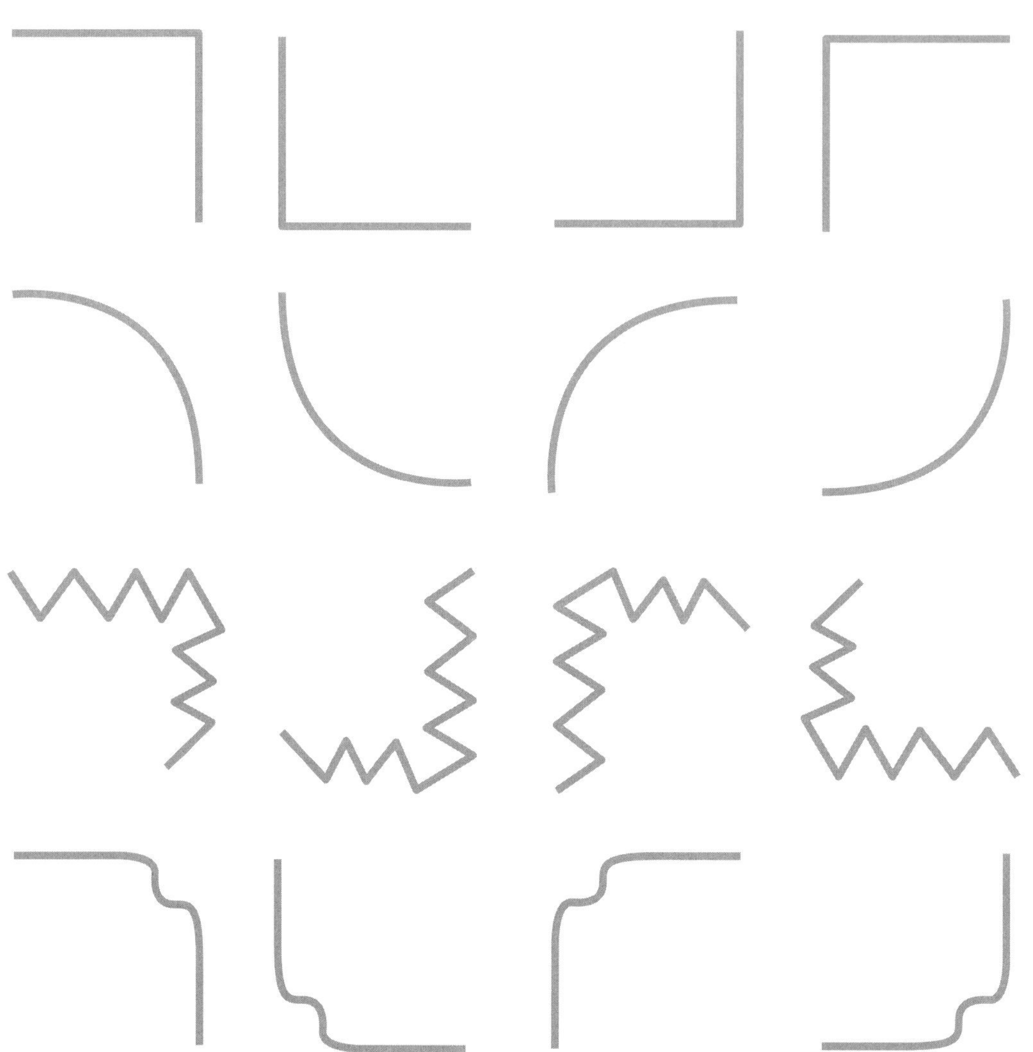

edges

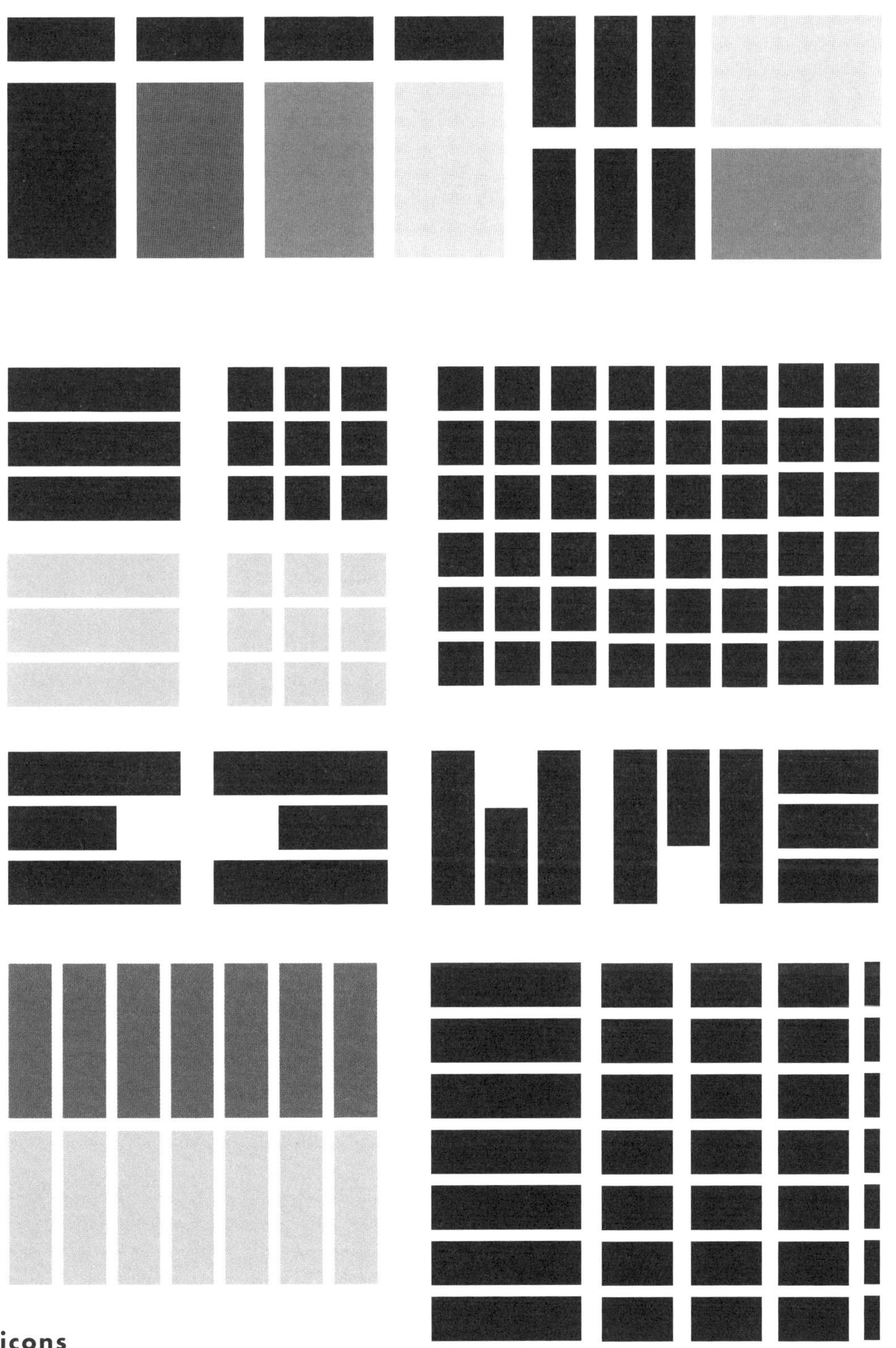

icons

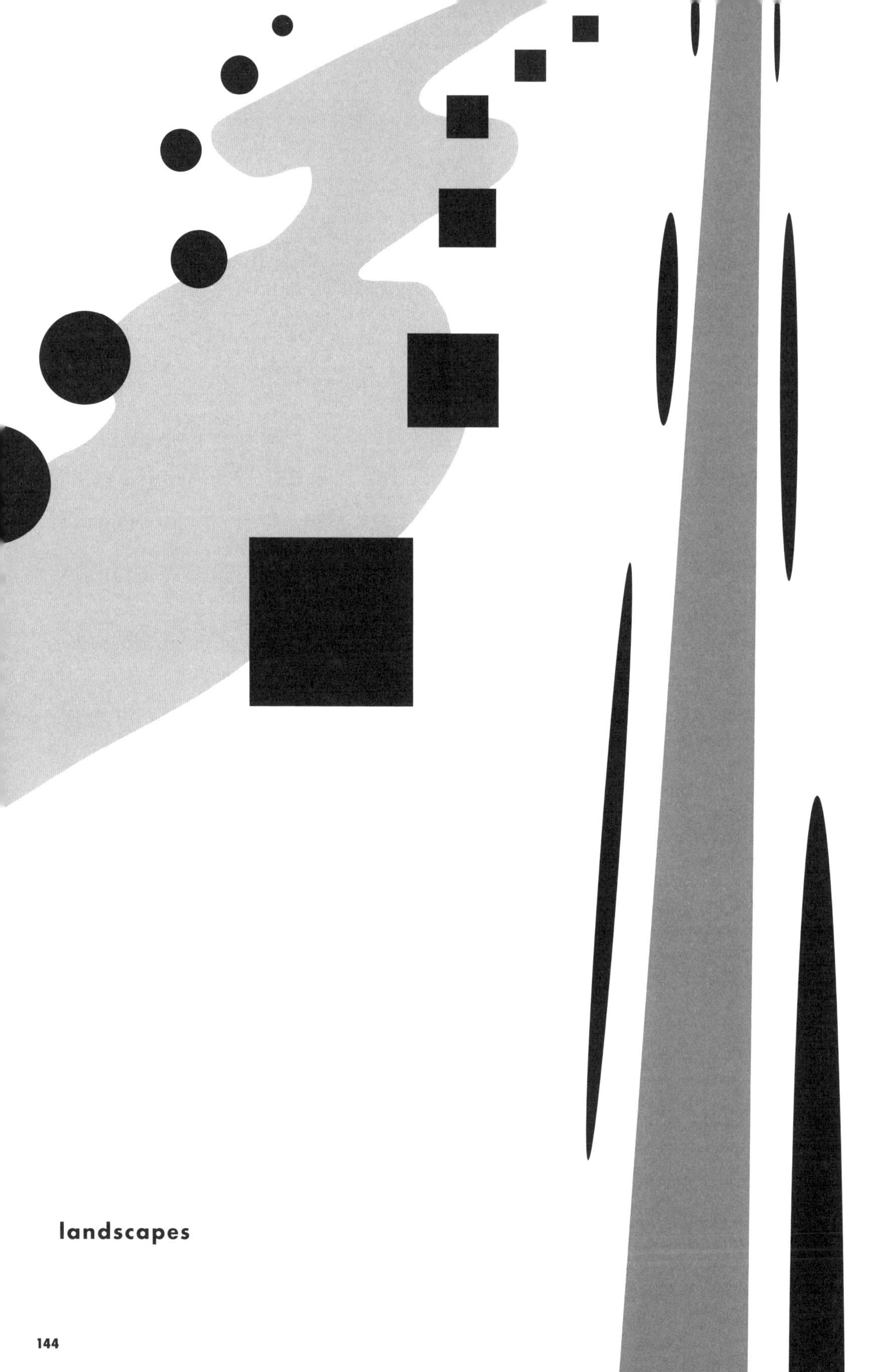

landscapes

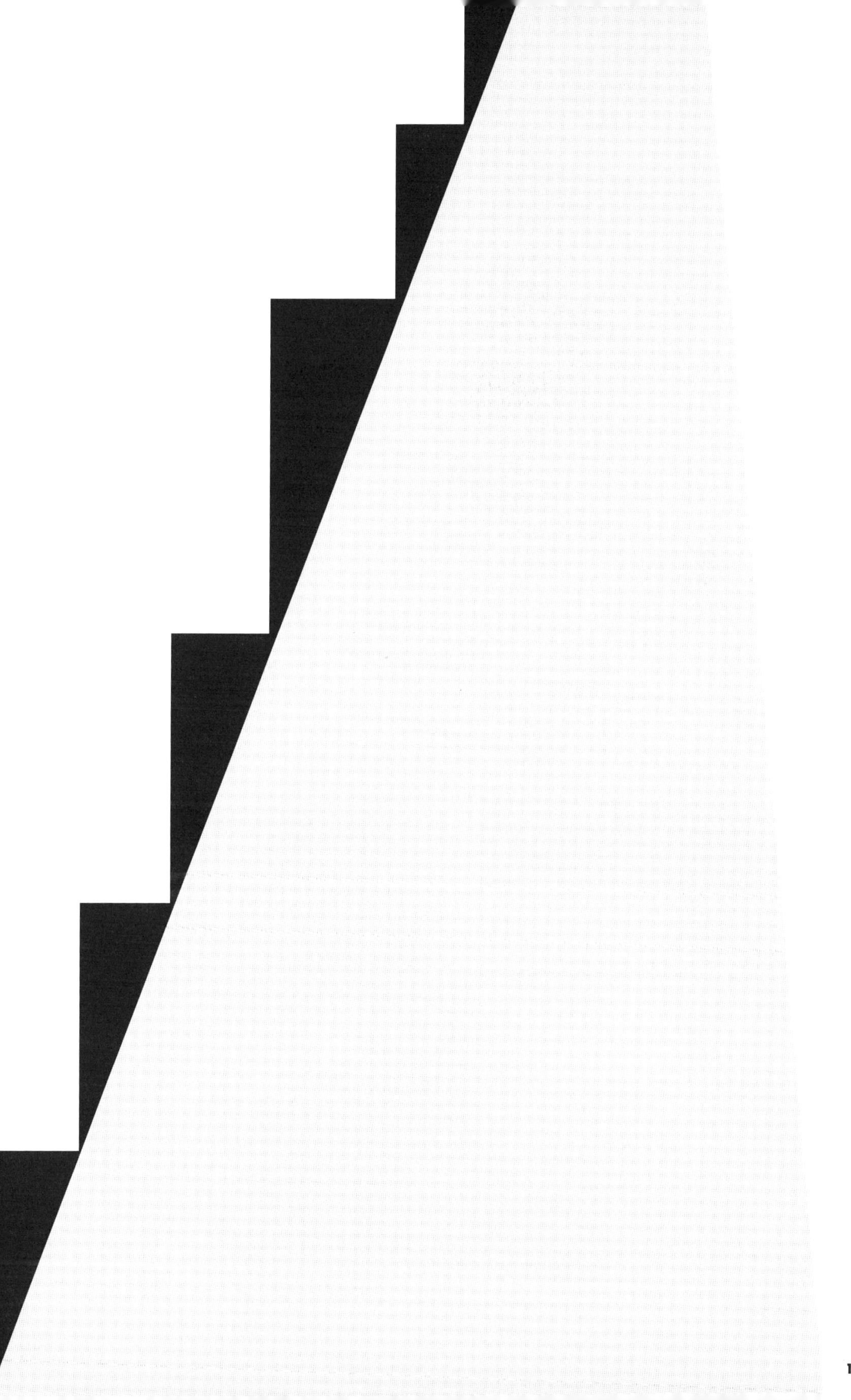

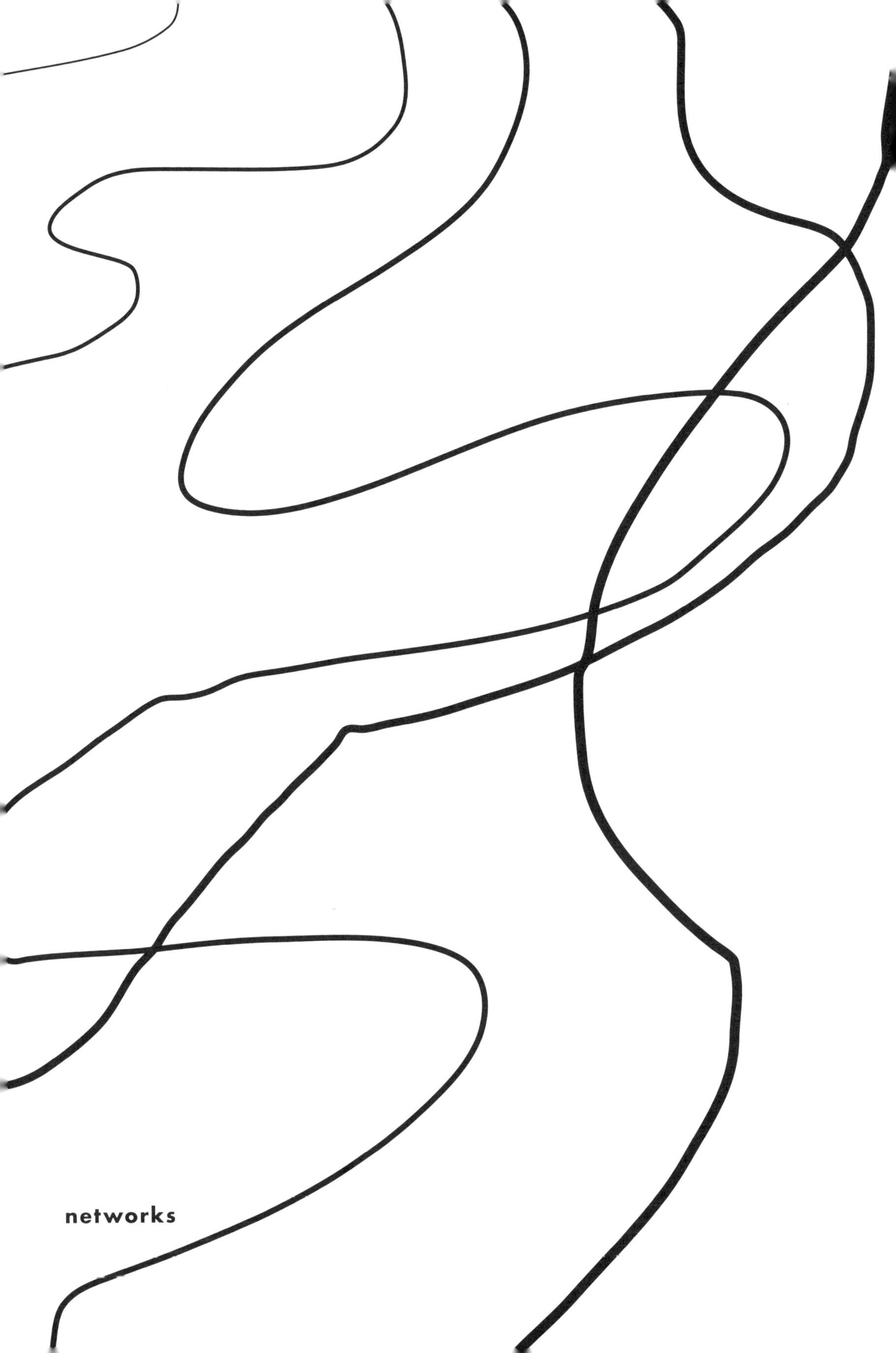
networks

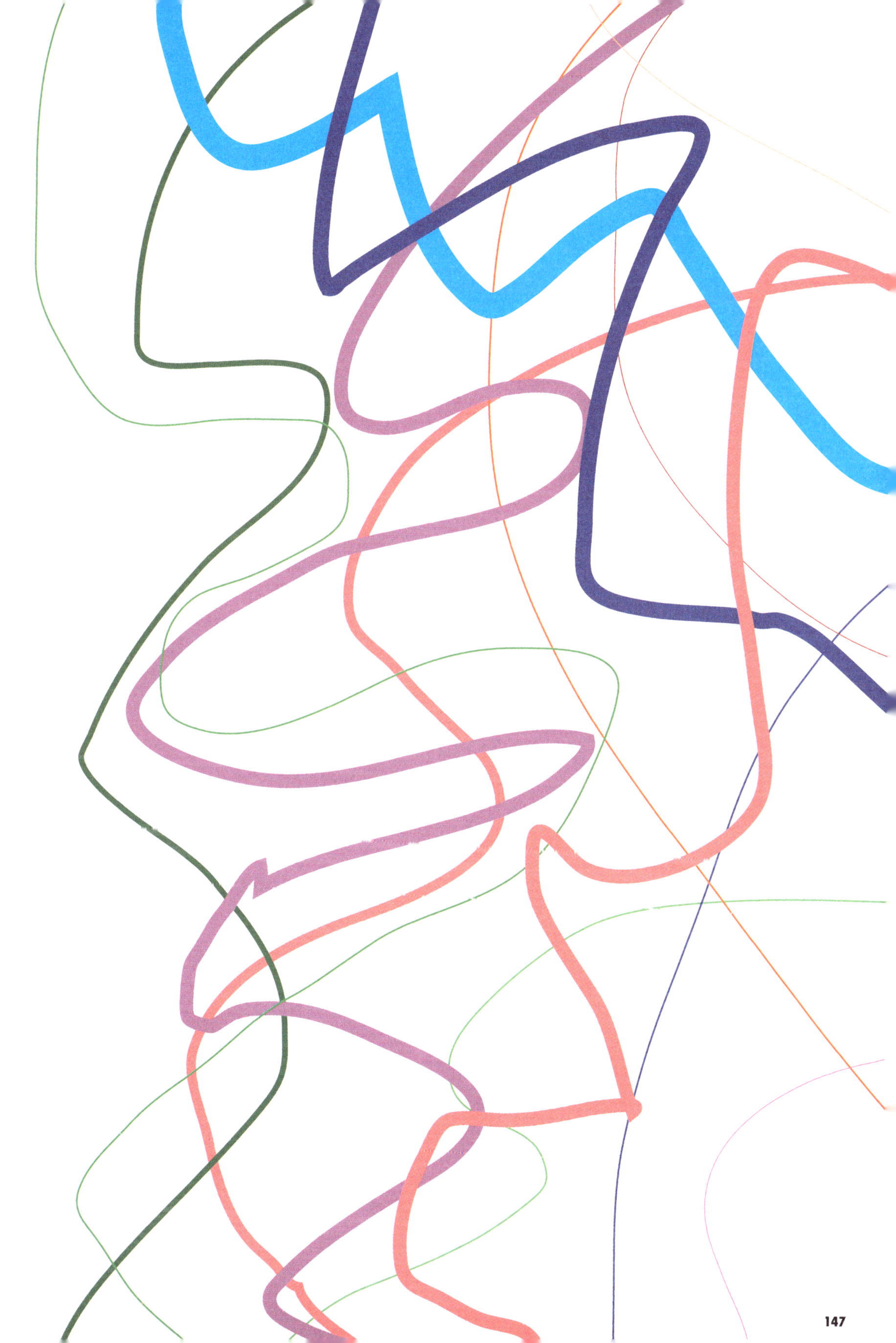

sketch, fold or cut here

exercise

Add shapes using pencils, markers or pens. Feel free to explore using other shapes from using the examples below. Also, feel free to add cutouts using color or black and white paper. Options are limitless!

sketch, fold or cut here

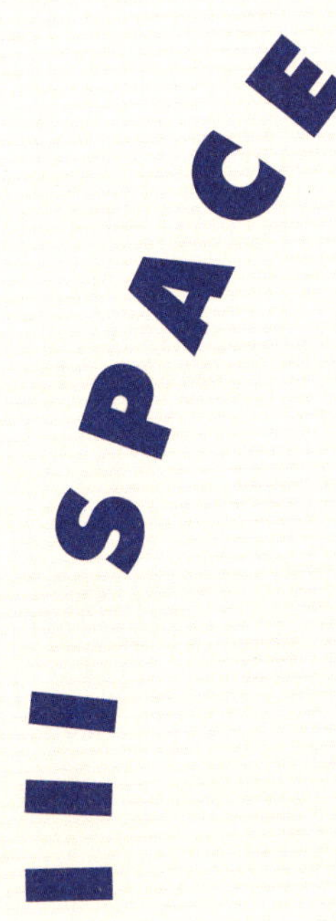
III SPACE

8. coordinates

Working with spatiality in the working area, whether is creating a sketch in a sketchbook or a final outcome of a digital project. Spatiality has several coordinates and the first level is X,Y,Z.

X stands for horizontal, Y for vertical, and Z for diagonal. X and Y work great in 2 dimensional outcomes. Meanwhile, 3 dimensional space is created through Z creates perspectives and distance that could be closer or further from the viewer. In addition, to add more dimensions it is important to create more values and that will create 4D, 5D, 6D, 7D, etc. All these require more space, and values can be added.

Thinking and creating in various hyperplanes is a great option to understand space. The 2D dimensional is the most successful one, but other dimensions should be more explored and engaged because as designers we have access to it.

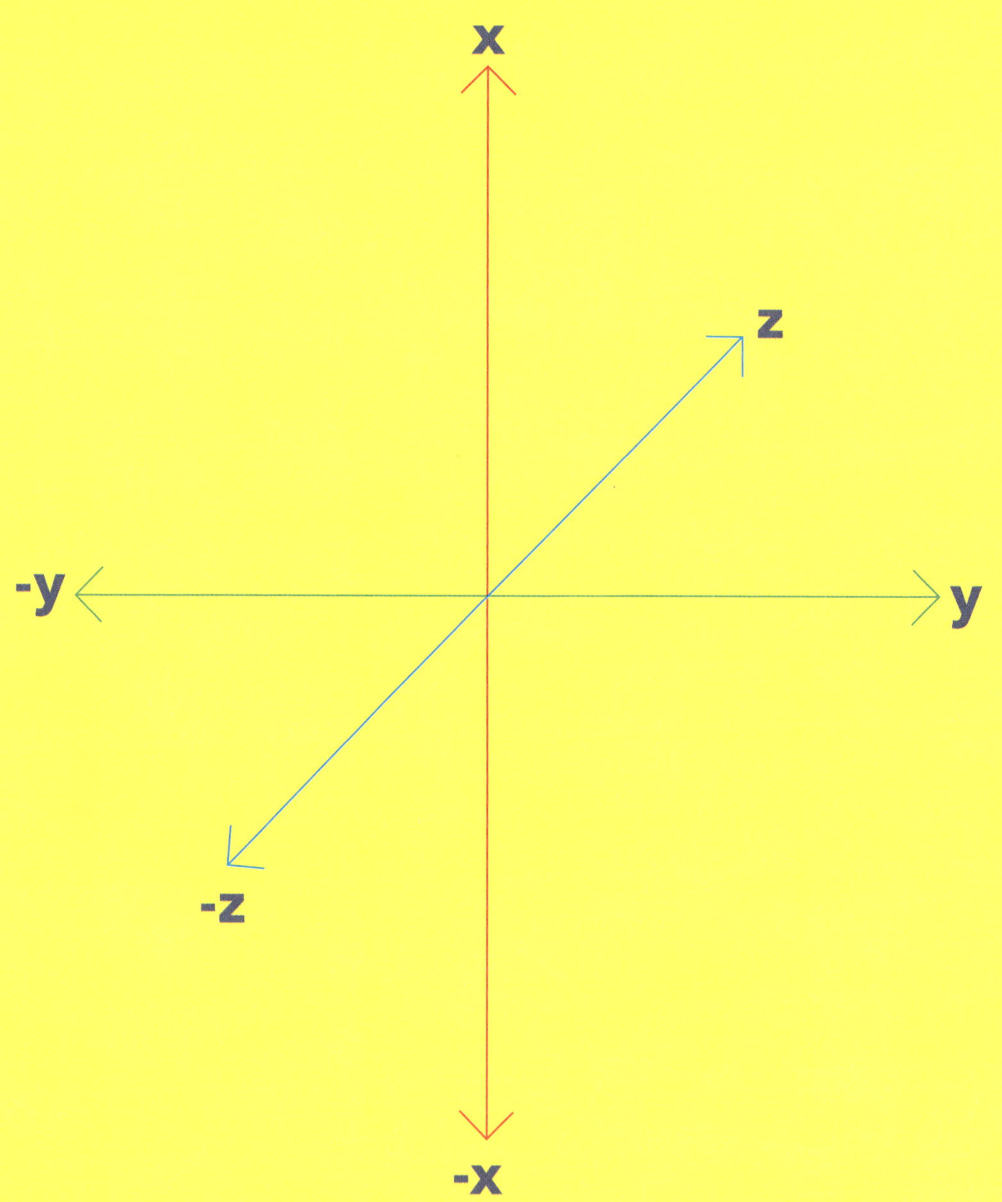
x
z
-y
y
-z
-x

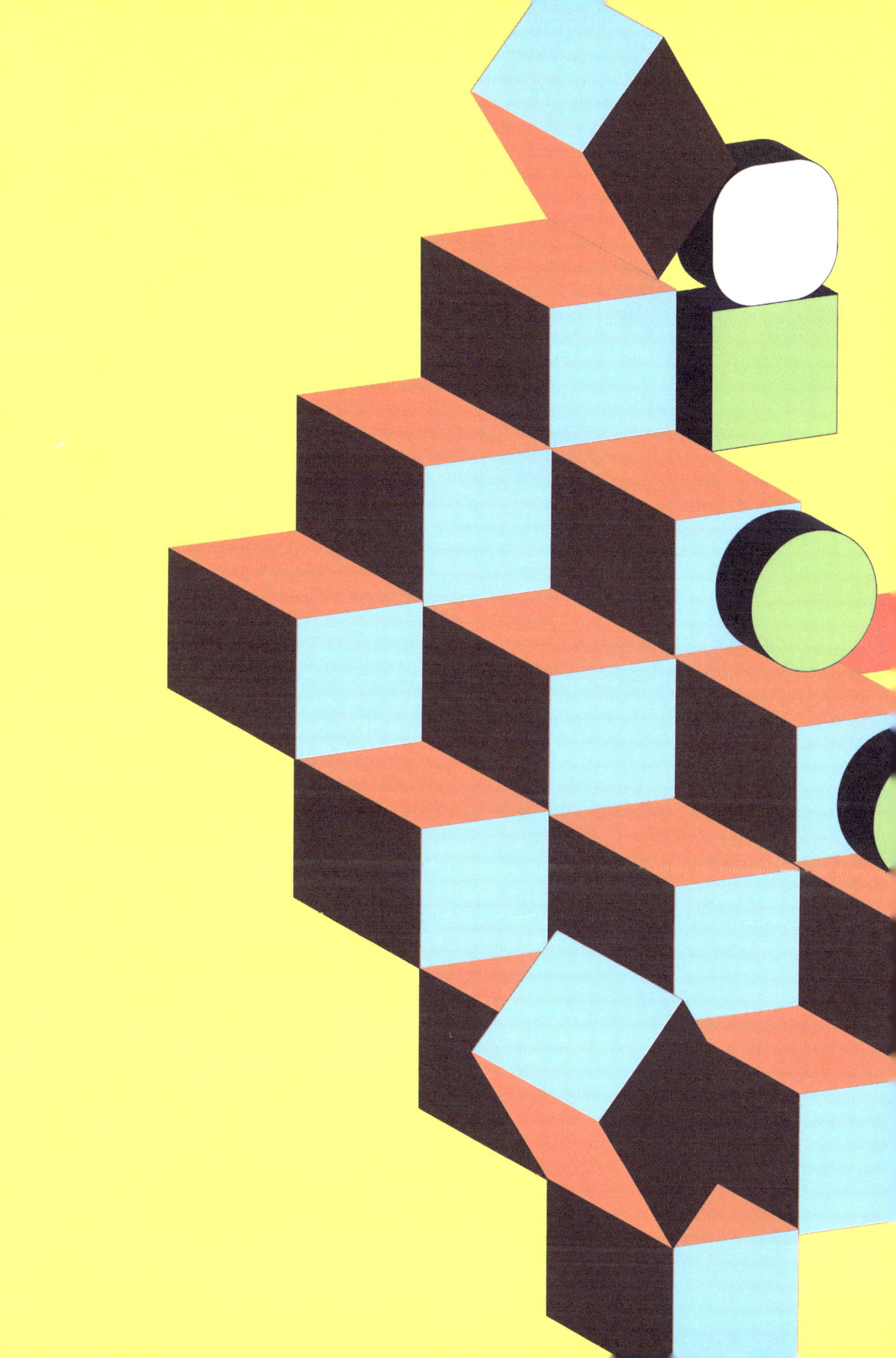

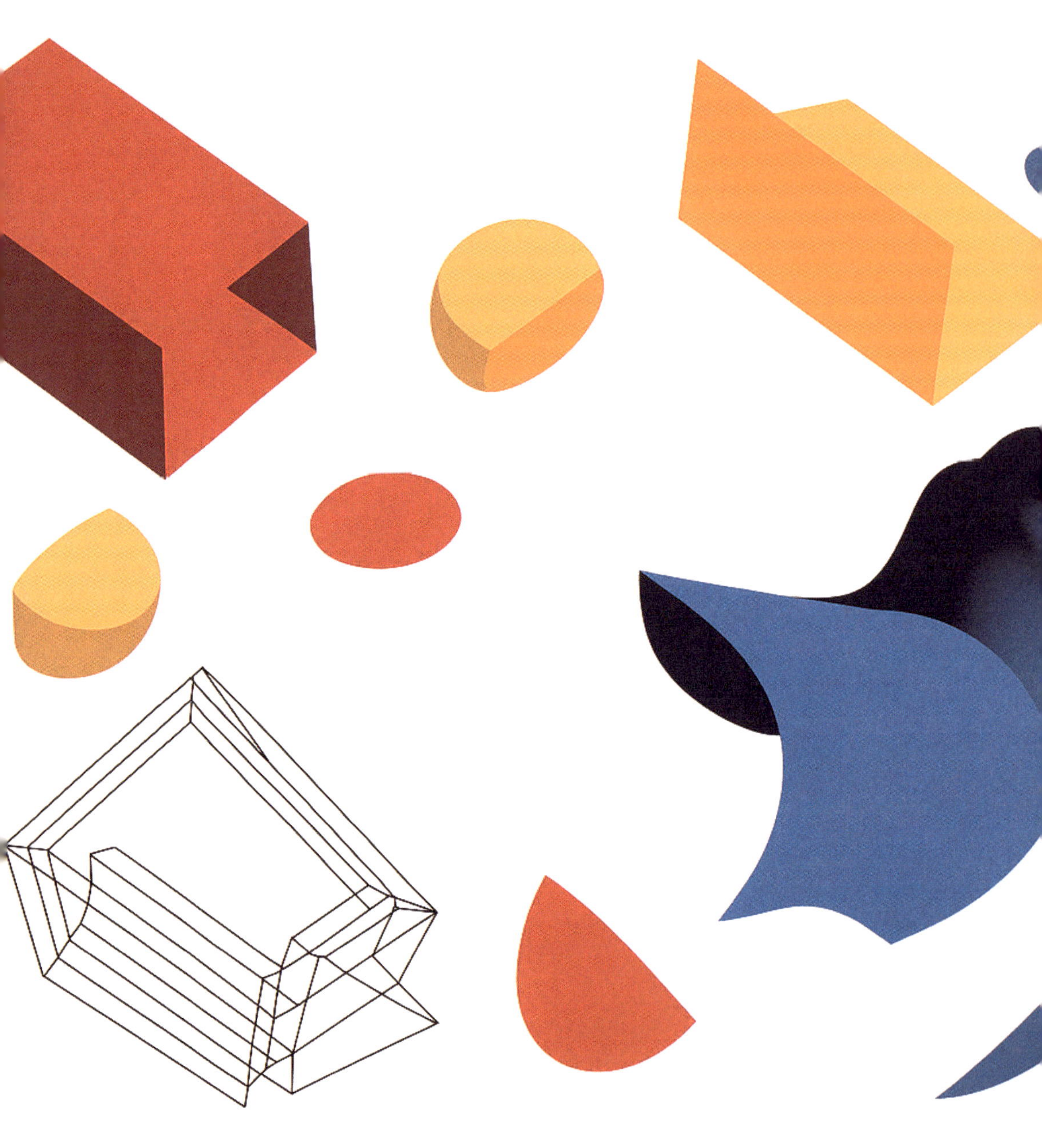

creating shapes in 3D space

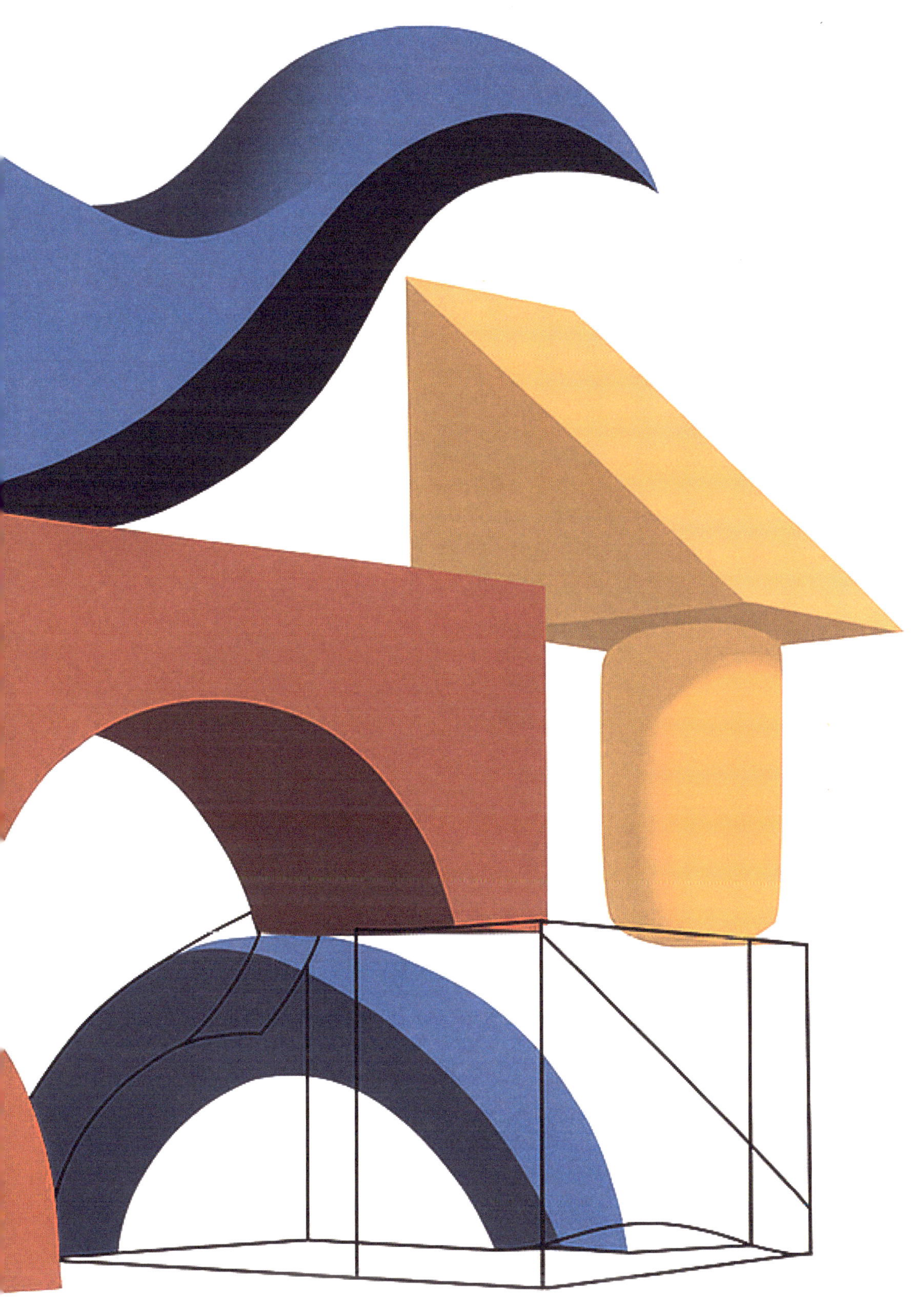

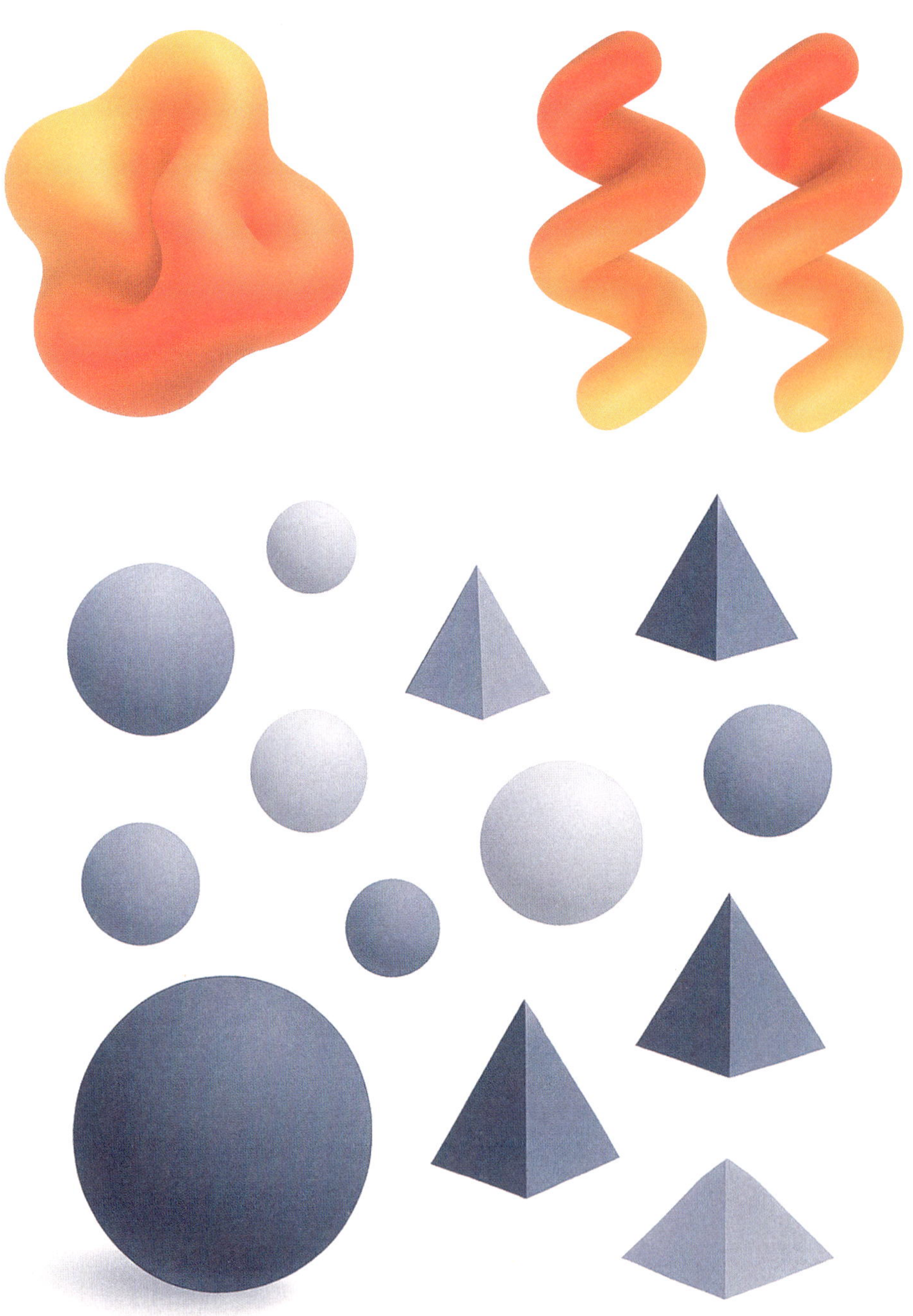

creating shapes in 3D space

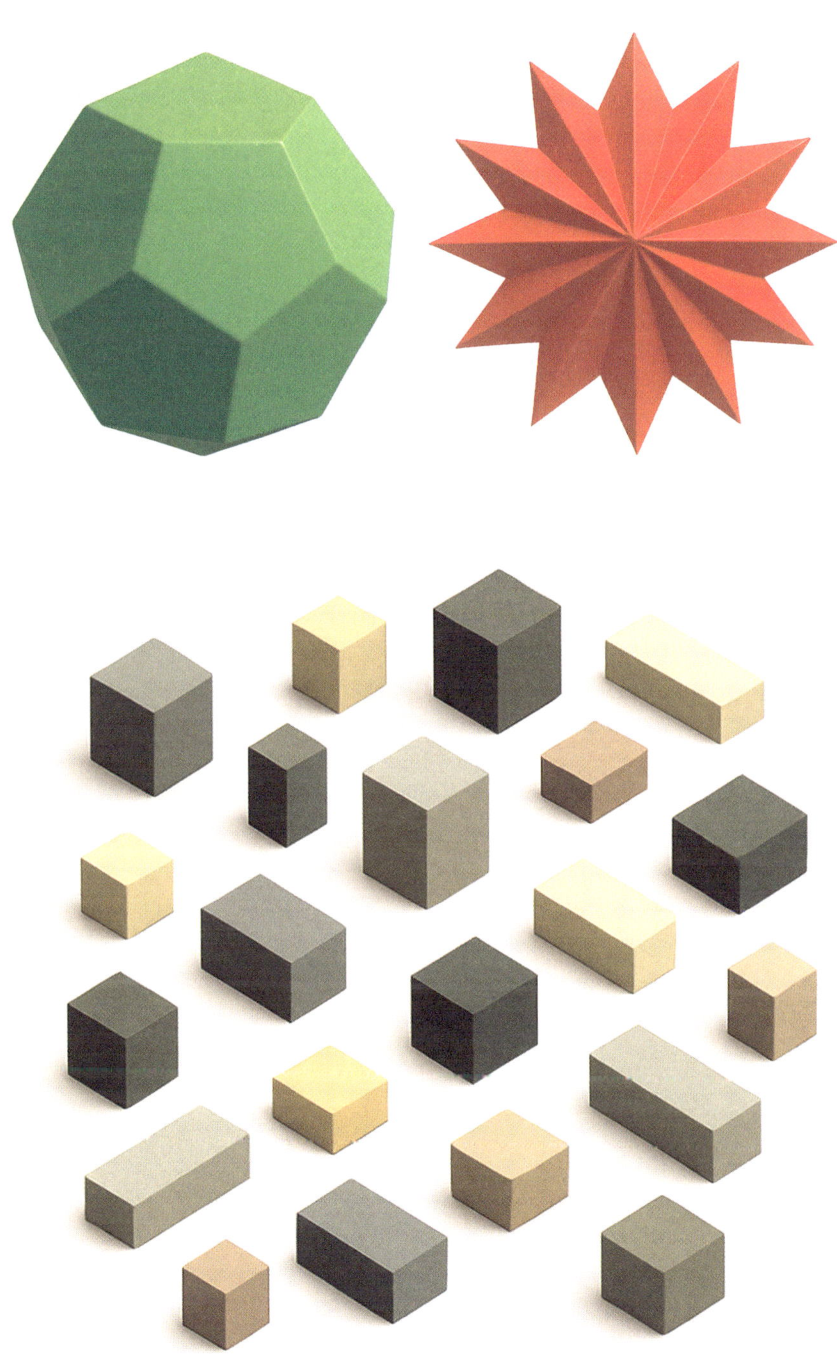

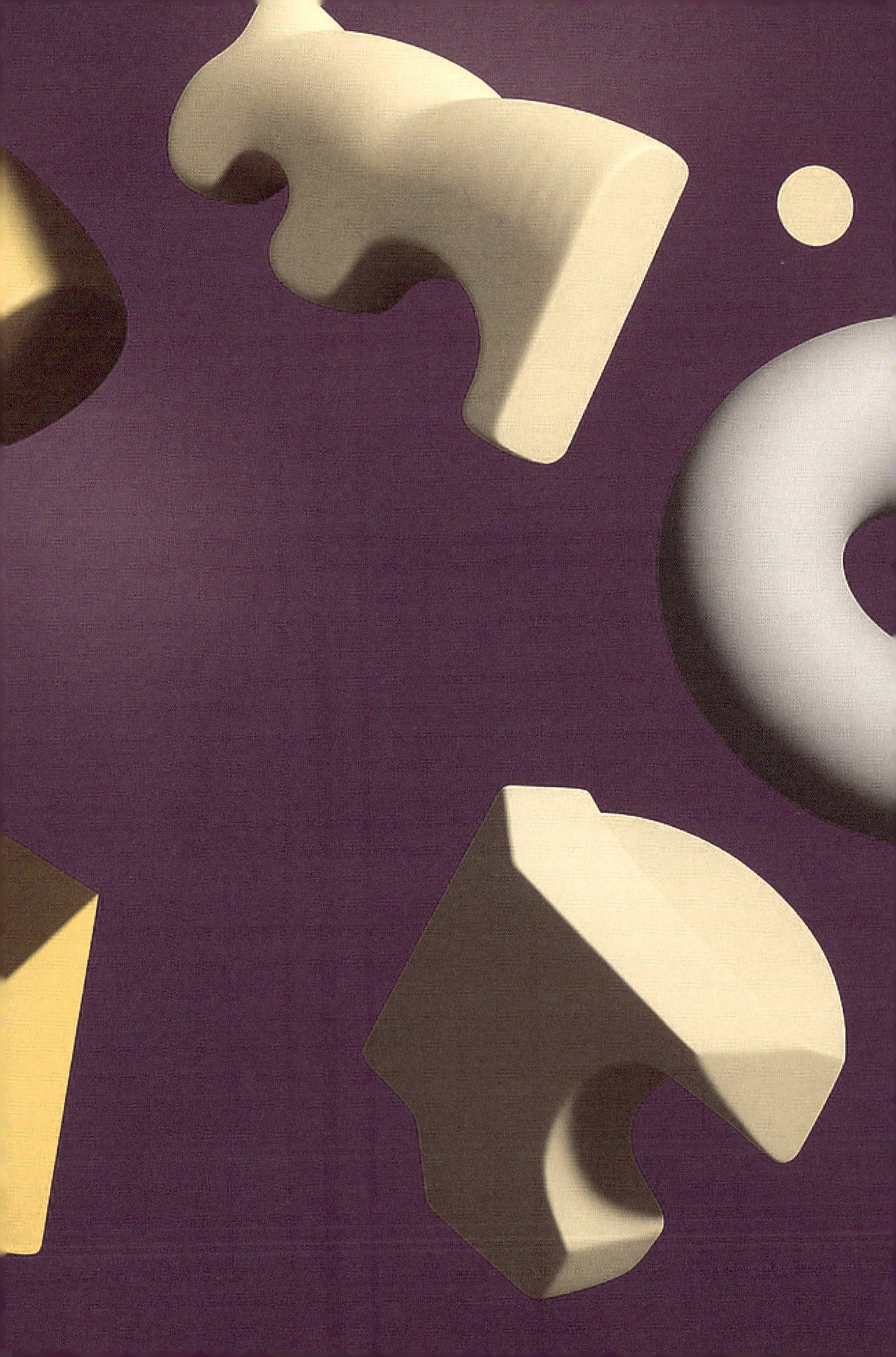

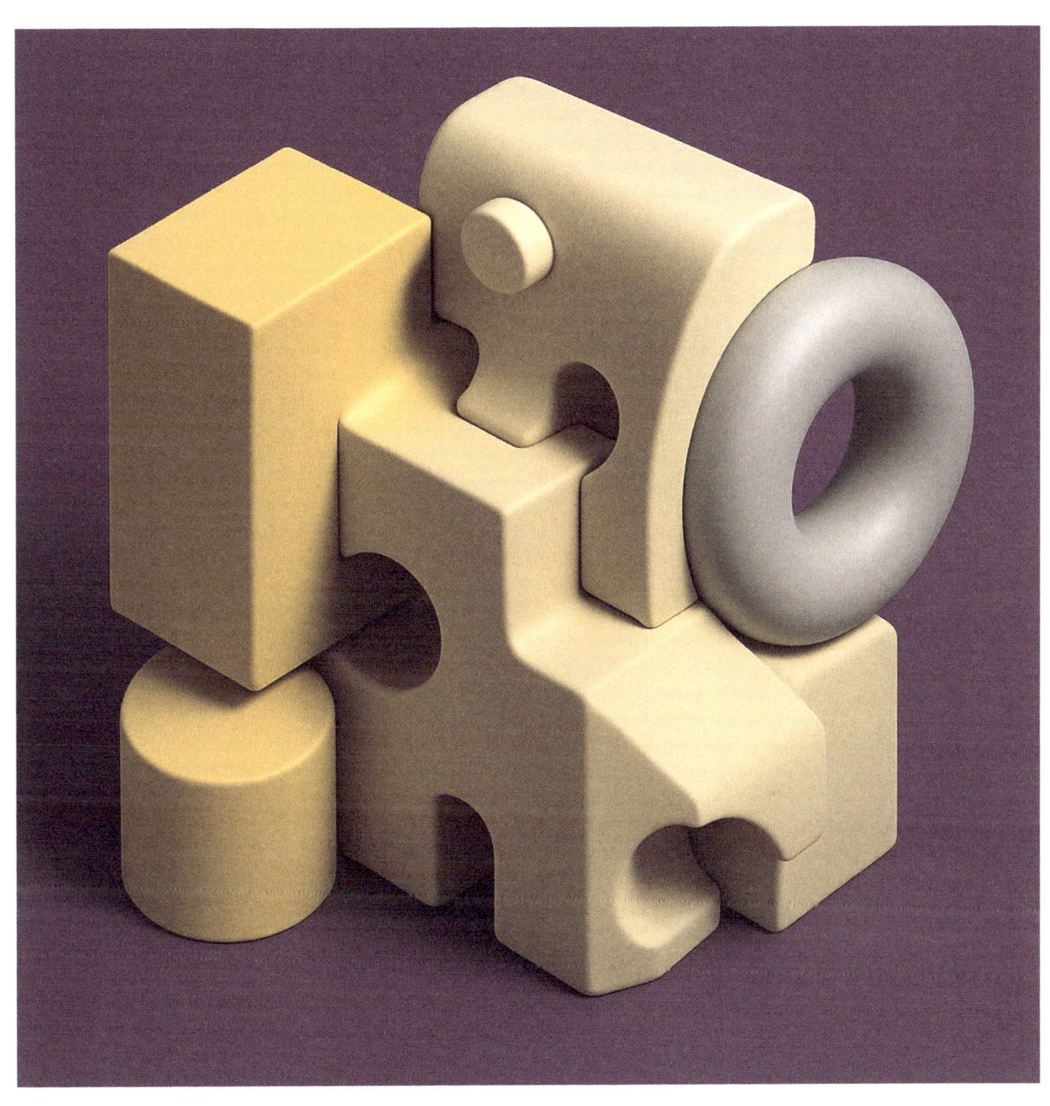

creating shapes using bright colors in 3D

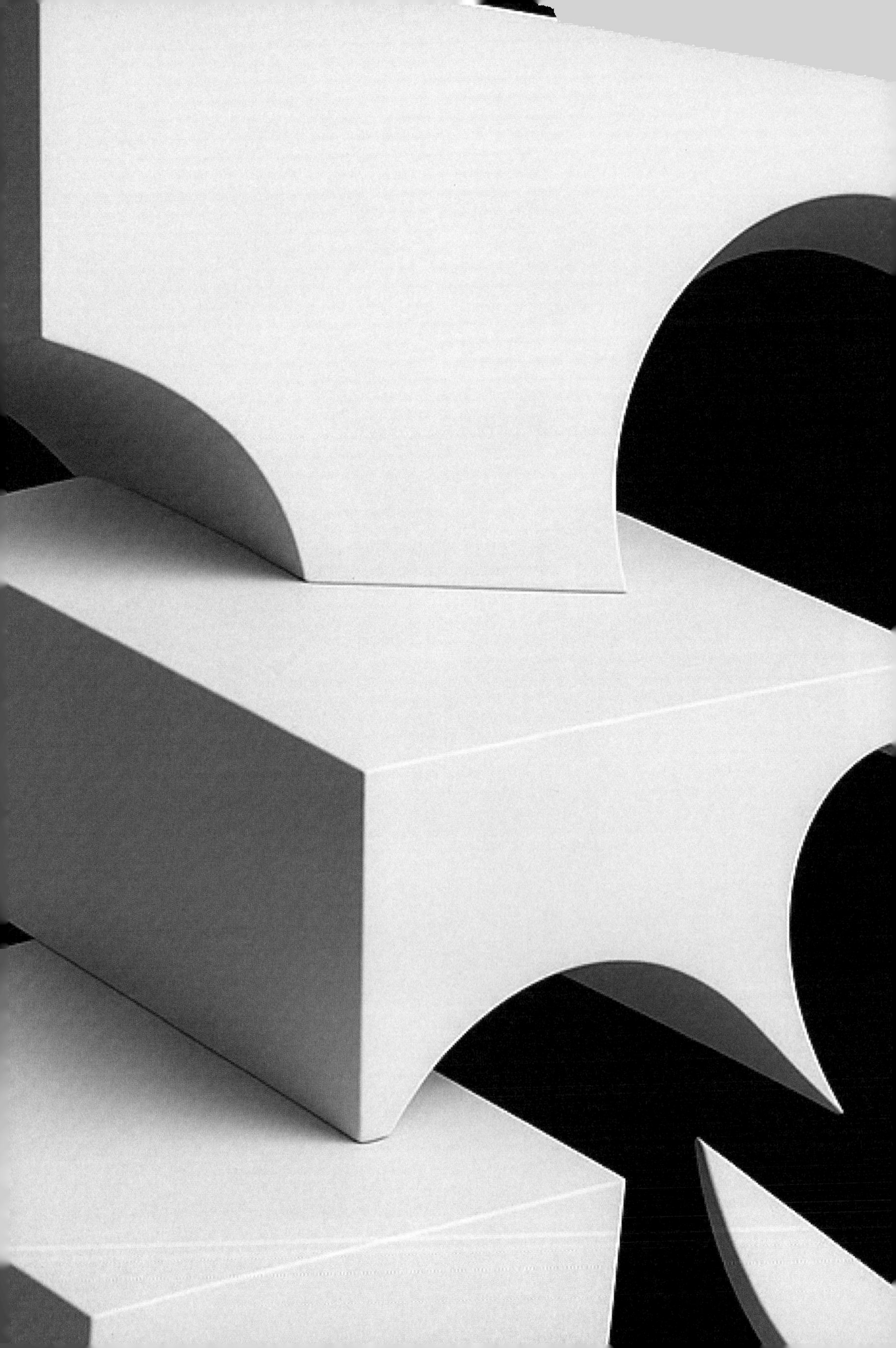

sketch, fold or cut here

exercise

Add shapes using pencils, markers or pens. Feel free to explore using other shapes from using the examples below. Also, feel free to add cutouts using color or black and white paper. Options are limitless!

sketch, fold or cut here

9. explorations

Understanding space begins with the familiar dimensions mentioned in chapter 8. When we enter the world of higher dimensions: 4D, 5D, 6D and beyond. Each new dimension adds layers of perspective, transformation, and relational complexity. Shapes like hypercubes, hypertriangles, and hyperspheres evolve from their simpler counterparts by being duplicated and connected across dimensions. A square becomes a cube, a cube becomes a tesseract and this logic continues infinitely, folding space in ways we can model, if not always visualize.

These multidimensional forms multiply in complexity with each step. A tesseract 4D cube has 16 corners, a 5D hypercube has 32, and so on. Shapes like the orthoplex a spiked structure made from opposing vectors and fractals infinite patterns within finite space show that dimensionality isn't just size it's about relationships, recursion, and structure. Fractals especially show us how space can be infinitely deep and yet bound by a visible form much like a galaxy or even human thought. Dimensional design isn't just geometry is art; it's a way of understanding systems, networks, and evolving forms.

Ultimately, working with dimensions means thinking beyond surfaces it's designing across planes of logic, emotion,

interaction, and time. As creators, we're not limited to flat pages or simple volumes; we have access to spatial frameworks that mirror how the universe builds itself. Whether sketching in a notebook or shaping complex digital systems, exploring higher dimensions opens the door to richer, more immersive design. It's infinite in possibility, yet beautifully structured a galaxy with an edge.

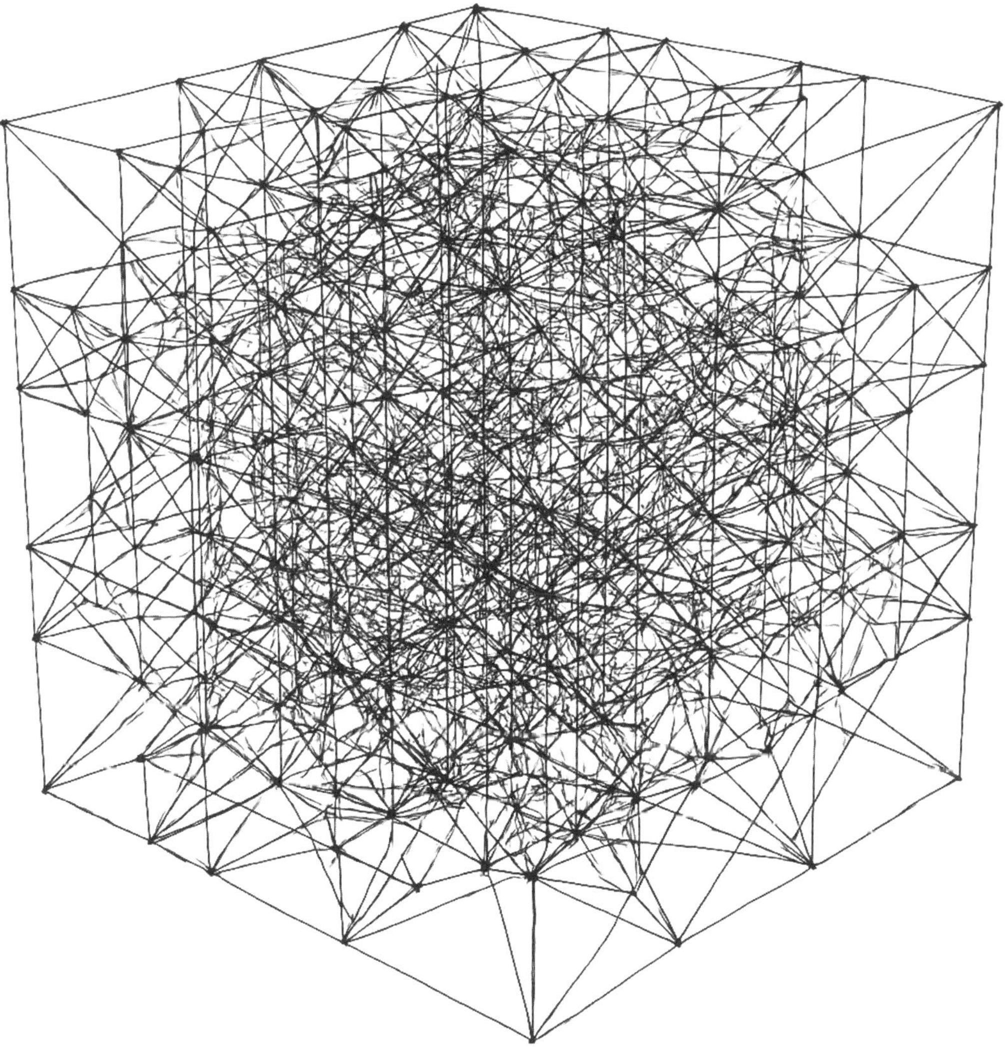

10D hypercube consists of 1024 vertices and 5120 edges

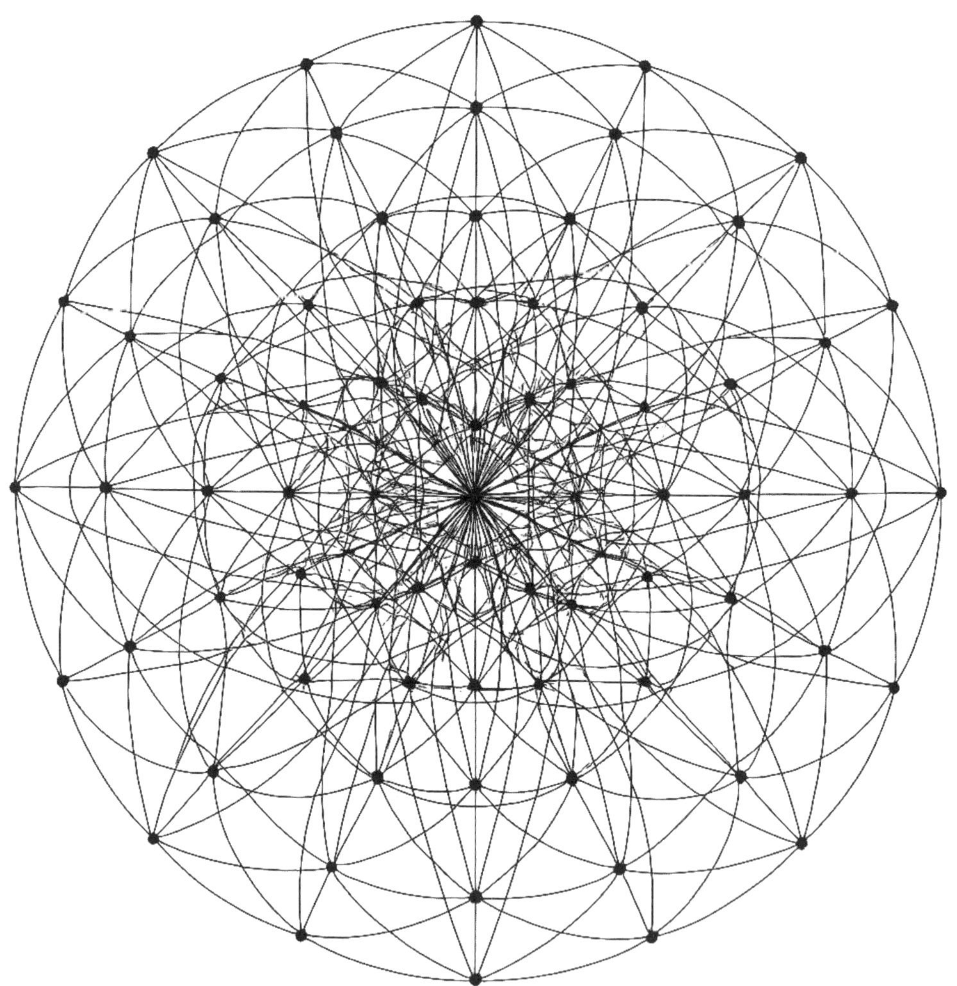

hypersphere 8D

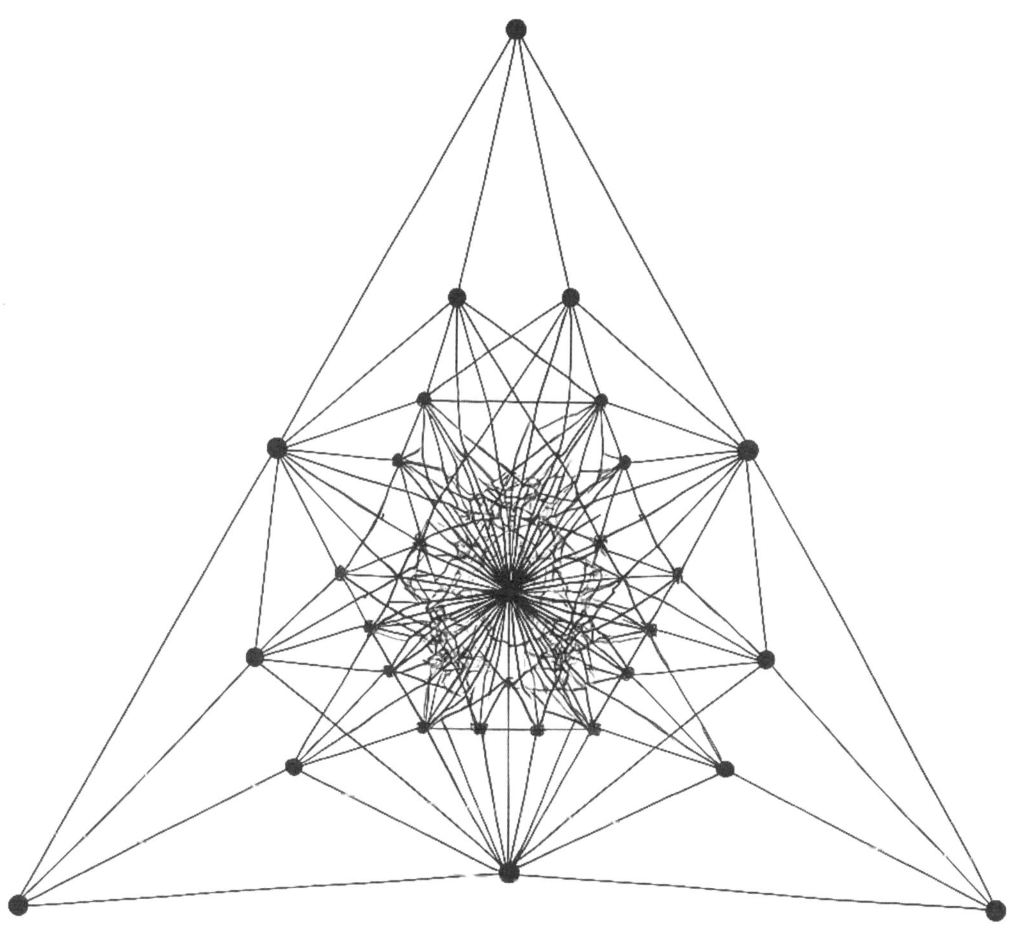

hypertriangle 6D

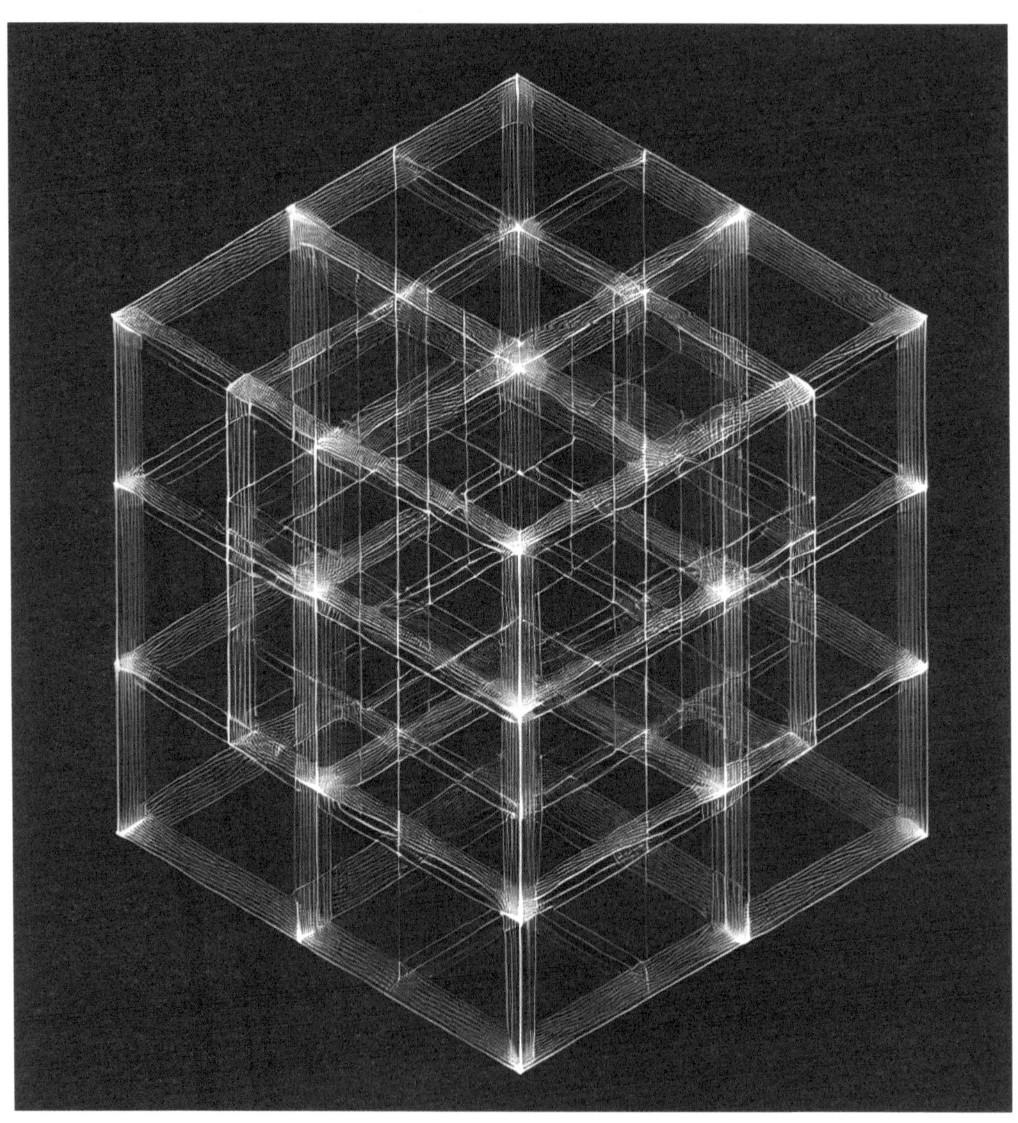

impossible shapes

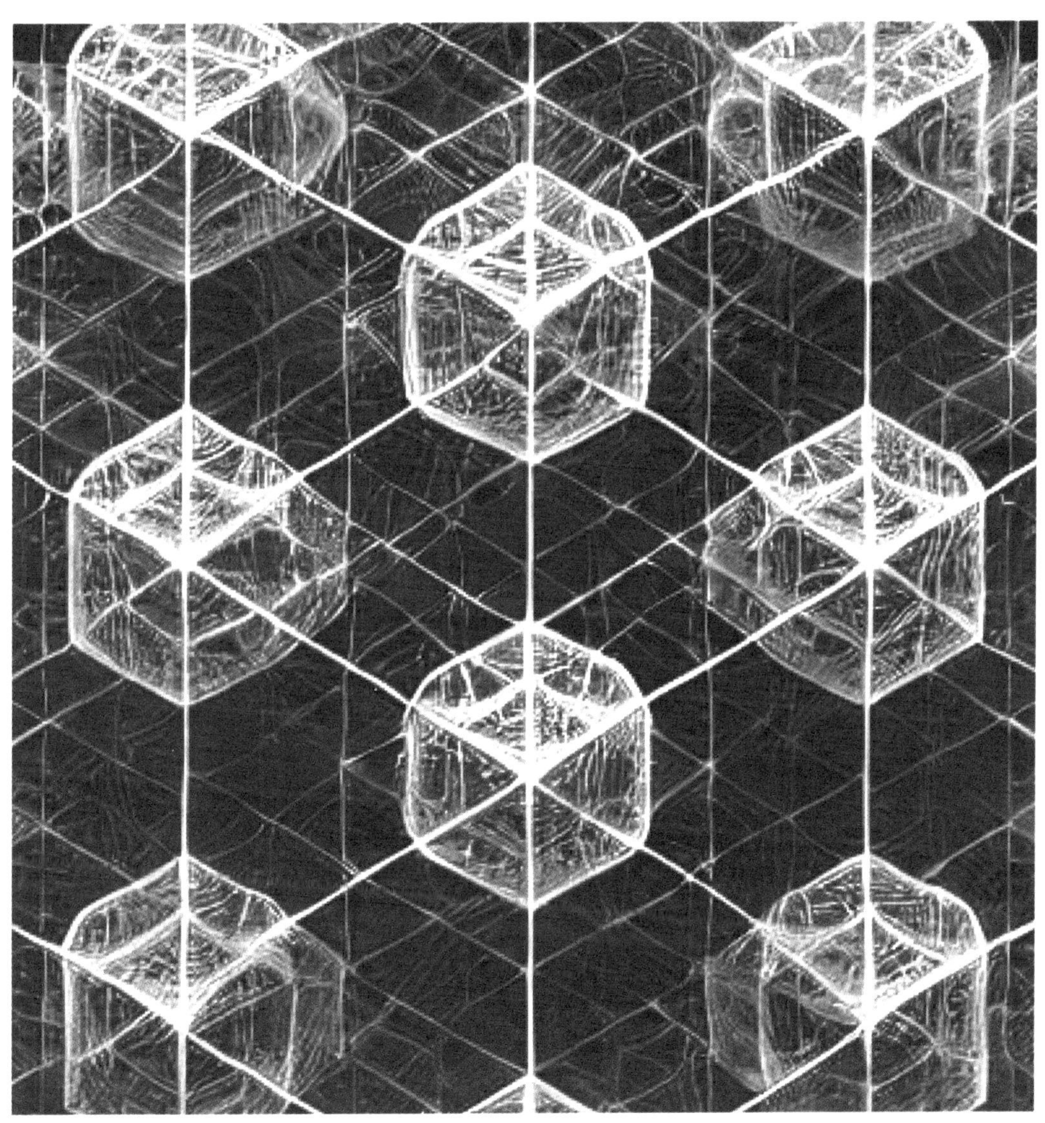

multidimensional shapes

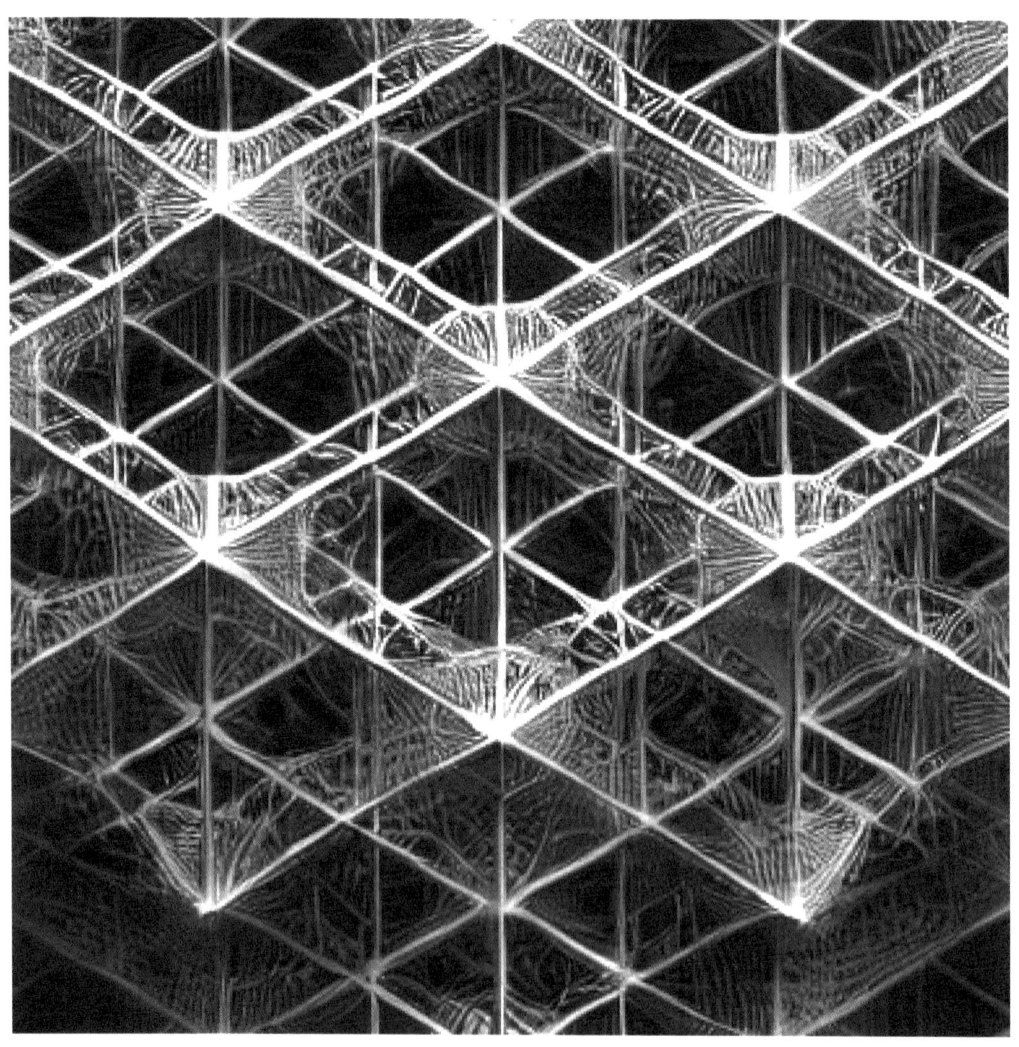

impossible fractals

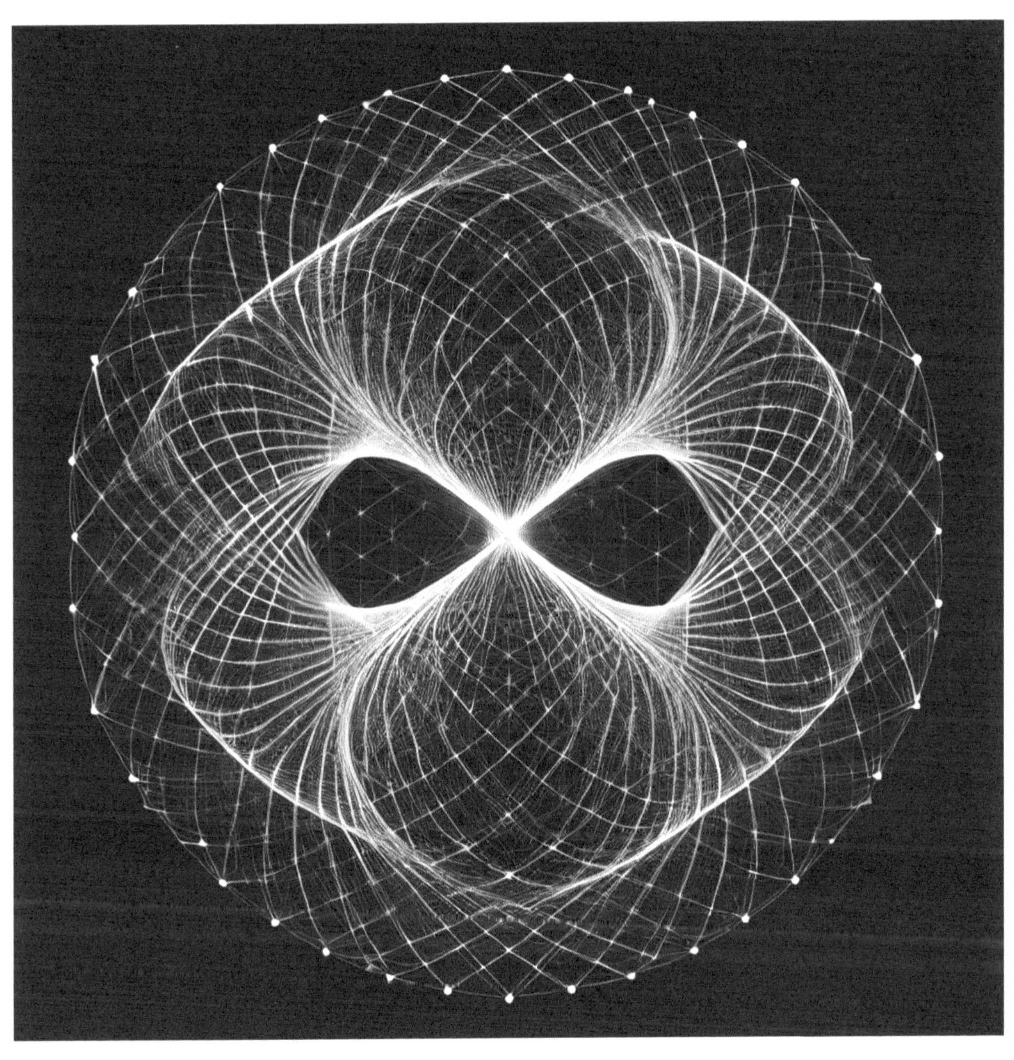

orthoplex 100D

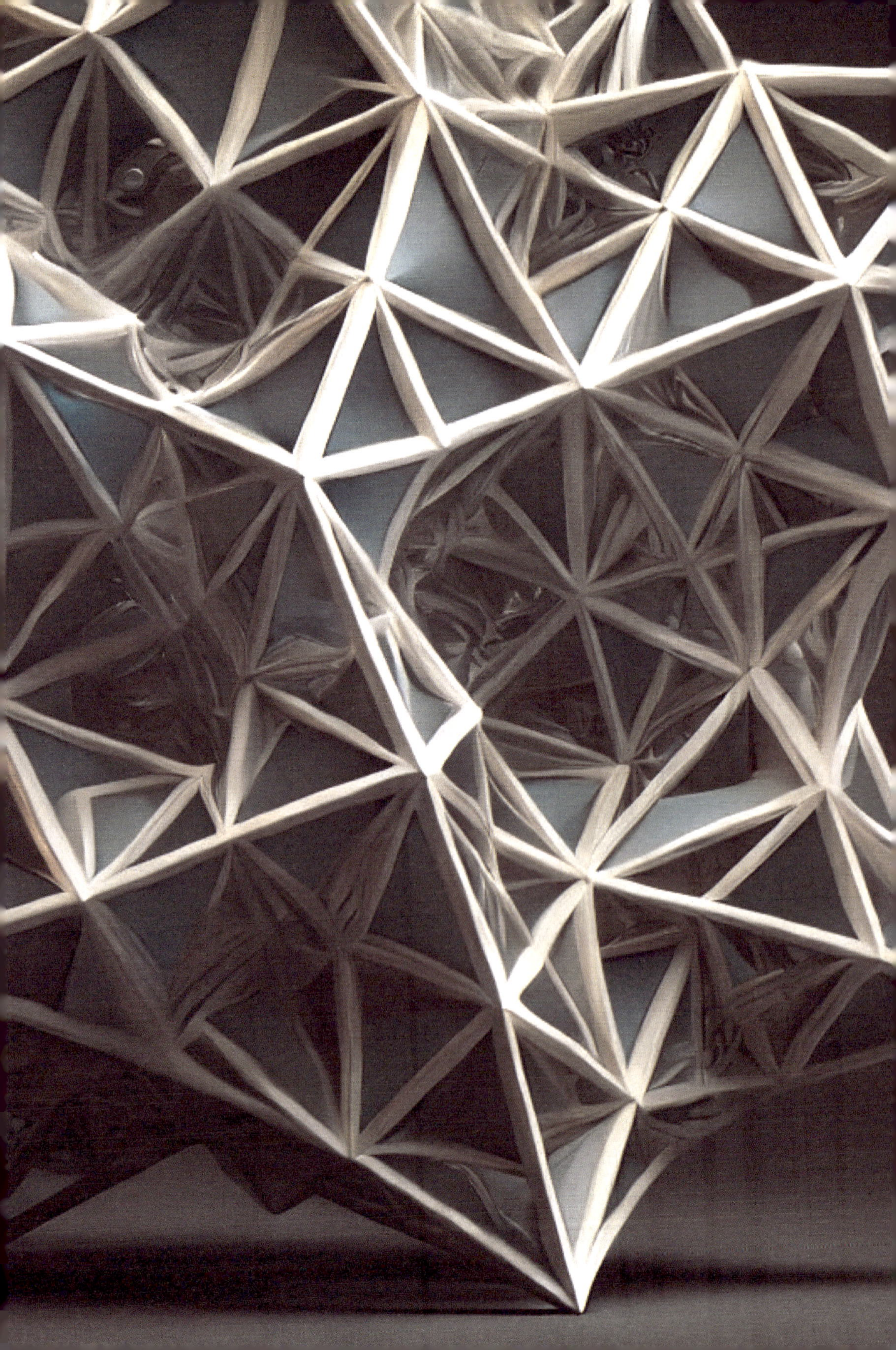

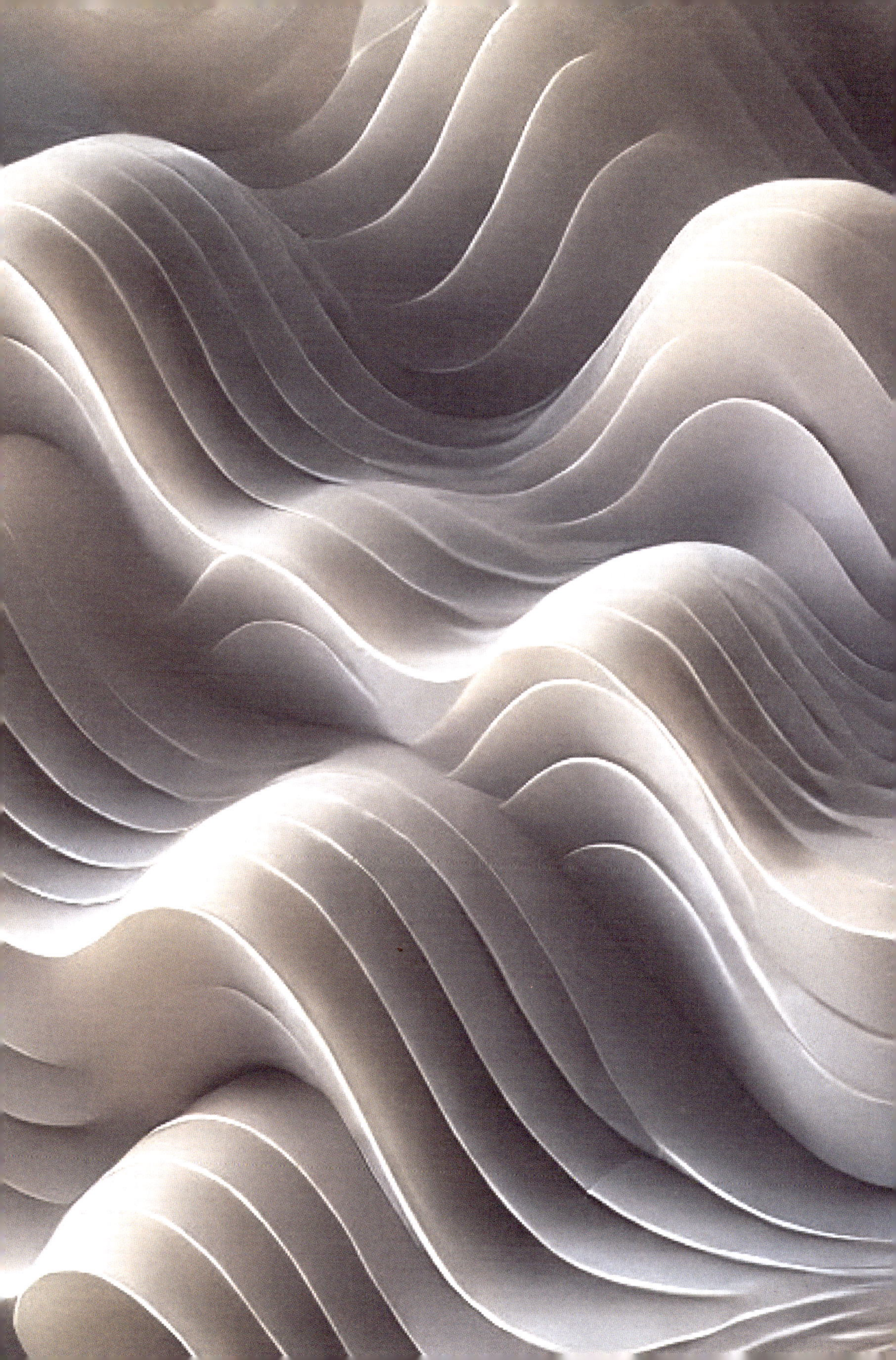

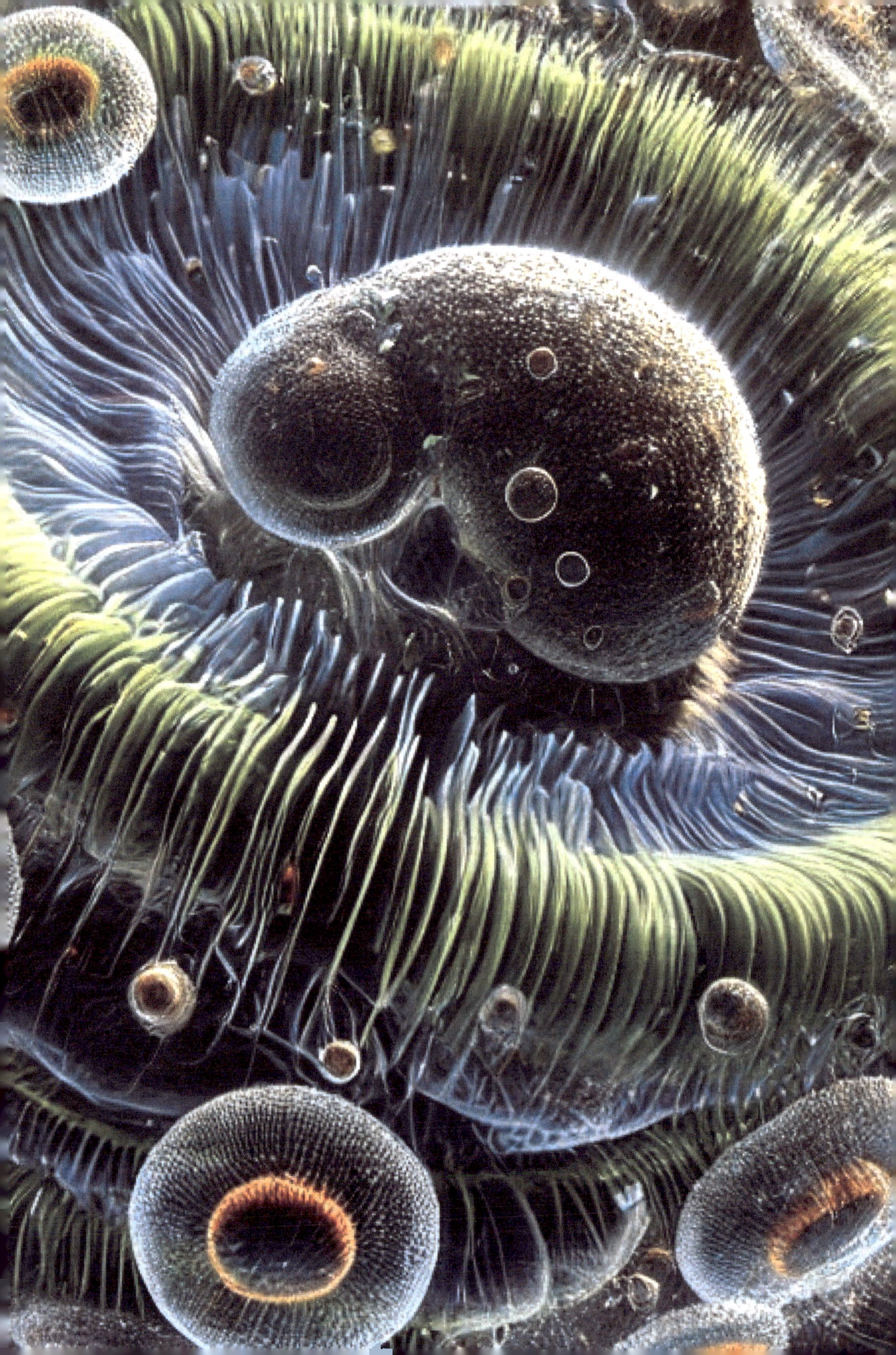

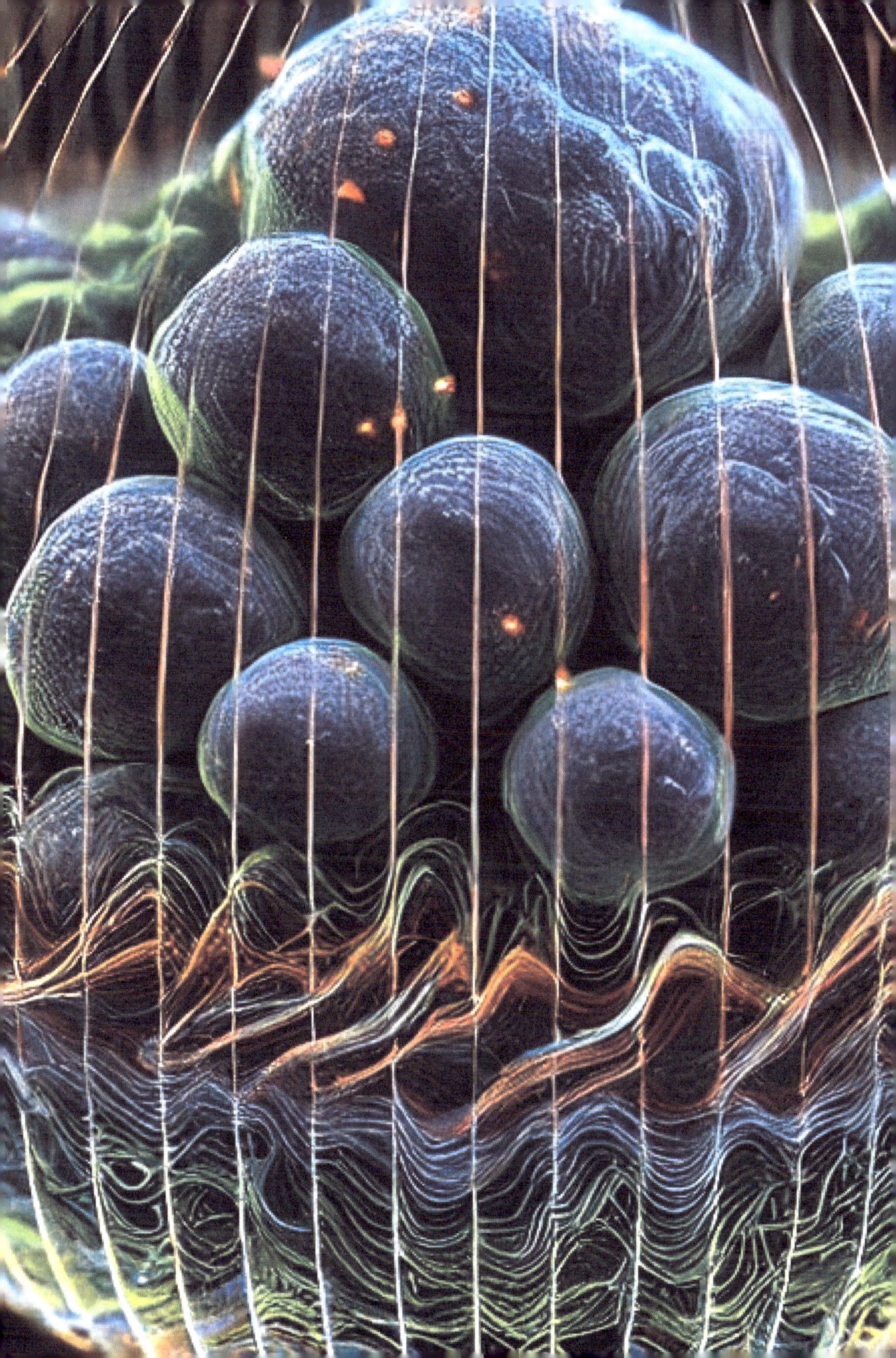

exercise

Add shapes using pencils, markers or pens.

cut or fold here

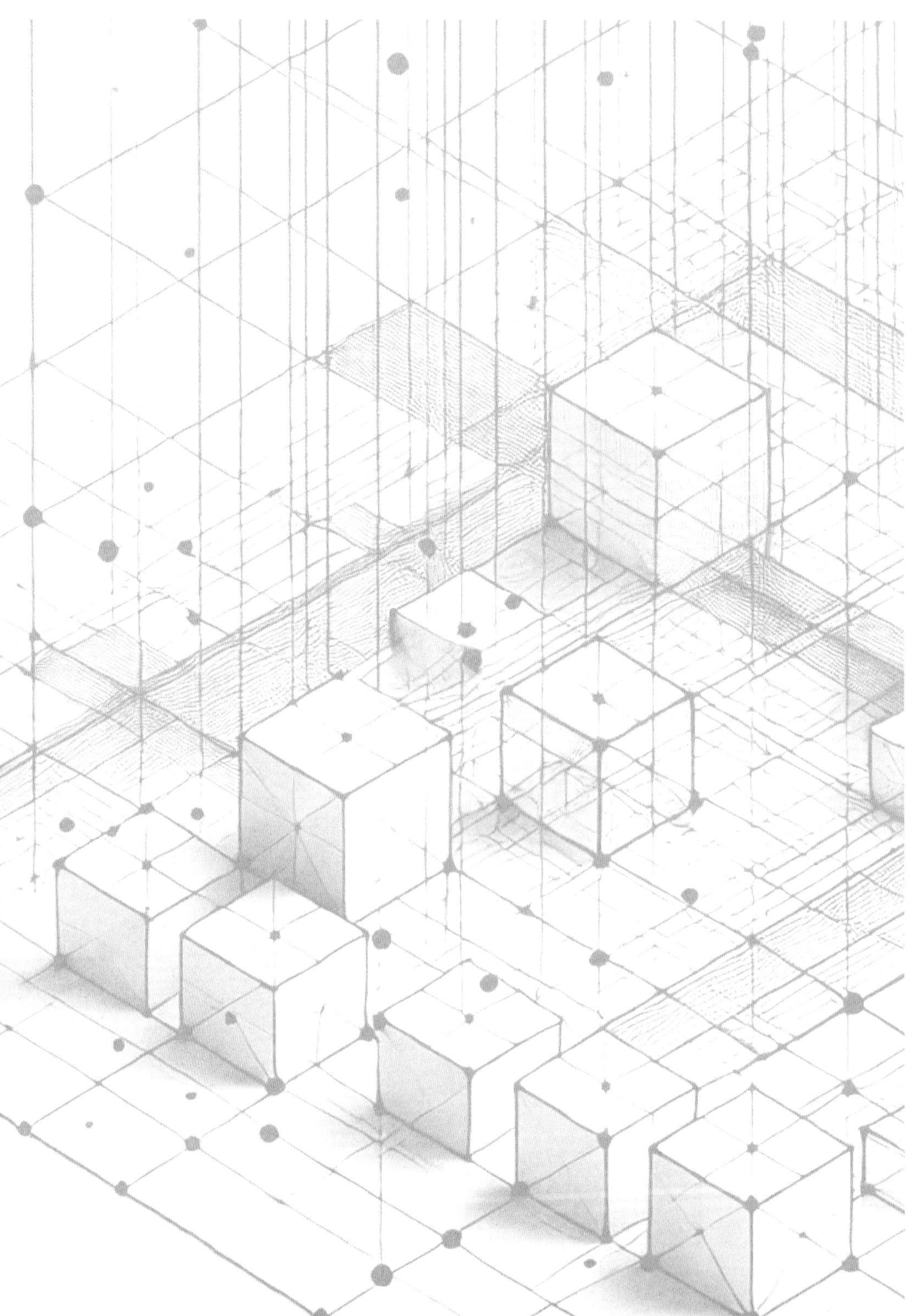

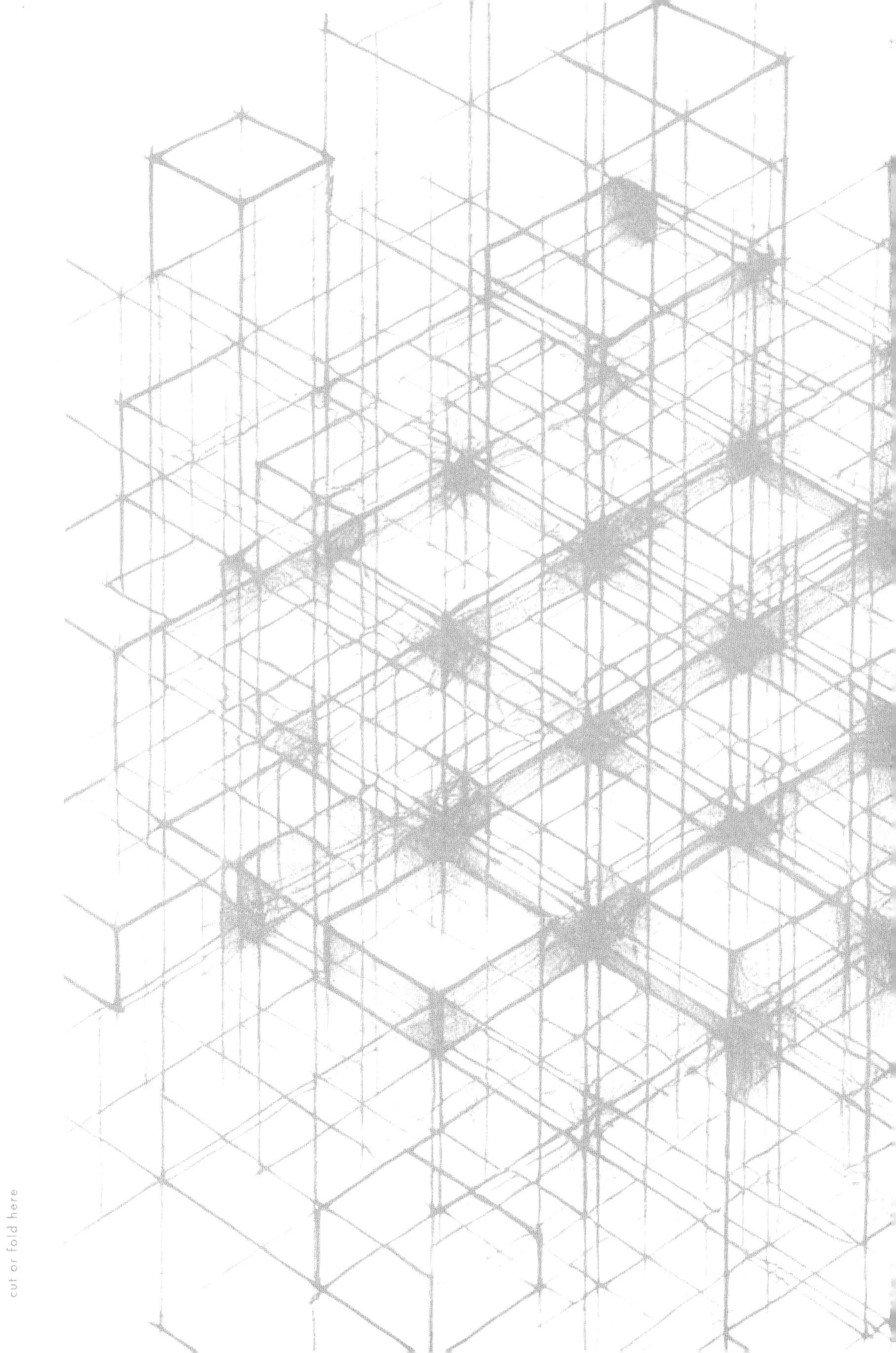

cut or fold here

feel free to take notes on these pages

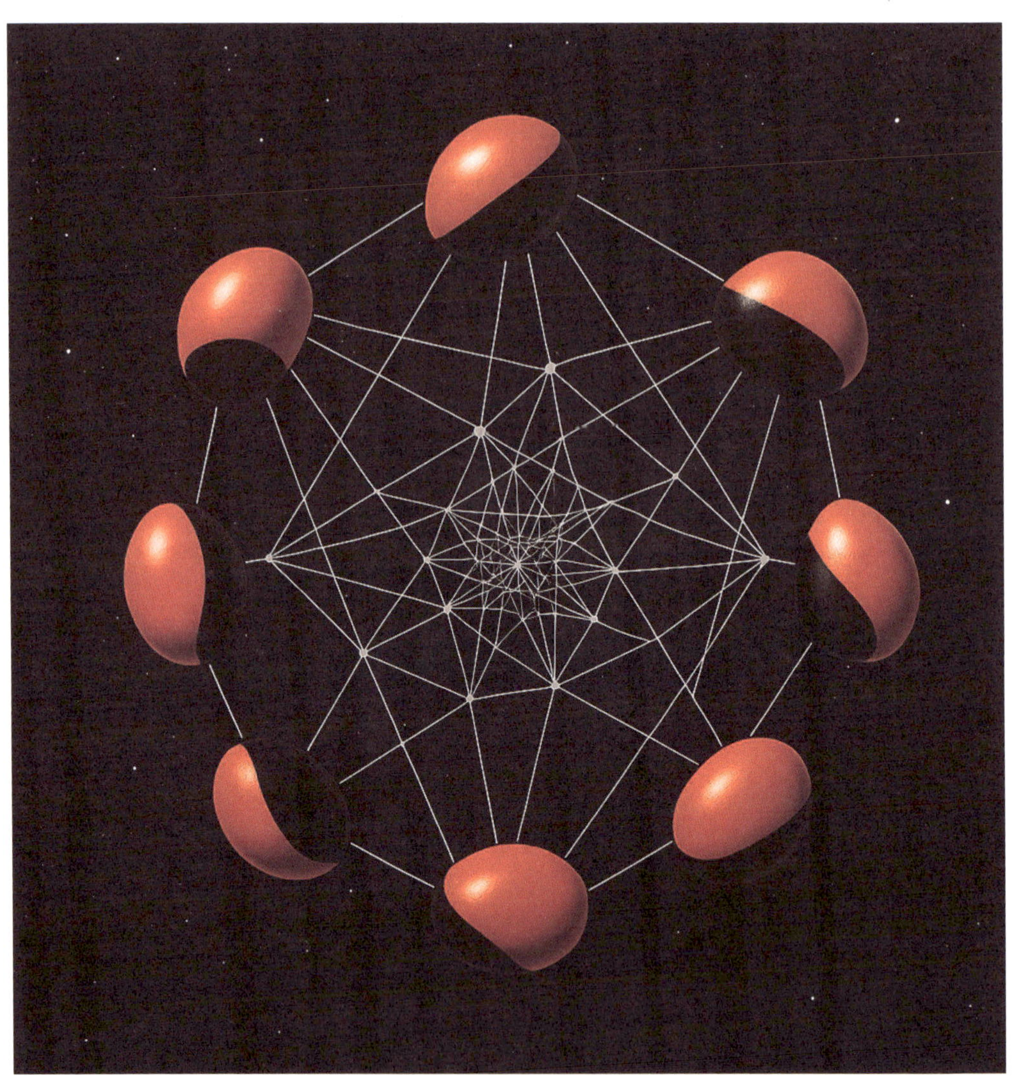

Thank you for taking the time reading this book and the image above is "hyperhuayrurus in space".